Cultural Diversity

To my parents, who have always been willing to argue with me about the social world – as a basis for the next argument

Cultural Diversity

Its Social Psychology

Xenia Chryssochoou

350 Main Street, Malden, MA 02148-5020, USA
108 Cowley Road, Oxford OX4 1JF, UK
550 Swanston Street, Carlton, Victoria 3053, Australia

The right of Xenia Chryssochoou to be identified as the Author of this Work has been asserted in accordance with the UK Copyright, Designs, and Patents Act 1988.

First published 2004 by Blackwell Publishing Ltd

Library of Congress Cataloging-in-Publication Data

Chryssochoou, Xenia.
    Cultural diversity: its social psychology / Xenia Chryssochoou.
        p.   cm.
    Includes bibliographical references and index.
        ISBN 0-631-23122-6 (alk. paper) – ISBN 0-631-23123-4 (pbk.: alk. paper)
        1. Pluralism (Social sciences) 2. Multiculturalism. I. Title.

HM1271.C487 2004
306–dc21   2003007538

A catalogue record for this title is available from the British Library.

Set in 10/12.5 Pt Rotis Serif
by Kolam Information Services Pvt. Ltd, Pondicherry, India
Printed and bound in the United Kingdom
by TJ International, Padstow, Cornwall

For further information on
Blackwell Publishing, visit our website:
http://www.blackwellpublishing.com

Contents

Foreword

Not long ago (yes, not long ago), I wrote to a Polish friend who had served as a guinea pig in a medical experiment: "Ah, it is so good to be a foreigner!" In one of her books, Germaine Tillon, who had met this girl in Ravensbrück, describes her at the same time as so carefree and so sad. Of course, it does not make sense to recall such memories after closing this book. But perhaps it does. It is strange, indeed, to read a well-documented book of unquestionable scientific value on issues that one has known for a long time and about things that one has first hand experience. It is so tempting to be able to formulate a general idea about one's own experience. But are we able to do so? Who knows?

Nonetheless, this memory came back to warn me that the concepts, the questions, the phenomena of acculturation are marked by history. They have a signification in and for their time. This is something that Xenia Chryssochoou has well understood, since she offers a clear and efficacious analysis of her time – postmodernity, if one wishes to call it so. She proceeds with simplicity and at the same time with great ability to define concepts and to present them to students, her future audience. Following her account, we can understand precisely, chapter after chapter, the questions associated with emigration, racism, discrimination of minorities, and the assembly of fragmented cultures.

Xenia Chryssochoou writes both with sensibility and intelligence about the molecular aspects, if one can call them that, of the nowadays generalized quest for identity and power, of the rights on one's own culture and, thus, about the wounds of acculturation, the obstacles that the "Other" needs to overcome to succeed in this quest. I do not know, in social psychology, another book more focused on this subject.

As far as I am concerned, I would say modestly that we learn a lot, even if we find a certain distance. It is a fact that I had sensed a long time ago: we are in the presence of an *ethnicization* – almost completed – of the representation of our society. Who is to blame if I cannot entirely share this representation? Except that before (yes, a long time ago), even as a refugee, we believed in a historical representation of our society and of a world able to change. Although the same problems were most probably at stake, the interplay of representations and languages gave them another experienced meaning. The right to one's own culture was a duty to tradition, and the duty to culture a right to emancipation.

The remark I have just made is not intended as a criticism. It aims simply to express the desire to make allowances for time, to make our vision become "Einsteinian" in a four-dimensional social psychology.

Needless to say, one of the major qualities of this book is the theoretical concern of its author, the best part being the application of the concepts of each theory and the elements on which it is based to a new domain: culture. It is a heuristic transfer that describes and explains the diversity of cultures. Is it a fact of our existence or the outcome of our actions? It is not important. Anyhow, we come to know this diversity through its symbols and its phenomenology.

This is why it is so difficult to know whether multiculturalism is *the* answer to the "malaises of civilization" or a provisional social contract between the acting minorities which responds, as I've written before, to their need for visibility, for social recognition. It was only in America that it was possible for me to observe a kind of parallelism between the differentiation of cultures and the dedifferentiation of society.

In a few words, the apostle Paul defines in plain language what Man is: "there is neither Jew nor Greek, there is neither slave nor free man, and there is neither man nor woman." To my knowledge this is the subtext of any text on multicultural identity. It goes beyond the diversity of cultures and the infinite differences between cultures. It seems to me that the author of this book shares this conviction, this sensibility. Let's hope that her book will find success with students, its audience, and all other readers.

Serge Moscovici

Preface

Six years ago when I joined the Department of Psychology at Surrey University I was asked to prepare lectures for a course on applied social psychology for second year undergraduate students. Fresh from my PhD obtained a year and a half before, I thought: "What do I know about applied social psychology?" But then I thought that if social psychology cannot say much about the societies in which we live then what is the point of it? The saying attributed to Kurt Lewin – "there is nothing more practical than a good theory" – rang in my head and I started preparing for my course with the enthusiasm of a novice. I probably chose a question for this course that was at the center of my preoccupations in terms of my recent move to Britain and in terms of my research interests. I entitled the course the social psychological dynamics of immigration and multiculturalism.

When, several years later, I was contacted to write a book on crosscultural psychology, I instinctively refused. There are good people in the field who have devoted time and effort to understanding crosscultural situations and devising methodologies to study them, and psychologists owe much to their efforts to decentralize our points of view. I was not capable of adding anything to this field. However, I had co-authored a chapter with Evanthia Lyons on crosscultural methodologies for a book on research methods (Lyons and Chryssochoou 2000) and the idea of crosscultural psychology was fresh in my mind and challenged me. Crosscultural psychology, to my mind, was looking at the impact of cultural diversity on psychological phenomena as we know them and giving us the possibility to redefine them. But what is cultural diversity in itself? How do people understand and use it to make sense of their experiences and explain the world in which they live? These were the questions I asked myself and the more I thought about them the more I thought that this is another way of studying cultural phenomena within the field of social psychology. So I based my outline for the book on this idea, which was also the one I used for the course: what can social psychology tell us about the culturally diverse societies in which we live?

Of course, cultural diversity is an area that includes other issues (gender, sexuality, disability, etc.), not only those based on race, ethnicity, and nationality, but the journey is hard enough without looking at all of them. Besides, I do not believe that one can do justice to all of them if one tries to understand them all with the same lens. Faced with a predominantly white, Anglo-Saxon, and female audience in my lectures, I chose to focus on race, ethnicity, and nationality as categories that assemble and differentiate people. I have learned a lot from interactions with my students in this course, both from their questions and from the way they positioned me as a foreign social psychology lecturer. This book owes much to them in many respects, and when I decided to write it I mainly started by talking to them. I wanted to tell them a story uninterrupted by the necessary theoretical frameworks that they needed to know, but which at the same time is informative and scholarly. I wanted to describe to them the journey of social psychology in modern times and societies and the light it sheds on different aspects of our lives. And storytellers are themselves part of the story, not mere relayers of a reality "out there." They contribute to the construction of knowledge. This is something that writers of textbooks usually forget when they claim to voice the scientific "truth" in simple terms for students to learn and give back at exam time. Anyone who has corrected exam papers knows that this is not how it happens. Students give back knowledge that they have assimilated and accommodated with their previous understandings and, perhaps, beliefs. In their essays and exams they *construct* knowledge; this is the knowledge they use outside the boundaries of the university.

I am not arguing here that there is no such thing as a corpus of knowledge that we are happy enough with in the sense that it satisfies the criteria the academic community has set up to evaluate research. It is precisely because there is such knowledge that I was interested in communicating it. However, I do ask readers of this book to bear in mind where I stand when I express these positions. That is the purpose of this preface: to provide some clues as to where I stand.

This book is addressed primarily to students and novices in social psychology. I hope I have taken care not to patronize them. I have tried to be simple, but not simplistic. I give my own opinions as well as those of others, particularly regarding definitions. In doing so I hope to make clear that different people say different things and propose alternative answers to questions and that this is an inherent feature of academic work. By quoting extensively from others (an uncommon feature in many textbooks) I also hope to provide an example of the sort of thing we expect in essay writing. I assume that readers understand the complexity of the issues involved and that problems cannot be solved with black-and-white answers.

I chose to present mostly classic approaches and key theories and paradigms of social psychology in the form of "theoretical snapshots," placed at the end of the book. This was done for four reasons: (1) because these theories are present throughout the book; (2) because their detailed description would have interrupted the story; (3) because I believe that a good knowledge of the pillars on which social psychology was built is essential to understand and critically discuss current debates; (4) because, as a reader myself, when I read a book outside the boundaries of my discipline I wish to have a quick reminder of where the jargon comes from. I hope, therefore, that these "snapshots" (abbreviated TS in the text) will be useful reminders throughout the book and perhaps more generally.

Similarly, I have provided definitions of key terms in the margins and used tinted panels to present some issues in more detail and to present empirical research by way of illustration. This presentation of empirical research serves three purposes. Firstly, it presents the different types of research methodologies that social psychology uses. Secondly, the research I have chosen is grounded in multicultural issues, originates from various countries, and concerns a range of different groups. Thirdly, it serves an educational purpose by showing students how to pick up crucial points when they read academic papers and try to recall the research they describe.

This book should not be understood as a huge literature review, either of social psychology or of cultural diversity. I have tried to present the issues in a succinct way and not to give masses of references. For each one of my chapters, a whole book could be written: I have therefore listed important publications for interested readers to use as keywords for their own searches. Similarly, the theoretical snapshots are exactly that: snapshots. Thus, I hope that my colleagues will excuse me if I haven't made reference to the whole body of their research.

Before you go on to read this book I need to make some final points. Although my own theoretical preferences are presented, I have chosen an eclectic approach in relation to theory. Some might say that this strategy runs the risk of presenting incompatible epistemologies. This is probably true. However, I have chosen to look at the state of the art in social psychology and see how it is "applied" to current culturally diverse societies. My starting point was the issue, not the theory, nor the methodology. I decided to look at the issue as a fox and not as a hedgehog, to use Moscovici's (1988c) metaphor.[1]

Having said that, there is no point hiding the fact that I did all this from my position as a Western researcher trained in European social psychology, and as an immigrant – firstly to France for nine years and secondly to Britain for another six. My experiences in both countries, as well as my socialization in Greece, heavily influenced my way of looking at and doing social psychology. The image of social psychology I present is through these lenses. I regret that I was unable to represent the body of knowledge developed in non-Western universities. I give due warning, therefore, that the social psychology presented in this book is Western and European. These are the societies I had in mind when talking about the issues of multiculturalism. I am pretty sure that multicultural issues in India, China, or Africa are of a different nature, despite their similarities. Pettigrew (1998a) set out to examine whether the knowledge social psychologists acquired from racial relationships in the US could be applied to those Western European societies facing immigration. In turn, we will need to look at whether the knowledge we have acquired in the Western word is useful in other multicultural societies around the globe. But that is a project for another book.

Having warned against the idea that "my world" is *the* world, I wish also to warn that in reading this book you might think that cultural groups are "objects" that exist "out there" and can explain differences and similarities between practices and people.

In order to communicate with readers I found it necessary to use the words "culture" and "cultural." However, I have written extensively about the dangers of reifying and essentializing categories that we have constructed in order to explain similarities and differences and to legitimize or change social relationships. Thus I wish to apologize if readers think that this book contributes to the reification of culture. My intention is to start a debate about commonly used concepts that are argued and understood in different ways.

The last point I wish to make is that I certainly do not believe that social psychology holds the keys to all the answers about this huge issue of cultural diversity. It is blindingly obvious that we need to tackle these issues from every perspective that the human and social sciences allow. I regret that I am not able to provide a multi-disciplinary approach in this book and I acknowledge this as a weakness. However, as Tajfel (1969: 173) says: "from the point of view of research in social psychology, this impossibility to encompass the problems within one study, however ambitious it may be, or within one discipline, does not mean that we have to sit and wait in a perfectionist contemplation." I think that this book can serve as a basis for discussion with non-Western trained researchers; equally, I hope that it can serve as a basis for dialogue with other social disciplines. The issue of cultural diversity, at least in Europe, has started to "bother" people. Therefore, it has triggered enough researchers to problematize it (Deaux 2000a).

I certainly am pleased to have been given the opportunity to think about and explore the links between social psychology and cultural diversity. After all these caveats, I wish you pleasant reading.

NOTE

1   In *La Machine à faire des Dieux*, Moscovici describes the researcher as a strange creature: half fox and half hedgehog. When the researcher tries to capture the mysteries of society, he or she behaves like a fox, exploring multiple paths and methodologies. However, when it comes to explaining the data, the researcher becomes a hedgehog and refuses anything that contradicts his or her vision.

Acknowledgments

Now that this book is finished I would like to acknowledge all the people who contributed to it directly and indirectly.

In writing this book I have been talking to my students. I would like to thank them for inspiring me with their questions during lectures.

The ideas of Serge Moscovici and Henri Tajfel have been a true inspiration for me and I hope that my "internal debates" with both of them are evident in this book. Like many social psychologists in Europe and elsewhere, I am grateful for their passionate construction of European Social Psychology, and for their commitment to understanding and theorizing the mysteries of conflict and social change. Very modestly I would like to acknowledge their contribution to my way of thinking and doing social psychology.

In many respects this book owes a lot to Jean-Claude Deschamps, who I observed "doing" social psychology. I've learned a lot from him and this is a good opportunity to thank him for it.

People at Blackwell Publishing gave me their trust and I would particularly like to thank Sarah Bird and Lindsey Howarth for their enthusiasm, support, and patience. I hope that they are satisfied with the outcome. I would like also to acknowledge the support I had from Karen Wilson, Will Maddox, Joanna Pyke, Rhonda Pearce and in particular from Jack Messenger, who had the hard task of copy-editing.

Part of this book was written during a sabbatical spent in New York. I would like to express my gratitude to Kay Deaux for hosting me at the Graduate Center at CUNY and for "opening doors" for me. My friend and colleague Gina Philogene was instrumental to my visit in New York and I would like to take the opportunity to tell her that her friendship means a lot to me.

In New York I stayed at the C. L. R. James Institute. Jim Murray, its director, should be acknowledged for facilitating my stay and for helping me get to grips with the city and its atmosphere.

The Department of Psychology at the University of Surrey has been my intellectual home during this period. I wish to take this opportunity to acknowledge the support I received from all members of staff. In particular, I would like to thank Glynis Breakwell for giving me time, opportunities, advice, and support; the research committee for supporting my application for a sabbatical; and Chris Fife-Schaw for his support as a senior colleague and head of department.

My friends and colleagues at the Social Psychology European Research Institute – Julie Barnett, Adrian Coyle, Moira Dean, Mick Finlay, Peter Hegarty, Catherine Mills, and Clare Twigger-Ross – deserve my gratitude for providing me with a warm and intellectually challenging working environment. In particular, Evanthia Lyons has been a fierce critic, a source of support, a colleague with whom to discuss, and a friend. I am thankful to her for all of that.

I also thank my PhD students, Yukiko Kuwahara, Spyridoula Ntani, and Tina Rothi, who are all doing research in issues relating to cultural diversity and have been a source of inspiration and ideas.

Very special thanks go also to Alison Pike for allowing me to get things "off my chest" when I needed it, to Martyn Barrett for the pleasant way he introduced me to new projects, and to Mark Bradshaw for insisting that I shouldn't take myself and my book too seriously.

My friends in Guildford – Mark Chenhall, Birgitta Gatersleben, and Joe and Jenny Param – fed me well many times and I would like to thank them for taking care of me during the tough period of writing.

I wish also to thank my friends in Greece, France, Canada, and elsewhere for making my world culturally diverse and for being patient with my lack of availability during this project.

I've shared the "pain" of writing with my dear friends and colleagues Margarita Sanchez-Mazas and Julie Antypa, whose friendship is so important to me.

Matt Kemsley, Thanassi Panayiotopoulos, Catherine Mills, and in particular Lesley Storey "proved" their friendship by going through the pages and checking the English. I am profoundly indebted to them. I am also grateful to Spyridoula Ntani, who gladly helped me with the referencing.

Over the years, I had the pleasure to count Themis Apostolidis and Chiara Volpato among my friends. The discussions I had with both of them about social psychology and the world are precious to me. It is impossible to express how much I owe to them both. I hope they both know how I feel. I would simply like to thank them for reading and commenting on my manuscript and for being a constant source of support and encouragement.

I would like also to acknowledge the presence of Elena Paul, my childhood friend, who recently reappeared in my life. She and her family provided me with a comforting space. Her friendship means a lot to me and I hope that as an immigrant herself she will find the book interesting.

Finally, I need to acknowledge that I have been blessed with the love and support of my family. My parents, Dimitris and Eleni Chryssochoou, my sister Vivi, and my late grandmother have been there all along. I do not have enough words to express my love and gratitude to them.

Introduction

Mural in Dalston Lane, East End, London.

The fact that people move to live in different places from where they were born is as ancient as the world. This book is not about *why* people move, but about *what* happens when they move. For example, what does the movement of people mean for the social organizations that are created? What does it mean for the social and symbolic relationships that develop and for communication between people?

We will discuss what it means for people to leave environments that, although they were difficult, poor, or even dangerous, were familiar to them, and what people feel when they find themselves in places about which they know very little. We will look at what happens in those societies to which large numbers of people move and how their inhabitants view the newcomers. We will examine how the relationships between those already there and the newcomers evolve and what this contact means in the long run for the community. Finally, we will seek to understand the conditions under which people of different cultures and backgrounds can live peacefully together within the same political organization, and under which conditions conflict is more likely to arise. By means of these discussions, we will try to understand what holds our societies together and makes them cohesive, how societies exercise control, and what produces movement and change.

We will look at all these issues through the eyes of a social psychologist. This, of course, does not mean that the only way of looking at these questions is a social psychological one. It just means that we will follow the particular way social psychology has of researching these complex phenomena. I hope this book will reveal the kinds of issues to which current multicultural societies give rise and will convince you that it is worth looking at them through the lens of social psychology.

What is Social Psychology About?

Social psychology is a discipline in the social sciences and usually finds its institutional niche within psychology departments. I want to avoid giving a formal definition here. I hope that what social psychology does will become clear as you go through the pages of this book. Yet, if I were to give a brief description, I would say that what makes social psychology distinct is a combination of what it studies, how it studies it, and the level of explanation it seeks. Social psychology is interested in studying the relationship between the individual and society. Thus, some of the questions that social psychologists try to answer concern

- how people understand and construct their social reality;
- how they feel in their environment;
- what motivates their actions;
- how and when they act together;
- the consequences of these actions;
- how people and groups influence each other;
- how people and groups produce knowledge, norms, and artefacts.

In brief, social psychology is interested in understanding *how people are transformed by society and how they transform society.* As Moscovici (2000: 114) puts it, "the field of social psychology consists of social subjects, that is, groups and individuals who create their social reality (which is in fact the only reality), control each other and create their bonds of solidarity as well as their differences. Ideologies are their products, communication is their means of exchange and consumption and language is their currency."

What makes social psychology distinct as a discipline is not only its object, but also its way of looking at it. Moscovici (1988b, 2000) suggests that what differentiates social psychology from the related disciplines of psychology and sociology has been its efforts to understand the conflict between the individual and the social, along with its particular way of looking at this relationship. Within a social psychological framework, the relationship between the individual (as ego/organism) and the social object needs to be studied through the relationship between this individual and a social subject (an Alter that can be real, symbolic, represented, an individual, or a group). For example, if we were to look at how people (individuals) develop a European identity (object), a social psychological perspective would suggest, for instance, that one might look at how and whether other memberships (i.e., national, regional, political) intervene in this process.

Social psychologists use different methods, including experiments, observational methods, surveys, interviews, and focus groups, to answer their questions. As methodology is not the main focus of this book, however, I will not expand on the technicalities of these methods. Nonetheless, as you read this book you will see different examples of research and get a flavor of the various ways social psychological questions can be answered.

What is more important than the method used is the level at which the answer is given. Doise (1984, 1986, 1997) suggested that researchers should accept that there are different levels of explanation and that they should make a special effort to integrate them (panel I).

For example, we could look at the dynamics of multicultural societies at different levels. We could be interested in understanding the psychological processes that facilitate people's adaptation to different environments or that would make people more tolerant of diversity (intrapersonal level). Alternatively, we could look at whether personal contacts and friendships with people of a different ethnicity, religion, or race make people more accepting towards others from different groups (interpersonal level). We could also ask whether the status of the different groups within a given society and the asymmetric relationships between them condition the way these groups coexist (positional level). Further, we could also study how beliefs about what constitutes a nation, or how the norms regulating the distribution of common resources (material and symbolic), influence perceptions and acceptance of other people and groups (ideological). There is a lot of social psychological research on these issues and on many other similar questions. Being able to articulate and integrate these levels is currently the goal of many social psychologists.

Panel I   Social Psychological Levels of Explanation (Doise 1984, 1986, 1997)

- *Intrapersonal:* the explanation resides in the individual. This type of explanation concerns the individual (cognitive) processes organizing human experience.
- *Interpersonal and situational:* the explanation resides in the situation and the interaction between people. This type of explanation concerns the dynamics of the social relations in which people are involved.
- *Positional:* the explanation resides in the position, the status, of the people or the groups involved.
- *Ideological:* the explanation concerns the role of general social beliefs and social relations between groups.

Social Psychology and the Study of Multicultural Societies

Social psychology has its origins in the early years of the twentieth century. Its findings do not necessarily concern humankind throughout history but, rather, meet the requirements of our modern society. Many of the current theoretical discussions of social psychology developed after World War II. Social psychologists were appalled by what happened during this war. The violence, the atrocities, the Holocaust, all motivated social psychologists to understand the psychological processes and the social conditions that could lead people to such extreme behaviors. Among other things, they have looked at processes of social influence, at processes leading to obedience to authorities, at prejudice, discrimination, and intergroup conflict. They have used a variety of methods (laboratory experiments, surveys, and qualitative techniques) to investigate what it is in the relationship between the individual and the social that can produce situations of such conflict, hate, and rejection between groups that people could torture and kill. Today, these lines of research are still being developed.

Historically, this research took place in a world divided between more or less homogeneous or homogenized (at least in Europe) political structures (the nations), yet also in a world that was divided between two blocs, West and East. This powerful divide was objectified in Europe by the existence of the Berlin Wall. These divisions have for generations shaped the way people thought about the world and their own place in it and the way people acted.

Nowadays these divisions are challenged. The fall of the Berlin Wall in 1989 and the reunification of Germany have symbolized the end of the old East–West divide. In addition, the Treaty of European Unification (Maastricht 1992) has signaled that nation-states will not be the only political organizations of note in the twenty-first century and that the relationship between a nation and its citizens might change. Further, technological advances and easier travel have created opportunities for people to move across boundaries. These new sociohistorical conditions are in many respects

Panel II   Globalization (Castles and Davidson 2000)

Globalization refers to current trends in the economic sphere. Economic activities are carried out by transnational companies on international markets. More and more regional markets, such as the European Union or the North American Free Trade Area, try to facilitate the free movement of capital, goods, and labor across national borders. These economic relations beyond national borders call for the development of supranational institutions in order to regulate them. European integration constitutes an attempt to produce such regulators. The European Court of Justice, the United Nations, and the World Trade Organization are also such attempts. Their existence is one of the trends that characterize globalization.

Nevertheless, according to Castles and Davidson, although transnational economic activity is a central aspect of globalization, it is not a new trend. The pre-World War I era, for example, could equally be characterized by worldwide markets that consolidated the economic empires of many European countries. What is new today is the speed at which information is transmitted and economic activities take place. The new information technologies have radically changed the way people communicate, work, trade, and produce. This rapidity of information transmission, which calls for fast reactions, is a central characteristic of today's global societies (Wicker 1997).

summarized by the term "globalization." Globalization is an over-used word in everyday media and political discourse. To start our discussion, let's look at Castles and Davidson (2000), who make explicit the trends encapsulated by "globalization (panel II)."

Globally regulated transnational economic activities challenge the democratic process. A growing concern exists about democracy and human rights at an international level, as people begin to feel that these global trends deprive them of control at a national level and make global institutions unaccountable.

These sociohistorical conditions are producing new relationships among individuals and groups. They demand that people review the way they see the world and as a consequence the way they define themselves. It should not therefore be surprising that identity and identity politics have acquired a prominent position in lay, political, and scientific discourse.

Our task will be to explore how changes in sociohistorical conditions affect the way people understand and construct their social environment and the ways people act upon this environment. We will look at this interaction between the individual and social phenomena throughout this book. We will, for example, discuss the role social psychological phenomena (such as identity and motivations) play in organizing how people understand the world and act upon it. At the same time, we will discuss how social phenomena shape the functioning of psychological mechanisms. Our aim is to discern the principles of this interaction between the individual and the social in order to understand the functioning of our societies and the constitution of culture (Moscovici 2000).

Cultural Memberships and Understanding of the Social World

Social psychological research aims to capture the interplay between social thinking and sociohistorical dynamics in order to understand how societies function and how culture is produced. But what is culture? It is important to define the concept in order to understand its impact on psychological processes, structures, and behavior.

There is a big debate in psychology and more generally in social and human sciences about how to define culture (panel III). In some definitions the concept of culture includes behavior, in the sense that our behaviors are expressions of our culture. Other definitions emphasize that participating in a culture means having common understandings (shared meanings) of our world.

However, along with trying to find a consensual definition of this concept, the main argument of researchers in psychology is to highlight how important it is to take into account the cultural context in which psychological studies were conducted (Jahoda,1984, 1986, 1988; Moghaddam, Taylor, and Wright 1993; Smith and Bond 1998). They are right to point out that human experiences are linked to the social context in which people live. One of their first arguments was that psychologists

---

Panel III What is Culture?

Culture consists of explicit and implicit patterns, of and for behavior acquired and transmitted by symbols, constituting the distinctive achievements of human groups, including the embodiment in artefacts. The essential core of culture consists of traditional (i.e., historically derived) and selected ideas and especially their attached values. Cultural systems may on the one hand be considered as products of action, on the other as conditioning elements of further action.

(Kroeber and Kluckholm 1952: 181)

Moghaddam, Taylor, and Wright (1993: 2) define culture as the human-made part of the environment.

Culture includes all that has worked in the past and become a shared perspective, transmitted from generation to generation (Triandis 1997: 334).

Culture is an interactive process with two main component processes: the creation of shared activities (cultural practices) and the creation of shared meaning (cultural interpretation) (Greenfield 1997: 303).

Culture is a relatively organized system of shared meanings (Smith and Bond 1998: 39).

should not generalize their findings to all cultural contexts; nor should they impose assumptions derived from their cultural environment on other cultural contexts.

A key issue in this debate concerns whether psychological functioning and human behavior are universal or culture specific. Most psychological models were developed in North America and Europe. Quite rightly, the question arose as to whether such findings could be generalized to other contexts. Replication of studies outside the North American context has not always been successful (Amir and Sharon 1987). Furthermore, when studies were conducted in different contexts, researchers observed variations in the phenomena examined. These facts strengthen the arguments of crosscultural psychologists, whose research focused on understanding the role of culture in psychological processes and mechanisms.

What aspects of psychological functioning can be generalized to the whole of humankind? Could culture be a factor that explains psychological and behavioral differences among people and societies? What is the impact of culture on human behavior? Does culture *cause* human behavior in a way that allows us to predict it? These are some of the questions that concern crosscultural research.

This line of research has focused on culture for what it did and not so much on what it actually was. Although these issues are extremely important, for the sake of our own discussion here, let's step out of these debates. Instead, let's consider culture as the outcome of the relationship between the individual and the social, and treat the word "culture" as an inclusive term that supposes common meanings, understandings, and practices among people in a culture.

Sharing a culture means that people have a common way of viewing their relationship with the social and physical environment, a common way of institutionalizing their relationships, of communicating their thoughts and emotions, of prioritizing their activities, of dividing tasks and resources, of attributing value, honors, and power. In other words, it means that people have shared views about the world and how it functions, and they are aware that they do. People have a sense of belonging to a collectivity with a common way of thinking about the world. However, having common understandings does not mean that every single person has the exact same view about social reality. What is important from a social psychological perspective is not how many others think like ourselves, but the fact that we believe that others do think that way. As Jodelet (1989: 50) remarks, "the social connotations of knowledge are not based on their distribution among several individuals but on the fact that each person's way of thinking is marked by the fact that others think likewise" (my translation). The idea that others think like us consolidates our beliefs and makes them more powerful. Further, it gives us a feeling of togetherness. Both these things make culture important for people.

People of the same culture share common systems of social categorization and common understandings about the status, meaning, and relationships of these categories. At the same time, belonging to specific categories organizes people's thoughts about the world. People's views are shaped by their social relationships and their position in a given society and culture. Thus, categories such as nationality, gender, class, race, religion, etc., since they signal our position in society, also shape our understandings, beliefs, and practices. In turn they acquire their meaning within cultural contexts. This meaning is constructed through communication and processes of social influence. We will explore how lay knowledge is constructed and shared when we discuss social representations and processes of social influence.

For the moment, we should bear in mind that culture is not only important in debates among social scientists, but it is also important for lay people. Its importance rests on the fact that culture means a way of experiencing our relationship with the world, along with our belief that this way of thinking and doing is shared with others.

Cultures flourish from our recognition that they represent a set of beliefs, modes of thinking and practices that are peculiar to them and different from others. Some cultures are more inclusive (e.g., Western culture), others refer to a small group of people (e.g., Basque culture), but each one of them is important for its members because it represents the way they construct their social reality and provides them with action alternatives.

Within this perspective, there are as many cultures as there are shared ways of giving meaning to the world and to our actions. Scientists and lay people talk, for example, about Western and Eastern cultures, about the Mediterranean culture, the Celtic culture, the black culture, but also youth culture, working-class culture, and so on and so forth. Culture becomes another way of categorizing people based on observed differences in beliefs, practices, and behaviors. Sometimes culture is confounded with nation, at other times with religion, race, and economic and social development, or a combination of these categories (panel IV). All these criteria, along with location and time, help people to draw boundaries and to unite and separate people.

Panel IV   Ethnicity, Nationality, Race, and Citizenship

Defining ethnicity, nationality, race, and citizenship has proved to be a difficult enterprise and has interested many scholars in the social sciences (Sollors 1996). The reason is that each definition presupposes a theory: a theory of ethnicity, of the nation, of race, or of citizenship. It is beyond the scope of this book to discuss these different social theories. What interests social psychologists is how these categories are used in everyday interactions. In other words, what is their function in everyday life? The way these categories are used is also part of theories: lay theories, commonsense theories or, as we call them, *social representations* (TS1) (Jodelet 1989; Moscovici 1961/1976, 2001). Social psychology is interested in uncovering these theories and understanding their logic in order to be able to explain people's actions and behaviors.

What we mean by ethnicity, race, nationality, etc. is socially constructed. In other words, people share a definition of ethnicity, race, and nationality and this knowledge is the result of their everyday interaction with the social world. This interaction includes people's discussions with their family, friends, and colleagues, the newspapers and books they read, the television they watch, the films they see, the Internet. Our theories about the world are the result of processes of social influence and communication and depend also on our different memberships, and on our previously acquired beliefs and values. Thus the meanings of ethnicity, nationality, race, and citizenship are social constructions that depend on our different positions in the world. It is therefore hazardous to try to define them. The following brief definitions seem to have the agreement of many social scientists and coincide with everyday usage. However, I acknowledge that these definitions can be contested and challenged.

- *Ethnic, ethnic group:* from the Greek word εθνος (ethnos) meaning nation, people. It defines a group of people that have certain characteristics of civilization in common, in particular a community of language and culture. Ethnic groups are defined by real or mythical descent and are supposed to share a common history and experience. In modern societies the phrase "ethnic groups" is used to describe cultural minorities within a nation-state.
- *Race:* a category used to differentiate people on the basis of phenotypic differences such as the color of skin. Its relationship with ethnicity has been a matter of wide debate. Of particular interest has been the question as to whether ethnicity and race are synonymous and overlapping concepts, as to whether race is an aspect of ethnicity, or whether the two concepts describe different things.
- *Nationality:* often used interchangeably with ethnicity. Most often it refers to one's membership of a nation-state or of a group that aspires to be a nation-state (e.g., Scottish nationalists). Depending on whether one refers to an ethnic or a civic conception of the nation, nationality can be equated with ethnicity or citizenship.
- *Citizenship:* defines the legal membership of an organized political entity such as a national state. It concerns the relationship of the individual with this organization and includes the rights and duties of the citizen and his/her expectations from this organization (protection, welfare, etc.). Citizenship refers mostly to the nation-state. However, with the event of more global groupings there is also a question about other types of citizenship (e.g., European citizenship).

One of the main functions of these categories is to confer a social position on individuals and therefore to contribute to their identity. Thus, from a social psychological point of view, what interests us is what people mean when they refer to these categories, how people conceptualize the relationship between them, how and when they use them, and with what consequences.

Culture defines membership of a community of like-minded people. If culture constitutes a community of people with common ways of thinking and experiencing the world and thus with common practices, the question that we need to ask is whether people with diverse cultures can coexist harmoniously in time and place under the same political and social organization. This is also the question that modern multicultural societies are called to answer.

Beliefs About Acculturation: The Coexistence of Different Cultures Under the Same Political and Social Organization

When people who were born and socialized in different cultures start living together they have to adjust to the novelty of "the Other" and their ways of thinking about the world. The Other represents an alternative, a challenge to our habitual way of seeing things, the way we think about the world and ourselves. As we will see later, people use comparison to evaluate themselves. Festinger's (1954) social comparison theory argued that when people make these comparisons they choose others that are more or less similar to them. What happens when the Other is from another culture? How are we going to evaluate ourselves in relation to "Them"? Whose way of seeing the world is one to follow?

Usually, those who are in a majority – either of number or through real or symbolic power and/or material resources – manage to establish their view of the world as the strongest position. They might argue that their way of perceiving and doing things is the "golden" way, that tradition and history have proven them correct, and that there is no reason why they should change. Thus, they say, if other people want to be part of their group, all they need do is abandon their traditions and follow the majority's cultural rules. Others might consider that entry to their group is only possible through birth, so that even if people adopt their group's traditions, customs, and way of life, they could never become full members of the group. Still, they are happy to have newcomers in their country as "guests," insofar as these newcomers make an effort to follow the majority's cultural goals. Others might say that people should publicly conform to the cultural norms of the country as established by the majority, but in private they can follow their own cultural norms. Finally, there is also the possibility that in the private sphere each group keeps its own ways of thinking and doing things, but in the public sphere they contribute toward building a common way of seeing the world – a new culture. What I have just described here are the ways in which people think about **acculturation**.

> **Acculturation**
>
> Acculturation comprehends those phenomena which result when groups of individuals having different cultures come into continuous first-hand contact with subsequent changes in the original culture patterns of either or both groups.
>
> (Redfield, Linton, and Herkovits 1936: 149)

How will newcomers or those in a minority position react to the challenge of a new culture? Some might refuse to accept the culture of the majority and hang on to their own culture. Others might be willing to abandon their cultural norms and adopt the culture of the majority. Another option might be to keep their own culture but also accept new elements of the culture that they have just encountered. Finally, they might find themselves between cultures, "rejecting" both new and old ones. Gordon (1964) proposed that, during their lifetimes, members of cultural minorities moved slowly towards accepting the majority's culture. Their progression is along a continuum, starting with the maintenance of their own culture and ending with the adoption of the majority culture. The midpoint of this continuum is *biculturalism*. Gordon's model considers bicultural individuals to be in a transitory period and that if they want to adapt successfully in the new environment they should assimilate to the new culture. This model of acculturation is called *unidimensional* because it assumes that mainten-ance of one's own culture and adoption of the majority culture are mutually exclusive options, or opposite poles of one dimension.

Berry (1990, 1997a, 1997b, 1999, 2001) suggested that acculturation involves two major issues. The first issue concerns whether cultural maintenance is considered important and whether the culture of origin should be preserved. The second issue concerns whether contact with other groups (mainly the culturally dominant group) and participation in the larger society are undertaken (panel V). Berry's model is

Panel V   Strategies of Acculturation

Contact and participation	Culture maintenance	
Cultural minorities: Is it considered to be of value to maintain relationships with the larger society?	*Cultural minorities:* Is it considered to be of value to maintain one's identity and characteristics?	
Larger society: Is it considered to be of value to have contacts with other cultural groups?	*Larger society:* Is it considered to be of value that immigrant groups maintain their cultural identity and characteristics?	
Yes Cultural minorities Receiving society	Yes Integration Multiculturalism	No Assimilation Melting pot or pressure cooker
No Cultural minorities Receiving society	Separation Segregation	Marginalization Exclusion

Source: Berry (1990, 1997a, 1997b, 1999, 2001)

(*Continues*)

Panel V (*Continued*)

Bourhis, Moïse, Perreault, and Senécal (1997) proposed a reformulation of questions referring to cultural maintenance and contact-participation. Their suggestion made the questions more specific towards immigrants and aimed to avoid a possible discrepancy between a question that measures attitudes (cultural maintenance) and a question that measures behavioral intentions (desirability of contacts with the native-born community). In particular, they reformulated the question of contact in order to ask directly whether people wished to adopt the cultural identity of the receiving community. They propose the model below:

Contact and participation	Culture maintenance	Is it considered to be of value to maintain the immigrant cultural identity?
Is it considered to be of value to adopt the cultural identity of the receiving society?	Yes	No
Yes	Integration	Assimilation
No	Separation	Anomie Individualism

Further, Bourhis et al. proposed to distinguish between those individuals who have problems in identifying with the identities of their cultural ingroup *and* of the native-born group, and those individuals who reject both identities because they prefer to be seen as individuals rather than members of a cultural group. According to Bourhis et al., the former are more likely to experience cultural alienation (anomie), whereas the latter are influenced by an ideology of meritocracy and are following an individualistic strategy.

bidimensional because it considers that cultural maintenance and cultural participation are different dimensions. The way people respond to these two questions leads to a typology of acculturation strategies.

The question from a social psychological point of view is how to understand which factors will shift the decision one way or another. One factor that might influence newcomers' acculturation strategies concerns the relationship they have with their cultural group. Of particular importance might be the norms of this cultural group. Some groups value the maintenance of bonds between their members. In this case the community is part (at least symbolically) of the process of individual decision making. In these communities, individual decisions and actions are influenced by the norms and beliefs of the community: "what people would say" constitutes an important factor when making a decision about one's personal life. In other groups, people are more independent in the way they conduct their lives. As we will see later, whether one belongs to a group with a "collectivistic" or an "individualistic" belief-system influences the strategies of acculturation that one might choose. It could be more difficult to abandon one's culture when one belongs to a group with collectivistic beliefs. Furthermore, groups become important for people because they provide them with a sense of belonging and a way of perceiving themselves. Thus, it might be extremely difficult for some people to abandon a group that is important for self-definition. When a cultural group gives a sense of identity to its members it is very difficult to "leave" it unless this identity is successfully replaced with another. To do this, not only should the person be willing to adopt the values, beliefs, and ways of behaving of the new group, but also the other members of the group to which the person aspires to belong should recognize him or her as one of them. For example, I might want to become French and adopt the values, beliefs, and ways of living of the French people. However, if French people do not recognize me as French I will not have succeeded in my acculturation strategy. This is the case for many North Africans living in France, and similarly for many people of Asian or African-Caribbean origin in Britain. Finally, distancing oneself from the *ingroup* can be considered to be an act of disloyalty that people accept with difficulty. Therefore, we should not assume that people in a new cultural environment are completely free to choose to abandon their cultural identity. Many factors influence the acculturation paths that people follow. These issues will be further discussed in chapters 1, 3, and 4.

Another factor that might influence strategies of acculturation relates to the beliefs of the receiving community. The immigrant-receiving community has expectations about how newcomers should be accommodated and what strategies they should adopt. These expectations therefore construct the framework for possible acculturation strategies. For example, if the immigrant-receiving community does not allow people to maintain and express their cultural identity, this option, although still possible, is weakened. Immigrant-receiving communities' beliefs about acculturation interact with their perception of their own national and cultural identity and their attitudes towards Otherness. Thus, the presence of cultural minorities might push the majorities into reconsidering and reshaping who they are. It is not self-evident that majorities would be willing to change the way they perceive themselves. These issues will be discussed further in chapters 2, 3, and 4.

Acculturation strategies are not an issue that concerns the cultural majorities and minorities separately. The beliefs of all the communities interact and shape the acculturation process. The wishes of the minorities and the expectations of the majorities set the scene for acculturation to take place. Changes can be observed in both majorities and minorities, as well as in the overall community. In chapters 3 and 4 we will be concerned with this interaction and its consequences for the relationship between cultural majorities and minorities.

Finally, beliefs about acculturation define the overall ideological milieu that influences the state's policies about acculturation and immigration. How people feel about acculturation and diversity, as well as their level of tolerance for different understandings and practices, has an impact on the policies that governments put in place. Of course, this relationship is not unidirectional. People's beliefs influence policies, and policy measures in turn impact on people's practices and beliefs. Understanding this interplay between attitudes, representations, and policies is vital in order to understand how societies move and change without disintegrating. If, as we said earlier, the way we see the world really is changing in response to the trends of globalization, it is important to understand the impact of these changes on people's identities. Identity is an issue that becomes extremely important in plural societies. Researchers have used the concept of identity to explain people's actions, and it has seeped into commonsense and everyday discourse, so that people use it to justify their actions. I would argue that our point of departure in social psychology is to understand the interplay between different forms of knowledge (scientific, lay, religious, etc.). How people perceive themselves, what they claim they are, how they are recognized to be, how they are evaluated by others, together constitute a particular form of knowledge that might "filter" their understanding of the world and influence their actions. Identity summarizes this knowledge. Thus, it constitutes a key issue for multicultural societies in which questions of "who people believe they are" and "who they believe they are not" establish the boundaries between communities. This is discussed in chapter 4 alongside issues of beliefs, representations, citizenship, and social change.

Thus this book will look at culturally diverse societies, first from the point of view of cultural minorities (chapter 1) and then from the point of view of cultural majorities (chapter 2). These chapters will discuss the social psychological consequences of changing cultural environments and receiving new populations. People assume that when people live in culturally diverse communities there is an increased potential for intergroup conflict. We will discuss this issue – along with theories of conflict and how to reduce it – in chapter 3. Then, in chapter 4, we will discuss nationalism, identity, and citizenship. I hope these chapters will equip you with the social psychological theories and empirical findings that are useful for understanding plural societies and give you a taste for social psychology and the motivation to explore its theories and methods.

One of the most important points in this book is that acculturation, the peaceful coexistence of different cultural groups, and the development of plural societies depend on the social context of encounter. Thus, it is important to put our findings into context and avoid generalizations that might not be applicable to every encounter. We must, for example, take into account the sociohistorical factors defining minorities (i.e., colonization, issues of race, European unification, etc.). Furthermore, it is vital to consider the sociohistorical factors defining the climate of the encounter and, in particular, how the beliefs of majorities and minorities interact and how the reasons behind the encounter can influence its development. Throughout the book, I try to use examples of research from different contexts. Further, in chapter 4, I discuss issues relating to the model of the European nation-state that was founded on the concept of homogeneity of culture. I also present issues relating to the European Union, which aims to integrate different national groups. In addition, I discuss the North American and Australian experiences of multicultural societies founded on immigration and subject to continuing processes of ethnic diversification. Homogeneity or diversity, devolution or centralization, democracy and representation, individual and collective rights and duties are all issues at stake in these societies. They are also at the heart of debates among social scientists. I do not claim here to present definitive answers to these questions. To do that one would need the joint endeavours of sociologists, political scientists, economists, historians, cultural anthropologists, social psychologists, and generally all social scientists. Rather, I attempt to give a flavor of how a social psychologist discusses these issues and show how social psychological processes are embedded in historical and social factors. In particular, the aim is to discuss how people's understandings and actions influence the social context.

Such a discussion aims, on the one hand, to help social psychologists put their theories and findings into context and thus help them to challenge and develop them. I will be pleased if this book contributes to debates in social psychology and opens new paths of enquiry that might help the discipline meet the sociohistorical challenges it faces.

On the other hand, this presentation can be seen as a social psychological contribution to the wider debate among social scientists. The expertise that social psychologists have acquired about how people deal with unfamiliarity and psychological threat, about the conditions that can lead to conflict and its reduction, about what motivates people's actions, how they deal with power and status asymmetries, and how they construct theories about the world, can be a very powerful tool in understanding the new social reality.

Ultimately, this book aims to look at how theories and empirical findings within the social psychological literature can inform the dynamics of current societies characterized by cultural diversity and plurality. I hope you find it enjoyable and intellectually challenging.

Chapter 1

Moving Into New Environments: The Perspective of People Belonging to Non-Dominant Cultural Groups

Plate 1   Immigrant demonstration in Italy, July 2000. The banner says: "We claim more respect and dignity."

Outline

We will begin by discussing immigration and cultural diversity from the point of view of those who change cultural environments and those who find themselves in environments where they are a minority in terms of culture. In plural societies a cultural group might be in a minority position at a number of different levels (economic power, political power, numerical terms). Following Berry's (1997a, 1997b) suggestion, I will refer to these people as "culturally non-dominant groups" to emphasize their minority position within the larger society. I include in this term both people who recently migrated and people who are part of ethnic minorities.

Of course, the situation and the experiences of those who have emigrated recently and those who, although they are citizens of a country, belong to a culturally different group, are not identical. However, a common element in their life is that these people find themselves in a minority position in terms of their cultural background and a lot of their everyday experiences are linked to this fact. Thus, I will present some of the issues that are associated with this common experience from the point of view of social psychology. Naturally, when the issues concerning these groups differ, these differences will be pointed out.

A person may decide to relocate for various reasons, among them economic hardship, professional or educational opportunities, wars, conflicts and persecution, and reunion with family members (see panel 1.1). Research by Boneva and Frieze (2001) has suggested that personality factors might also be involved in the propensity to move, which would help explain why some people decide to relocate and others don't. Reasons for moving and personality factors significantly influence how people experience culturally different environments and how they acculturate. Although these questions are very important for the student of acculturation, they are not the main focus of this book.

Our focus here is what actually happens in culturally diverse environments and how people deal with this diversity. We shall begin with those who are in a non-dominant cultural group. Three issues will be raised to discuss cultural diversity from their point of view: (1) how people deal with change, manage unfamiliar environments, and cope with the threats that change brings to their self-evaluation and identities; (2) the challenges that culturally diverse environments generate for people's values, the retention of their culture, the way they see themselves and the world; (3) how members of non-dominant cultural groups deal with social mobility, and issues of power and discrimination. We discuss the opportunities that these people may have to become "full members" of the new society and prosper, and the social psychological factors associated with claiming civil, social, and political rights.

Panel 1.1   Immigrants, refugees/Asylum Seekers, Sojourners, Ethnic Minorities: Definitions

- *Immigrants:* people who voluntary move to another country with the intention of making their life there and staying permanently. Second-generation immigrants are people born in a country from parents who emigrated.
- *Sojourners:* people who voluntarily move to another country without the intention of living there permanently.
- *Refugees/asylum seekers:* according to the Geneva Convention, adopted in July 1951, the status of refugee is accorded to a person who due to "well-founded fear of being persecuted for reasons of race, religion, nationality, membership of a particular group or political opinion, is outside the country of his/her nationality and is unable, or owing to such fear, is unwilling to avail him/herself of the protection of that country; or who, not having a nationality and being outside of the country of his former habitual residence is unable or, owing to such fear, is unwilling to return to it." These people are seeking asylum in safer countries.
- *Ethnic minorities:* culturally different groups of people within a nation-state. Their presence might be due to immigration or to particular links with the specific nation (for example, members of ex-colonies). These people are usually citizens of the nation-state. Second-generation immigrants are also considered part of this group.

According to Berry et al. (1987), non-dominant cultural groups vary in relation to how much they want cultural contact and whether or not such contact is a result of their movement to a new environment:

WILLINGNESS OF CONTACT

MOBILITY	VOLUNTARY	INVOLUNTARY
SEDENTARY	Ethnic Groups	Native Peoples
MIGRANT	Immigrants Sojourners	Refugees

From Berry et al. (1987)

   In Italy there is another term for foreign people: *extracomunitari*, which means "people from outside the European Union" and refers to immigrants in general. This term is interesting because it signifies an extension of the ingroup boundaries to include people from the EU, but also highlights clearly the exclusion of everybody else.

Managing Change, Unfamiliar Environments, and Experiences: Acculturation as a Major Life-Change Event

Undoubtedly, migration is a major change in a person's life. Whatever their reasons for migrating, people leave behind loved ones, familiar environments, and lifestyles. They also lose their position in their immediate environment, their community, and their country. They are referred to as immigrants, refugees, asylum seekers, foreigners, etc. They are faced with new values, new practices and ways of living, and they may not know why people behave as they do and how they themselves should behave. They may feel indignation and disgust toward some practices and become anxious in social situations. Often, they can experience prejudice and discrimination. They may feel that they have lost control of their lives and experience helplessness. In such contexts people need to understand, to cope, to rebuild their lives. This is described by Oberg (1960) as "culture shock." The idea of culture shock, however, has been criticized because it seems to imply that acculturation is solely the problem of newcomers, who should try to adjust, and because it stigmatizes those who do not make this adjustment successfully (Bochner 1986).

Researchers have argued that when changes can be relatively easily accommodated, acculturation can be considered as a learning experience (Berry 1980, 1992, 1998; Bochner 1986; Brislin, Landis, and Brandt 1983; Furnham and Bochner 1986). People learn about their new environment and accommodate new behaviors in accordance with this understanding. In other cases the experience of migration is more difficult, it affects people's health, and they suffer from **acculturative stress**.

Berry (1997a) provides a comprehensive practical framework for acculturation research. This framework emphasizes both structural group-level factors (such as the situation in the society of origin, the ethnic **ingroup**, and the society of settlement) and process features, namely how people experience acculturation and how they cope with the stressors linked to this experience.

A number of factors (at an individual level) prior to or during acculturation moderate this experience and influence the process of acculturation. In panel 1.2 I have slightly modified Berry's framework to emphasize acculturation as a meaning-making experience that concerns major changes in people's lives. It is precisely how people make sense of this experience and how they deal with change and unfamiliarity that influence their own psychological adjustment and participation in a sociocultural environment (Ward 1997). At the same time, their presence and their actions also transform this environment.

This framework avoids the word "adaptation" because it somehow signifies that there is a very concrete reality to which people have to adapt. Acculturation can be viewed, as Schönpflug (1997) suggests, as a migration-induced process of

Acculturative stress

A reduction in health status (including psychological, somatic, and social aspects) of individuals who are undergoing acculturation, and for which there is evidence that these health phenomena are related systematically to acculturation phenomena.

(Berry et al. 1987: 491)

Ingroup

Social psychological jargon qualifying the group or social category to which one belongs or with which one identifies. Similarly, "outgroup" qualifies the group or social category to which one does not belong or with which one does not identify.

individual development where identities (ethnic, national, etc.) are formed. The effect of acculturation on people's identities should not be underestimated. However, acculturation can also be seen as a process of social change in which the culture of origin is reinterpreted and reconstructed (Horenczyk 1997), and in which the so-called receiving sociocultural environment is also changed by the presence of different cultural groups and their relationships. On the one hand, we need to consider the huge diversity of immigrant experiences (Pick 1997); on the other hand, we need to target dominant cultural groups as well (Kagitçibasi 1997). These dominant groups are not monolithic and we should not underestimate the complexity and variability of receiving society's attitudes (Horenczyk 1997).

I suggest that there are shared understandings alongside individual variations in the way people experience acculturation and deal with unfamiliarity. This meaning-making process and the "coping" that it requires apply to both non-dominant cultural groups and dominant ones. The coexistence of different cultures under the same political institution changes the way people see themselves and the world, and induces social change. Social representations theory (Moscovici 1961/1976, 1984, 1988a, 1998, 2000, 2001; Jodelet 1984, 1989; Doise 1990) has provided social psychologists with a theoretical framework to understand how people deal with unfamiliar events and environments, and how through communication and social influence they construct shared understandings and common practices that produce culture (TS1).

Our work as researchers of acculturation from a social psychological perspective should be to understand how people comprehend and cope with change, how they integrate novelty into more familiar frameworks, and how these understandings guide their actions.

Loss of status, the need to survive, and self-evaluation in a new environment

One of the major changes that migrants face is a change in their status and material circumstances. Migrants need to find ways of surviving in the new society. The most obvious hurdle is the need to make a living. The experience of migration inevitably redefines frames of reference and calls upon people to reposition themselves within them. Who are they in relation to this new society? Often, the receiving society defines them by their common condition as immigrants, refugees, or asylum seekers, or by opposition to the native-born population, describing them as foreigners or in relation to their ethnicity or nationality. For example, when I first moved to France, for a long time I was not introduced to people simply as a friend, but as the "Greek friend" of the speaker. The attribute "Greek" qualified my position. In addition, people lose the position they held in their society of origin, perhaps in relation to their family structure or their profession. It is not uncommon, for example, for Polish immigrants working in Greece as painters or cleaners to be qualified computer engineers or architects. Recently, medical schools in Britain started offering conversion courses for refugees who

Panel 1.2

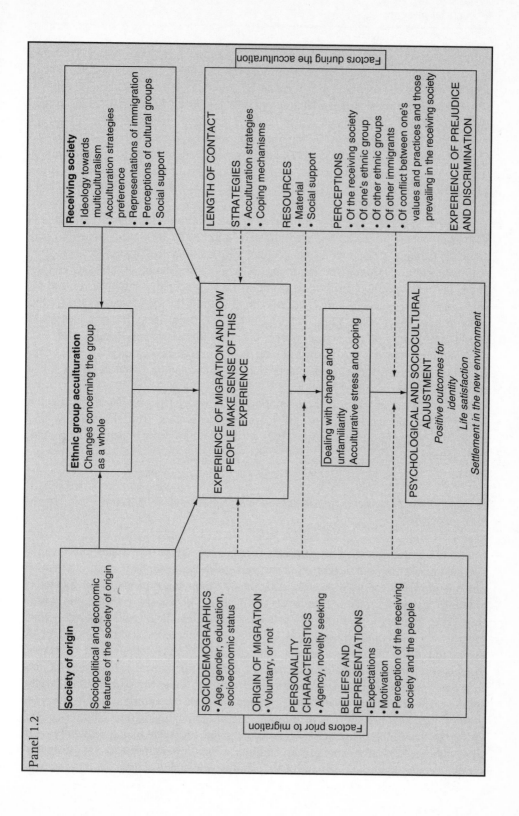

Society of origin

Sociopolitical and economic features of the society of origin

Ethnic group acculturation
Changes concerning the group as a whole

Receiving society
- Ideology towards multiculturalism
- Acculturation strategies preference
- Representations of immigration
- Perceptions of cultural groups
- Social support

Factors during the acculturation

EXPERIENCE OF MIGRATION AND HOW PEOPLE MAKE SENSE OF THIS EXPERIENCE

LENGTH OF CONTACT

STRATEGIES
- Acculturation strategies
- Coping mechanisms

RESOURCES
- Material
- Social support

PERCEPTIONS
- Of the receiving society
- Of one's ethnic group
- Of other ethnic groups
- Of other immigrants
- Of conflict between one's values and practices and those prevailing in the receiving society

EXPERIENCE OF PREJUDICE AND DISCRIMINATION

Dealing with change and unfamiliarity
Acculturative stress and coping

PSYCHOLOGICAL AND SOCIOCULTURAL ADJUSTMENT
Positive outcomes for identity
Life satisfaction
Settlement in the new environment

SOCIODEMOGRAPHICS
- Age, gender, education, socioeconomic status

ORIGIN OF MIGRATION
- Voluntary, or not

PERSONALITY CHARACTERISTICS
- Agency, novelty seeking

BELIEFS AND REPRESENTATIONS
- Expectations
- Motivation
- Perception of the receiving society and the people

Factors prior to migration

were qualified doctors or health professionals, so that they could practice in the UK. Thus, in the new environment that defines them as the Other, migrants need to redefine and evaluate themselves.

According to Festinger (1954), people need to establish an accurate evaluation of themselves, their abilities and opinions. When there are no objective means to do so, this evaluation is made by comparing themselves to similar others. According to Festinger's social comparison theory (TS2), people will avoid comparisons with dissimilar others. The process of social comparison therefore contributes to the formation of social groups by defining "similar people" and increasing the pressures for homogeneity. Festinger also acknowledges, however, that when belonging to a group is especially attractive or when people cannot avoid the comparison they might also compare themselves to dissimilar others. In some cases, these comparisons can be damaging for self-evaluation.

People may use different points of comparison. They can compare their current situation with how they were in the past or how they aspire to be in the future (temporal comparisons). They may compare themselves with other individuals (interpersonal, intragroup, or intergroup comparisons). They may also compare their group to other groups (intergroup comparisons). They may also compare themselves with an abstract standard, a norm, or an ideal (Brown et al. 1992). Comparisons can have different directions: *upward* when the point of comparison is better than oneself, *downward* when the point of comparison is worse than oneself, and *lateral* when the point of comparison is of equal status.

People use these different comparisons strategically, pushed by motivations of self-enhancement or self-evaluation. Social psychologists have tried to clarify the conditions under which each comparison is more likely to happen. It has been argued, for example, that temporal comparisons are more likely to happen later in life (Suls and Mullen 1982; Brown and Middendorf 1996). Wilson and Ross (2000) suggest that people use temporal comparisons when they want to gratify themselves (a self-enhancement motive) and comparisons with others when they want to evaluate themselves.

It is not obvious how people of non-dominant cultural groups will actually choose to compare themselves. A temporal comparison might indeed enhance their perception of themselves if their situation before migration was worse, but it can be problematic for those who have reduced status by migrating, as in the case of the Polish immigrants mentioned above. In multicultural environments it is difficult to predict how self-evaluation will occur. Who is the appropriate point of comparison: people from the same cultural background or people in the receiving society; the culture of origin or the new culture? What are the dimensions along which the comparison takes place?

We know that when they have the opportunity people tend to select the dimensions of comparison in a way that allows them to be seen in a better light (Lemaine 1974; Lemaine, Kastersztein, and Personnaz 1978). We also know that the importance people place on the dimensions of comparison can be used in subtle ways to put others in an inferior position. Sometimes people emphasize their difference from others when in fact what they mean is that they are better than them (Mummendey and Schreiber

1984). This strategy depends also on the status of the groups under comparison (Mummendey and Simon 1989). However, some of the studies referred to here have been conducted in a laboratory setting. In real life people might not have the opportunity to select the dimensions along which to compare themselves; instead, dimensions can be imposed on them by more powerful groups (Deschamps 1980; Deschamps, Lorenzi-Cioldi, and Meyer 1982).

Hinkle and Brown (1990) argue that particular people and groups might be less inclined to use social comparisons as a strategy for evaluation – that they might instead evaluate themselves using abstract norms (models/norms of lifestyle). It is equally possible that social comparison as a means of self-enhancement is more important for the Western cultures in which most research has taken place. Even if people use abstract standards as points of reference, we need to keep in mind that these norms are socially constructed. Thus, the setting of criteria and the value attributed to comparative dimensions are part of a power-game of social negotiation. Members of non-dominant cultural groups are clearly disadvantaged in setting their criteria for self-evaluation.

Personal–group discrimination discrepancy

The tendency for minority group members to perceive a higher level of discrimination directed at their group as a whole than at themselves as individual members of that group.

(Moghaddam 1998)

Another issue requiring clarification is whether people will prefer to use personal comparisons or group comparisons. In a study involving former East and West Germans, Kessler, Mummendey, and Leisse (2000) showed that evaluations of one's personal or group material situation depended on different sets of comparisons. They also confirmed the well-known phenomenon of **personal–group discrepancy** in perceptions of discrimination (Taylor et al. 1990; Taylor, Wright, and Porter 1994).

They conducted a longitudinal study in Germany, after unification, asking East and West Germans to evaluate their material situation in comparison to either individual or group targets. They found that East Germans (who are believed to be and usually evaluate themselves as being inferior to West Germans in relation to material conditions) judged their personal situation as better than the group of East Germans as a whole. West Germans (considered to be the advantaged group) believed that at a personal level they had less privileges than West Germans in general. This research establishes more evidence that social comparisons form the basis for evaluation of status. Furthermore, it highlights the fact that the choice between comparing oneself as an individual and comparing oneself as a group member has consequences for the evaluation of one's position. This is a significant issue for people belonging to non-dominant cultural groups.

However, the crucial question is whether groups are important for people's identities. We should be careful not to forget that, just because our research is about multiculturalism and our participants have been chosen for their cultural memberships, it does not mean that these people consider their ethnic/religious/cultural group as *the* group important for self-evaluation. Finlay and Lyons's (2000) study with people with learning disabilities found that "learning disability" was not a salient category for self-description and evaluation, although people were aware of belonging to it. People with learning difficulties did not use this categorization when comparing themselves to others, despite the fact that parents and carers used it and despite the fact that this membership characterized their everyday life and activities. We can hypothesize that migrants and members of non-dominant cultural groups might not regard the categories that others assign to them as important for self-evaluation. We have some evidence, for example, that Muslim male immigrants in Britain do not wish to refer to themselves as "immigrants" because accepting this label implies settling for life there – a decision they have not yet made (Stickland 2002). People have a variety of categories to which they belong and a variety of identities. The assumption that they will use the one that homogenizes them as members of non-dominant cultural groups, or immigrants, denies them all their other identities. This is an issue that we need to keep in mind throughout this book.

Evaluating one's position in a multicultural environment is a complex issue. On the one hand, the context imposes new criteria, groups, and people to be compared with. On the other hand, it is difficult to know which identities and which dimensions will become important for self-evaluation. In order to understand how people and groups will position themselves, we need to conduct research in such a way that it gives us a clear picture of the context, the shared understandings and norms, and the factors that might differentiate these understandings. One of the issues that we need to investigate is what are the possible threats to people's identity arising from their migration and from being members of a non-dominant cultural group.

Threatened identities

Psychological threat with regard to identity is an issue that has attracted the attention of social psychologists. The concept of threat is used very often without clarification, but I believe we can identify two types of identity threat. The first type relates to self-evaluation. It occurs when – for whatever reason – people have no positive feelings about one or more of their self-descriptions or self-categorizations. The second type occurs when the way people perceive themselves is disrupted by changes in life which demand accommodation and a reevaluation of self. The first type of threat has been a core issue for social identity theory (TS3); the second type concerns identity process theory (TS4). Both theories assume that when one's identity is threatened one will engage in a series of coping strategies to eliminate the threat.

Drawing upon social identity theory (SIT), we can hypothesize that being a member of a non-dominant cultural group will threaten an individual's identities and will lead them to engage in a series of strategies for coping. They will either adopt a strategy for individual mobility and try to enhance their own position, or they will engage in strategies of social change in order to ameliorate the position of the whole group to which they belong. SIT is particularly interested in those identities that are linked to membership of social groups and categories. Thus, ethnic, religious, and national memberships, as well as being an immigrant, a refugee, an asylum seeker – in general, a member of a non-dominant cultural group – are of particular interest to those who work within this theoretical framework. The focus of their research will be to evaluate the salience of these identities for people's self-description, to measure the value they attribute to them, and to assess the consequences of people's identifications for inter-group relations and social change. The underlying assumption of this theoretical framework is that in order to avoid the psychological consequences of negatively evaluated identities, people will engage in particular actions that can trigger inter-group conflict. Thus, the social psychological processes involved in the choice of strategies to overcome a negatively evaluated social position can help us understand how people perceive the relationships between groups in a particular context and what are the consequences of these perceptions for social change. Later in this book we will discuss these strategies in relation to acculturation.

Drawing upon Identity Process Theory, it is possible to see the change that accultur-ation implies as a major threat to one's identity. People have to deal with this change, accommodate it in the way they perceive themselves, and reconstruct a sense of self that is no longer threatened. Timotijevic and Breakwell (2000) (panel 1.3) looked at how refugees in Britain from the former Yugoslavia dealt with this major change in their lives and the threat that it represented.

Panel 1.3   Migration and Threat to Identity (Timotijevic and Breakwell 2000)

Research question

The study set out to investigate the identity threats to those people from the former Yugoslavia who moved to Britain following the war in their country. These people are in an extreme situation because the country of which they were citizens ceased to exist as a result of the war. As well as leaving behind familiar places, possessions, friends, and family, these people have no homeland to which to return and have experienced the devastating consequences of war. They faced major changes in their lives. Under these conditions, how do migrants experience threat? What attempts do they make to adapt to enduring change?

Theoretical framework

Identity process theory (TS4)

Method

In-depth interviews analyzed with interpretative phenomenological analysis (see Smith, Osborn, and Jarman 1999; Willig 2001).

Participants: 24 people from Bosnia, Serbia, and Croatia were interviewed in the London and Birmingham areas.

The *interview schedule* included questions about people's decisions to move, perceptions of the receiving country and the native country, interactions with the

British and the ethnic community, and perceptions of the receiving community concerning the home country and life-satisfaction.

Results

Three major themes emerged from the analysis:

Attribution of responsibility and claims of self-efficacy
- Their exile, due to a major conflict, and the disappearance of their homeland made people feel helpless and threatened their self-efficacy and self-esteem.
- Being able to attribute the responsibility for the conflict to external causes was a major issue that helped participants to regain self-efficacy and self-esteem.
- Going through this situation increased their self-worth and made them feel more independent.

Category negotiation to achieve continuity and self-esteem
- The conflict challenged the boundaries and the meaning attributed to different categories such as "Yugoslav," "Croatian," "Serb," "Bosnian," etc. People have to renegotiate their national/ethnic identities, what the categories mean, and how they apply them in order to maintain a sense of continuity. The analysis showed that people have different ways to restore a threatened sense of continuity.

Categories and distinctiveness
- A major issue for participants was how to position themselves in Britain. Who are they? Different labels could apply to them: foreigner, immigrant, refugee, guest, etc. These categories are associated with meanings, some of which are linked to prejudice. How should they refer to themselves in the new situation? New identities need assimilation–accommodation.
- People may feel too distinctive or not distinctive enough. The fact that they are a minority may heighten their distinctiveness, or they may experience a loss of distinctiveness when they are lumped together in an over-inclusive category (e.g., refugees, immigrants) that masks individual differences and experiences. How should they restore optimal levels of distinctiveness? (See chapter 4 on optimal distinctiveness theory.)
- The use of categories to describe themselves revealed the acculturation strategy (marginalization, separation, etc.) that participants used (see panel V).

General discussion

This research shows the impact of violent and unpredictable events on identity. The threat that these people experience seems to be chronic and demands constant restructuring of their identities. Participants negotiated the meaning of identity categories at an individual level to establish continuity at an inter-individual and intergroup level, to respond to distinctiveness requirements, and to balance relationships with the receiving society and their ethnic group, in order to regain self-efficacy and self-esteem.

Definition of values

An enduring belief that a specific mode of conduct or endstate of existence is personally and socially preferable to alternative modes of conduct or endstates of existence. Values, once internalized, are standards for guiding action and as standards are employed to influence values, attitudes, and actions of others.

(Rokeach 1968: 160)

Values are desirable transsituational goals, varying in importance, that serve as guiding principles in people's lives.

(Schwartz 1996: 20; see also TS5)

Values are cognitive social representations of basic motivational goals, varying in importance, which serve as guiding principles in people's lives.

(Roccas and Brewer 2002: 98)

We have discussed here the different threats that people's identities face in a culturally diverse environment. An unfamiliar environment can also pose another type of threat: the challenge that it represents to people's beliefs and values.

Transmitting and Retaining One's Cultural Values, and Challenges to Perceptions of the World and of the Self

Challenges to the transmission of values and culture reproduction in culturally diverse environments

In the introduction we discussed the question of retaining one's original culture in relation to strategies of acculturation. Here we are interested in the challenges that culturally diverse environments pose to cultural reproduction. Cultures reproduce themselves by transmitting core values and beliefs from generation to generation.

Children are socialized within these value systems and parents and schools are the primary channels for this communication. However, in multicultural environments there might be conflicts between a family's values and the values promoted by institutional education. Young people are sometimes caught between their family's values, practices, and expectations and the values of the wider society. Similarly, parents might see a conflict between their own values and the ones that are required in order to get on in the new environment. This conflict can increase the intergenerational gap that normally exists between people and their offspring. Does migration influence value discrepancies between generations beyond intergenerational effects?

Knafo and Schwartz (2001) (panel 1.4) looked at how immigration impacts on the value transmission process, at value similarity, and how consistent parental messages appear to be in Soviet-born families that recently migrated to Israel, compared to Israeli-born adolescents and their families.

Panel 1.4   Value Socialization in Families of Israeli-born and Soviet-born Adolescents in Israel (Knafo and Schwartz 2001)

Research question

This research concerns the processes of value transmission in immigrant families. An underlying assumption is that children of these families may receive conflicting messages from their parents and the social environment. The situation of acculturation may affect the values that the parents transmit to their children, the values that the children perceive from their parents and how consistent they are with parents' behaviours, and the extent to which children accept these values. Also, research needs to take into account the possibility that the higher similarity between immigrant children's values and their non-immigrant peers than the value similarity with their parents may reflect a generation effect.

The research aimed to assess perceptions of value consistency, acceptance, and similarity of values with parents among immigrant and non-immigrant families.

Theoretical framework

Theory of integrated value systems (TS5)

Method

Participants: Soviet-born immigrant adolescents and at least one of their parents; Israeli-born adolescents and at least one of their parents.

Materials: A battery of questionnaires administered by a researcher who visited the family following their agreement. The measures included the value portraits questionnaire.

Results

- Independently, immigrant-status parents valued more conservation and self-transcendence values than their children, while children valued more openness to change and self-enhancement values than their parents.
- Immigrant children where more similar to their native-born peers on conservation and on openness to change values than they were to their parents. This might be a generational effect.
- However, beyond generational effects it seems that immigration increases the distance between adolescents and their parents. The difference between immigrant children and their parents was greater than the difference between native-born children and their parents on openness to change and conservation values.
- Immigrant children perceived a greater inconsistency in their parents' values over time and between what the parents said and what they did.
- Although there were differences between parents and children when the researchers compared them in groups, these differences disappeared when the comparison looked at the differences between parents and children taking them as dyads within a family.

General discussion

This research highlights the fact that immigration affects the process of value transmission in some areas and not in others. Perhaps the impact is on values

(Continues)

Panel 1.4   (*Continued*)

that are related to the immigration experience, such as openness to change. However, when we look at within-family value priorities the similarity between parents and children seems unaffected, in the sense, for example, that more conservative parents tend to have more conservative children. This can be explained by the fact that immigration affects both parents and children in the same direction, and although we can observe a gap at a group level this gap disappears at a family level.

The context of Knafo and Schwartz's study is interesting because both groups share a culture based on a common religion and live in a country where religious affiliation is important for self-definition and everyday interaction. There are also other factors that might influence intergenerational value transmission in multicultural environments. Phalet and Schönpflug (2001), for example, compared Turkish families in Germany with Turkish and Moroccan families in the Netherlands. They found that, after controlling for educational status and gender, parental values are selectively transmitted in different acculturation contexts and that transmission depends on parental goals such as conformity, autonomy, and achievement. In addition, the intensity of transmission varied across ethnic groups (more intense in Turkish than in Moroccan groups) and across receiving societies (more intense in Germany than in the Netherlands). To explain their results, Phalet and Schönpflug suggest that parents would feel less motivated to pass on their values in societies where they feel secure in their access to social rights and services, as in the Netherlands. Perceptions about the openness of the receiving society can influence the strategies of acculturation of immigrant groups through the process of value transmission. The structures of the receiving society, however, are not the only factors that explain variation among ethnic groups in relation to values transmission. Nauck (2001) compared the value transmission process of five different groups of migrant families (Turks, Greeks, and Italians in Germany, German repatriates from Russia, and Jewish immigrants from Russia to Israel). He found considerable variation among ethnic groups within the same environment regarding values transmission and their willingness to retain their original culture. His results indicate that the Turkish families in Germany, the German repatriates, and the Russian Israelis live in peaceful but segregated coexistence with the majority. In addition, the intensified social contacts between Italian and Greek families and members of the receiving society do not necessarily lead to more assimilation and the abandonment of original cultures. An important factor that seemed to influence this process was the educational level of the parents. However, contrary to what is the case for native populations, the educational level of the parents did not seem to influence their children's success in school, but the degree to which the original culture was maintained. Contrary to expectation, the higher the parental educational level, the more it was likely that the family's original language would be retained. These results demonstrate the complexity of the process of value transmission and retention in acculturation contexts. The migration history of a group, its position within the social structure of the receiving society, and its history of relations with the majority are probably factors that interact with the educational level of the family and impact on acculturation. We can only think of general acculturation patterns and then research their applicability to different cultural groups, in different contexts.

We have seen the types of conflicts that can arise *within* migrant groups in relation to values. Another type of conflict that can occur is between minority and majority cultures. Whose cultural values are "better"? We have seen that groups "fight" symbolically to establish the value dimensions according to which everybody is supposed to compare themselves for self-evaluation (TS2). Young Asians and their families in Britain may blame British culture for having lost its family values and for the drinking habits that it promotes. On the other hand, British families may denounce the practice of arranged marriage that exists in some Asian communities. The British film *East is East* (1999) brilliantly reflects the value conflicts that young people of Asian origin face in Britain in relation to dominant cultural values. There are also conflicts that become serious societal issues. The situation of young Muslim girls in France, whose wearing of the veil in school was perceived as ostentatious and led to their expulsion, involved a serious conflict of values that compromised the education of women, trapped between family and societal values. Another example of serious conflict is the issue of female genital mutilation performed in some cultures, which is putting the health and future development of young girls at risk. These practices are unacceptable in Western societies, not only for health reasons, but also because of the position that they imply for women.

In conclusion, conflicts of values between generations within non-dominant cultural groups can intensify the difficulties of acculturation both for parents and young people. The consequences of value conflicts between different cultural groups will be discussed later in the book, in connection with the processes involved in intergroup relations. Non-dominant cultural groups also face challenges to the way they see social relationships and the way they perceive themselves.

Challenges to cultural orientations, self-perceptions, and representations of the collective

It has been suggested that entire cultures can be characterized by their value orientations (Hofstede 1980; Schwartz 1990, 1992, 1994; Triandis 1989; Triandis et al. 1988). Following Hofstede's (1980) work, cultures have been popularly distinguished in terms of individualism and collectivism (TS6). These orientations characterize relationships between individuals and the social environment, and promote different sets of values and practices. However, as Coon and Kemmelmeier (2001) (panel 1.5) point out, we should not ignore the variability that can exist within cultures in multicultural societies.

One of the consequences of being socialized in an individualistic or collectivistic oriented culture is the way people construct "who they are (panel 1.6)"

Panel 1.5 Cultural Orientations in the United States: (Re)examining Differences Among Ethnic Groups (Coon and Kemmelmeier 2001)

Research question

The authors highlight the importance of within-culture variability in individualism and collectivism and take issue with the assumption that ethnic groups' cultural orientation matches the orientation of the culture of origin. Ethnic groups are cultural minorities that have a different history and relations with the majority, different aspirations, and a different position in society. Thus, individualism and collectivism might be manifested differently among ethnic groups. This research aimed to examine levels of individualism and collectivism among ethnic groups in the United States.

Theoretical framework

Crosscultural research on cultural orientations (see TS6)

Method

Participants: Undergraduate students in the US who described themselves as European Americans, African Americans, Latino Americans, or Asian Americans.

Materials: Questionnaire including different scales of individualism/collectivism (Singelis 1994; Triandis 1995; Oyserman, Coon, and Kemmelmeier 2002).

Results

Using meta-analytic techniques the authors found:

- African Americans scored higher on individualism than European and Asian Americans.
- There were no gender differences on individualism.
- African Americans and Asian Americans scored higher on collectivism compared to European Americans, whereas Latino Americans did not differ from any other group and any differences were stronger for men.
- The low reliability of the collectivism scale for African Americans raises the question as to whether the notion of collectivism, as devised by researchers, applies to this group.

General discussion

This research raises some important questions. First of all, by definition, multicultural societies cannot be monolithic in terms of cultural orientation and it would be wrong to ignore within-culture differences. Secondly, it will be equally problematic to assume that ethnic groups endorse the cultural orientation of their society of origin. It is possible that levels of individualism and collectivism change as a factor of the unique experience of each group and its relations to the majority, and the strategies that group members adopt in order to acculturate and ameliorate their position. Another important factor in changing cultural orientations is the impact of the dominant orientation and the normative character that this orientation has due to its powerful position. Thirdly, the study highlights the need to reexamine the content of the concepts of individualism and collectivism by looking at the meaning these concepts have for different groups.

Panel 1.6   Culture and the Self

Social psychologists believe that an important factor influencing the cognitions, emotions, and behavior of individuals is how people perceive and feel about themselves. Markus and Kitayama (1991) and others (Cousins 1989; Laungani 1999) have argued that different types of cultures (individualistic or collectivistic) influence the way people construct the self. These different constructions impact on people's cognitions, emotions, motivations, and behavior.

In *individualistic* cultures that emphasize individual differences, that reward personal goals and achievements, and where social relationships are mainly characterized by competition (TS6), people see themselves as *unique* individuals, *separate* from others. These cultures favor an *independent self.*

In *collectivistic* cultures that emphasize positions and roles, that reward compliance with cultural norms, and where social relationships are mainly characterized by cooperation (TS6), people see themselves as *related to others* and *close to their group*. These cultures favor an *interdependent self.*

Markus, Mullally, and Kitayama (1997) describe the relationship between cultural orientations and the self as "patterns of cultural participation" and "selfways": characteristic ways of being a person in the world, as different representations of personhood.

However, although research has confirmed that individualistically oriented and collectivistically oriented cultures give rise to different ways of constructing the self, this clearcut definition of the self – and more importantly a deterministic approach to the relationship between cultural imperatives and self-construction – has been challenged.

There is evidence from within-culture research that individuals vary in their degree of individualism and collectivism (Coon and Kemmelmeier 2001; Green-Staerklé 2002; Oyserman 1993; Triandis 1994; Watkins et al. 1998). Furthermore, Cross, Bacon, and Morris (2000) argue that being interdependent means different things for people living in individualistic or collectivistic cultures. In a recent theoretical development (Vignoles, Chryssochoou, and Breakwell 2000) we also argue that identity principles such as distinctiveness might not be a characteristic

(Continues)

Panel 1.6   (*Continued*)

exclusively of individualistic cultures; rather, people draw their distinctiveness from different sources in accordance with cultural imperatives.

I would agree with Green-Staerklé (2002) when she concludes that "individualism and collectivism might not be expressions of psychological characteristics of members of national groups, but these dimensions express normative, collective, and societal imperatives from which people develop strategies of self-presentation and evaluation."

The way we perceive ourselves is linked to the culture in which we are socialized and is an important point in our discussion about cultural diversity. It means that who we think we are influences how we see the world; at the same time, how we see the world influences how we see ourselves.

This idea has both theoretical and practical consequences. At a theoretical level, it means that the social structure and the psychological organization of individuals are connected. If we accept that identity is the psychological structure that reflects social relationships at an individual level, I would argue, along with others, that knowledge about ourselves might be constructed through the processes of social representations (TS1). In other words, the cultural regulations and orientations that operate at the level of the meta-system, influence how our selves are organized.

At a practical level, this means that people in culturally diverse environments might have different ways of perceiving social relationships and different ways of positioning themselves in relation to them. Groups of people might disagree in their expectations about how relationships are regulated. The social structure might encourage different perceptions of those relationships and might emphasize different models of personhood. Thus, people's cultural orientations might provide them with different understandings of social relationships, of where they themselves stand and how they are expected to behave. Interviewed on a television program about marriage, a 10-year-old British Muslim said that he would like to make his parents proud of him by accepting the wife that they will choose for him, but he wasn't sure if he would like her or not. His relationship with his parents seemed more important to him than his relationship with his future spouse. He seemed to see his role and position as a son as more important in guiding his choices. This might appear strange to another culture. These perceptions reflect different "theories" about the world.

Cultural diversity is neither new nor problematic in itself. The "problem" (if it is a problem) is that people tend to think that conflicting approaches are harmful. As social psychologists have argued, divergence can be the source of creativity and innovation (see TS17 on minority influence) and blind agreement can lead to destructive decisions (see panel 4.2 on groupthink and blind patriotism). The questions we need to ask ourselves are about how these views of ourselves and the world are constructed, how they become shared in order to enable communication, what is the content of the worldviews they reflect, and what are their consequences for societal cohesion and change. These questions are not new, but they have become crucial for multicultural societies.

Culturally diverse environments bring to the fore the fact that different representations of the collective exist. These representations organize the way we form relationships with objects and people. Individualist and collectivist cultural orientations probably mean that different forms of societal organization are reflected in the cultural goals of societies. An analysis of interviews conducted with women in Britain and Japan (Kuwahara and Chryssochoou 2002) showed that, although Britain is considered an individualistic society, people described it as characterized by class divisions that ascribe status to people and determine their relationships, loyalties, identities, and opportunities for success. On the other hand, participants described Japan – usually thought of as a collectivistic society – as characterized by a powerful division between the public and private spheres. Individuality was very much valued by the Japanese respondents, although they are only "allowed" to display it within the private sphere. They believe, however, that this situation is changing because of alterations in the economic system. It seems that the way society is organized is reflected in cultural imperatives and in representations of the collective.

Some researchers consider that these representations of the collective are **universal and linked to human evolution** (Fiske 1991, 1992).

Others have focused on understanding the consequences of these representations for power relations within a given society (Lorenzi-Cioldi 1988, 1995). Of particular interest for us here are representations of groups as collections or aggregates, which reflect a different priority for relationships and are clearly associated with different levels of power. Lorenzi-Cioldi's research deals mainly with gender relationships. He suggests that powerful groups, at least within Western societies, are represented as a **collection** of individuals and prioritize interpersonal relationships between equal and free individuals. Groups that are powerless in a given society are more often described as an **aggregate** of interchangeable individuals who favor interactions as group members.

Thus, powerful groups are described as variable and powerless groups as homogeneous. For the student of cultural diversity, Lorenzi-Cioldi's suggestion has an important implication for individualism/collectivism. We need to ask ourselves if describing societies as collectivistic – in other words as societies that give priority to group encounters – assigns them a less powerful position than our own societies, which are characterized by individualism and, therefore, by variability and distinctiveness. As we have seen, cultural orientations and representations of the collective are of extreme importance for self-definition and social interaction.

From the perspective of non-dominant cultural groups the issue is crucial. These people are in a numerical minority and their minority status can be aggravated by the poor material conditions in which they live. Furthermore, because of this minority status, their cultural practices are challenged. On top of all this, their cultural orientation might confine them *symbolically* in a powerless position because they are

Relational theory

Relational theory suggests that there are four different types of models used in every culture to give meaning to social interactions. These models describe social relationships and are used as cognitive schemata:

Communal sharing
Authority ranking
Equality matching
Market pricing

To find out more, see Fiske et al. (1998).

Western representations of groups in relation to their power

The *dominant* groups are represented as a collection of individuals, with their own specificity. *The non-dominant* groups are represented as aggregates of individuals that are undifferentiated.

(Lorenzi-Cioldi 1988)

represented as interchangeable members of homogeneous groups, a representation that describes the powerless.

We have discussed here the challenges that members of non-dominant cultural groups face in relation to the acculturation process, how they manage change and unfamiliarity, how they evaluate their status, what are the threats to their identity and the challenges to their values and self-knowledge. In the next section I discuss how members of non-dominant cultural groups deal with issues of power, social mobility, and discrimination.

Becoming a Member of the "New Society": Dealing with Devalued/Minority Identities, Prejudice, and Discrimination

As already discussed, moving into a new society requires a reevaluation of the self and a repositioning within the new environment. However, this reevaluation is not the unilateral decision of the newcomer. It is obvious that the receiving society's evaluations and perceptions play a crucial role in determining the opportunities that are open to newcomers and to minority members. Let's examine the social psychological aspects of being a minority for members of non-dominant cultural groups.

By being in a minority position within the wider society, immigrants and other non-dominant cultural groups can develop a minority identity. This identity is based on their cultural difference. It is important to keep in mind that such minority identities can be sources of pride and mobilization for their members (Hutnik 1991). For example, French Canadians and Scots, even if they are cultural minorities where they live, often display pride in their identity and show their determination to protect their difference and resist homogenization. However, minority identities are often (but not necessarily) devalued. Being part of a devalued group reflects the position of the group on a socioeconomic scale and within a symbolic hierarchy of cultures. Throughout history groups have attempted to negotiate positions in a hierarchy of cultures and delineate the boundaries of civilization. Ancient Greeks, for example, claimed that whoever was not Greek (in terms of culture) was a barbarian. Today, there is a symbolic (sometimes more than symbolic) conflict between Christianity and Islam, and Muslims who live in countries with a Christian majority are often put in the difficult position of having to prove that their culture is civilized rather than barbarous. Immigrants are often viewed by members of the receiving society as "scroungers" who have come to benefit from available resources and not to contribute. The constant reminder that one belongs to a devalued group can have serious psychological consequences.

What are the psychological consequences of being a member of a devalued group? Research on stigma by Crocker, Major, and Steele (1998) provides some insights. First of all, members of a devalued group have to deal with this issue on a daily basis. Even when they

Attributional ambiguity

Ambiguity may characterize the attribution of causes to outcomes for stigmatized individuals because stigma may provide a framework for interpreting events in their life. When outcomes are determined or influenced by other people (prejudiced or not), stigmatized individuals may be ambiguous whether the outcome was due to their personal qualities or by reactions to their stigmatized status.

(Crocker, Major, and Steele 1998)

perform everyday tasks they might be reminded that they belong to a group that is not highly regarded in society. As Swim, Cohen, and Hyers (1998) remark, people's reactions to such situations can range from passivity and psychological withdrawal to a total separation from society. This is how members of non-dominant cultural groups can become progressively marginalized.

Dealing on a daily basis with a devalued identity may lead people to become oversensitive to the behavior of others and to how they are treated. Is the empty seat next to them on the train empty because nobody wants to sit beside them? Did they get their job through merit or because of a policy of positive discrimination? Attributing causes to events with certainty is a powerful need in all of us (TS7). When people with devalued identities try to explain others' behavior toward them they may not feel confident about their explanations. This phenomenon of **attributional ambiguity** (Crocker and Major 1989) can create problems in relationships and everyday interactions, and make people sensitive to rejection.

Rejection sensitivity

The disposition to anxiously expect, readily perceive, and overreact to rejection.

(Downey et al. 1998: 545)

When people assume they will be rejected it can prevent them from seeking interactions and fully taking part in society. Furthermore, as research into close relationships has shown (Ayduk et al. 2000; Downey et al. 1998), **rejection sensitivity** can operate as a **self-fulfilling prophecy**. Anxious people who expect to be rejected can act in aversive ways and generate reactions that confirm their initial expectations of being rejected.

Self-fulfilling prophecy

When beliefs and expectations about a situation or a person influence social interactions in a way that the outcomes or behaviors end up confirming the initial expectations.

Similarly, people belonging to devalued groups might experience stereotype threat.

Devalued identities are associated with a set of negative stereotypical beliefs about abilities, characteristics, and behaviors. People in non-dominant cultural groups are aware of these stereotypes and might be afraid that their behavior will confirm them. Anxiety about confirming a stereotype can have disruptive effects on the way people behave and become a self-fulfilling prophecy. In a series of studies, Steele and Aronson (1995) have shown that stereotype threat, when it refers to important dimensions

Stereotype threat

Is being at risk of confirming, as self-characteristic, a negative stereotype about one's group.

(Steele and Aronson 1995)

such as intellectual ability, can psychologically disrupt members of devalued groups to such an extent that it actually impairs their performance. Thus, African-American students under conditions that can generate stereotype threat in relation to intellectual ability (they were told that a test was diagnostic of intellectual ability) suppressed their performance in comparison to white participants. Under conditions where the threat was minimized they performed equally well or better than whites. Such research has shown that activation of a racial stereotype interferes with performance. Furthermore, activation of the stereotype is easily achieved. A simple question asking people to record their racial membership is enough to make the stereotype salient. Thus, the existence of negative stereotypes about a group may lead to behaviors that confirm those stereotypes (Crocker, Major, and Steele 1998).

Stereotype threat, fear of rejection, and avoidance of situations where the devalued identity is made salient can push people to disengage from a particular domain as a response to chronic threat. Major (1995; reported in Crocker, Major, and Steele 1998) found that the less African-American students reported to be engaged with academic performance and the less they valued doing well at school, the lower their actual grades were. This is not surprising. To succeed, one needs to be motivated and to think that the goal is worth pursuing. If members of devalued groups, aware of negative stereotypes, attempt to protect themselves from stereotype threat and possible rejection by disengaging from school and academic performance, they will underperform. As individuals, they then run the risk of being left behind in the educational system; as a collective, they feed the stereotypes about the inability of their group. We see here social psychological factors that interact with social conditions to impair people's development. It seems that people from cultural minorities who disidentify with the society in which they live can end up separating from it, becoming marginalized and prevented from making any valuable contribution.

Following social identity theory (TS3), awareness that one's social identity is devalued threatens self-evaluation both at a personal and at a collective level (Tajfel 1974, 1978, 1981; Tajfel and Turner 1986). When a devalued identity is conferred upon them, people engage in strategies to protect this part of the self that is attached to their social memberships (panel 1.7).

Panel 1.7   Social Identity Theory and Strategies for Coping with Devalued Identity

Social identity theory (see TS3) holds that individual or collective behavior depends on people's belief systems. When faced with a devalued social identity, those people who believe in the *permeability* of boundaries between groups (*social mobility belief system*) will choose a strategy of *individual mobility*. In other words, they will try to improve their status by becoming a member of the high-status group. The high-status group may encourage this strategy at a small scale for many reasons:

- By allowing some "passing," the high-status group provides evidence that it is doing something for members of the unprivileged group. Consequently, larger-scale efforts can be avoided.
- Members of the low-status group who pass into the higher-status group can serve as examples to prove that the boundaries between groups are open and that passing is possible. Consequently, structural conditions can remain unchanged.
- By promoting individual mobility belief systems, the high-status group "individualizes" the members of the deprived group and avoids overt conflict between groups.

Those members of devalued groups who succeed in passing into the higher group enhance their social identity. However, conditions for the group as a whole remain the same. For those who fail in their attempts at individual mobility, there is a high risk of marginalization: they may be unable to revert to their previous membership, either because they psychologically disidentify with it or because they are no longer welcomed by those they attempted to leave behind.

For those people who believe that the boundaries between groups are *imperme-able* (*social change belief system*) the choice of strategy to overcome a devalued identity depends also on the other perceptions of the structural social conditions. If they believe that the status asymmetries between groups are legitimate and that the situation will not change (stability), people are more likely to choose from among the strategies of *social creativity*. These strategies can make people feel better, but they do not change in the short term the sociostructural conditions that produce the status asymmetries between groups. These strategies include:

- *Finding new dimensions of comparison.* If the group is devalued in specific dimensions, members of the group might try to introduce other dimensions within which their group can be evaluated as being better. This strategy, if consistent, might change the social context in the long term by introducing new perspectives. Research on minority influence has shown how consistent minorities can bring change.
- *Redefining the value of the existing dimension of comparison.* For example, the movement "Black is beautiful" tried to change the perceptions associated with black skin and the black culture.
- *Abandoning the comparison with the high-status groups and looking for lower-status outgroups for comparison.* The high-status group may encourage this strategy because it serves the purpose of "divide and rule."

When people with a social change belief system perceive the asymmetric relations between groups as *illegitimate* and foresee *possibilities of change* (instability) they are likely to engage in *strategies of social competition*. These strategies might take normative forms such as civil rights activities and political lobbying, or non-normative forms such as terrorism, revolution, or war. If successful, these strategies are likely to change the social order and the relationships between groups.

However, it is important to keep in mind that the choice of strategy is not solely a matter of individual preference. It also depends on the belief systems of dominant *and* non-dominant groups, perceptions of the permeability of boundaries between groups, and the perceived legitimacy and stability of their relationship. Further-more, the choice depends on the personal status of the ingroup member, and the extent to which they identify with the ingroup.

According to the theory, immigrants and ethnic minority members faced with a devalued identity might try the following two options. Let's look at them in relation to the acculturation strategies discussed in the introduction.

A member of a non-dominant cultural group might opt for an individual mobility strategy if he or she believes that the boundaries between the groups are open. However, what do "open boundaries" mean in the case of culturally diverse societies?

They might mean that people could become full cultural members of the receiving society, leaving aside their cultural origins: in this case individual mobility would equate with a strategy of assimilation. They might mean that people have the chance to become citizens (with citizens' rights and duties) of the receiving society independently of their membership of a different cultural group and without having to abandon their culture: in this case a strategy of individual mobility becomes a strategy of integration. Thus, the same belief in the permeability of boundaries between groups might be interpreted in the first case as presupposing the abandoning of one's cultural origins, whereas in the second case this assumption is not made.

Furthermore, as we can see in panel 1.8, immigrants and receiving society members might have different ideas about whether assimilation or integration is preferrable.

If members of non-dominant cultural groups believe that the boundaries between groups are closed, they might engage in strategies of social creativity or social

---

Panel 1.8   Attitudes of Minority and Majority Members Towards Adaptation of Immigrants (Van Oudenhoven, Prins, and Buunk 1998)

Research questions

What do majority and minority group members think about the ideal form of adaptation? What kind of adaptation do Moroccans and Turks living in the Netherlands prefer? How does the Dutch majority evaluate the several forms of adaptation that Moroccan and Turkish immigrants may choose?

Theoretical framework

Berry's strategies of acculturation.

The immigrants

Most immigrants feel the need to have contact with the majority group, because this can help them to master their new environment.

Hypotheses
- Moroccans and Turks will be more positive toward integration and assimilation than toward separation and marginalization.
- Moroccans and Turks will have a preference for the integration strategy.

The receiving society

Majority group members like the fact that immigrants are inclined to seek contact with them. Dutch majority members would prefer them not to adhere to their own cultures, but to attempt to adapt to Dutch culture.

Hypotheses
- Majority group members would prefer assimilation and integration to marginalization and separation.
- Majority group members would prefer assimilation and marginalization to integration and separation.
- Assimilation would be liked most and separation least.

Method

Participants: 32 women and 62 men of Moroccan origin and 72 women and 131 men of Turkish origin, plus a representative sample of the Dutch population (N = 1844).

Material: Four different stories depicting a Moroccan or Turkish immigrant in the Netherlands (male or female to match the participant's gender) and providing information about the acculturation strategies of this character were presented to participants (each participant read only one story). Each story corresponded to one of the acculturation strategies (integration, assimilation, separation, marginalization). Immigrant participants were asked to specify whether they *identified with the character* whereas Dutch participants were asked to *estimate the percentage* of Turks and Moroccans in the Netherlands *who would behave like this character*. All participants were asked whether they liked the central character (affective responses) and whether other Moroccans/Turks in the Netherlands should behave in the same way (normative responses).

Results

The immigrants: The immigrant population in general showed more appreciation for integration. If the character in the story was described as having a considerable amount of contact with the Dutch and as considering his or her culture as being important, the participants:

- identified themselves more strongly with that person;
- felt more positively about that person;
- felt more strongly that Moroccans or Turks should behave like that person.

The receiving society: Respondents estimated that:

- The percentage of Turks/Moroccans who would like to maintain their culture was higher compared to those who did not. However, they had less positive feelings toward such a person and thought that other immigrants should not behave that way.
- The percentage of immigrants who have a great amount of contact with the Dutch was low. They felt more positively toward the story character that had greater contact with the Dutch and thought that other Turks/Moroccans should behave that way.

(Continues)

Panel 1.8 (*Continued*)

Thus, those adaptation forms that imply almost no contact with the majority are assumed to occur most often. However, minority members are evaluated more positively when they do not consider their original culture as important (assimilation).

General discussion

The main results of this study are that Turkish and Moroccan immigrants in the Netherlands prefer integration, whereas for the Dutch majority the most valued strategy is assimilation (although they also value integration). It is important for the majority that immigrants strive for contact and show appreciation and respect for their values.

There is a discrepancy between immigrant and receiving society's attitudes towards acculturation.

competition. Adopting a social creativity strategy might mean that people follow a policy of integration if they try to find new dimensions of comparison or change the values of the existing dimension. However, if their strategy is to select another out-group for comparison, they might already be in the process of separating themselves from the majority. In addition, separation is clearly the strategy of those belonging to non-dominant cultural groups who have chosen a strategy of social competition. There has been considerable debate, for example, within the Muslim community in Britain as to whether members should take active part in the public sphere of the country or live separate lives (Hopkins and Kahani-Hopkins in press).

As we have already seen, choosing one or another path of acculturation is not a matter of individual decision. Thus, dealing with a devalued identity is not a clear individual choice and every strategy has psychological consequences. Is it easy to change group membership? Research has focused mainly on the reactions of the dominant group towards those who choose to join it. Regardless of whether the strategy is accepted by the dominant group, the choice has psychological, symbolic, and material consequences for the person concerned. For example, those who express a wish to leave their group and join the culturally dominant group might be considered as renegades (Chryssochoou and Sanchez-Mazas 2000), or they might be marginalized and rejected by both communities. A Vietnamese student who has lived in Britain since the age of five said that her community regarded her as a "banana": yellow outside and white inside. She couldn't find her place in either the British or the Vietnamese community. At an individual level, it can be psychologically difficult to juggle with these considerations and find a place in society.

In an interesting field study within the framework of SIT, Blanz, Mummendey, Mielke, and Klink (1998) produced a taxonomy of the strategies that East Germans used in order to confront a devalued identity following the reunification of Germany. They suggest that strategies can be classified along two dimensions. The first dimension categorizes strategies according to whether they aim to (a) change the relationship between groups, leaving the groups unchanged; (b) change the object of the comparison (not entering, or avoiding comparison with, the dominant group); or (c) change the groups (altering the boundaries of the groups, or assimilating). The second dimension categorizes the strategies as either behavioral or cognitive. These suggestions comprise a useful tool for research in the area and their own research has cast some light on the meaning that the strategies have for members of devalued groups. However, the authors take care to point out that their research is based on a sample (East Germans) in a particular socio-historical context. This context is characterized by policies and ideological beliefs that influence the way people respond to devalued status. The authors conclude that "future research could also focus on whether strategies of the various response clusters might be predicted differently by variables such as the perceived legitimacy of the status inequal-ity, the degree of ingroup identification or the preference for a specific comparison object or comparison dimension" (ibid: 723). In other words, each multicultural context, each ethnic group, and the history of the relationship with the dominant group, might influence people's perceptions and thus their actions.

In order to predict the pattern of strategies that devalued group members will adopt, we need to understand how people make sense of their specific situation. Do they believe that the boundaries between groups are permeable? Is the relationship between groups legitimate? Will this relationship change in the future? These cognitive percep-tions are influenced by people's understanding of sociohistorical factors (the regula-tions at the level of the meta-system: see TS1). Actions arise from the interaction between these perceptions and the relative importance of particular groups for people's sense of identity. As research has shown for other low-status groups (Ellemers, Spears, and Doosje 1999), immigrants and ethnic minority members can respond to the threat of devalued identity by strengthening their identification with their cultural group (Phinney 1990). This can lead to a strategy of separation from the cultural environment of the receiving society. The level of identification with one's group, along with perceptions of factors that characterize the social context (such as permeability, stability, and legitimacy), guide people's choices of strategies in order to cope with a devalued identity (Branscombe and Ellemers 1998; Ellemers 1993; Lalonde and Cam-eron 1993) and impacts on their acculturation patterns.

Up till now we have discussed the consequences of a devalued identity and the strategies for coping with it. However, it is not just the consequences for people's identity but also the material and symbolic power issues that affect the condition of minority groups. Being in a minority might make salient issues of resource distribution between members of different groups; it might mean different opportunities for development and success; and it might produce feelings of resent-ment. In particular, members of minority groups may feel relatively deprived. Relative deprivation (TS8) is the feeling people have when they perceive a discrepancy between what they possess and what they believe they deserve and should be able to obtain. This feeling is the outcome of comparisons (TS2) between what one used to have and what one has now, or between what other people or other groups have and is desired. As Pettigrew (2002: 353) observes: "relative deprivation is a model social psychological concept, for it postulates a subjective state that shapes emotions

Reference groups

Groups that are used for social comparison and self-evaluation and that provide individuals with norms or standards. These groups are not necessarily the groups one belongs to.

False consciousness

The holding of false beliefs that sustain one's oppression.

(Cunningham 1987: 255)

System justification

The psychological process by which existing social arrangements are preserved in spite of the obvious psychological and material harm they entail for disadvantaged individuals and groups.

(Jost and Banaji 1994: 10)

Just world theory

According to Lerner (1977, 1980), individuals are motivated to believe that the world is a just and controllable place where people get what they deserve and deserve what they get. Thus, according to this belief, people are responsible for what happens to them and are rewarded for their efforts.

and cognitions and influences behavior." For non-dominant cultural groups and in particular ethnic minorities this issue is vital. Feelings of relative deprivation can arise if people perceive that they do not have the same rights or resources as other citizens, if they feel treated as second-class citizens. This feeling can be a powerful motivation for protest and mobilization if people realize that their group as a whole is deprived (fraternalistic deprivation). Civil rights movements in the US have arisen when the circumstances of the black population improved and people realized that their conditions and opportunities were lower than what they felt they deserved.

It might seem obvious that people will adopt strategies to overcome circumstances in which they are devalued. Sometimes, however, members of non-dominant groups accept their minority position and consider the dominant group to be superior. A seminal study by Clark and Clark (1947) asked 3–7 year-old white and black children to choose between different dolls: the one with which they identified, the one that they found beautiful, and the one they wished to play with. There was a tendency among black children, especially at younger ages, to choose the lighter-colored dolls. In my own research (Chryssochoou 2000b), investigating the construction of European identity, my Greek respondents often considered the category "European" as being a superior group of people, even in terms of IQ. The wealth of Western Europeans led people to make assumptions about the abilities of the group. Some respondents felt that other Europeans might not see the Greeks as part of the category "European." Thus, the more powerful groups manage to position themselves as "models" (Deschamps, Lorenzi-Cioldi, and Meyer 1982) and become **reference groups** (Hyman 1942, 1960; Merton and Lazersfeld 1950) for those who belong to less powerful groups. The **false consciousness** (Jost and Banaji 1994) that some members of minority groups develop legitimizes and **justifies the social system**. Thus, a system of social inequalities can be considered as just, even by those who are suffering (see Jost and Major, 2001, on the psychology of legitimacy).

The need to believe that one lives in a **just world**, in which opportunities are available and one has control over one's life, leads people to accept material, power, and symbolic inequalities even if they are suffering from them (Olson and Hafer 2001).

In such contexts the emphasis is put on individual differences and achievements, in the sense that people's outcomes are linked to their abilities and efforts. Thus, whoever does not achieve success is considered responsible and has only themselves to blame. Self-blame can be a psychological impediment to people perceiving the barriers that the social system places in the way of success. These beliefs are very powerful, at least in Western societies. They function as norms (**norm of internality**) or biases (**fundamental attribution error**) and guide our ways of thinking.

What does make people react to social inequalities? According to Taylor and McKirnan (1984) (TS9), changes in the structural conditions of society influence social psychological factors such as processes of social comparison (TS2) and social attribution (TS7). These processes impact on the perception of intergroup behaviors and on social action. In other words, what happens in society makes people change their targets of comparison when evaluating their own position, so that they attribute responsibility for their condition to different factors. Thus, perceptions about intergroup relations vary. For Taylor and McKirnan, intergroup relations follow five stages. Collective action is expected at the fifth stage when three conditions are present: (a) members of minority groups attribute their condition to the fact that they are discriminated against as a group; (b) members of minority groups evaluate their position using intergroup comparisons; (c) members of minority groups feel that they are responsible for their future and that they can do something about their condition collectively. We can conclude, therefore, that non-dominant cultural groups will fight for civil, social, and political rights when (a) they perceive that they are prevented from becoming full citizens because of their ethnic background; (b) they engage in intergroup comparisons with the dominant cultural group; (c) they feel able to take their future into their own hands. Collective action can take generally acceptable forms (e.g., lobbying, demonstrations, political representations) or non-acceptable forms (e.g., riots, terrorism).

Norm of internality

According to Beauvois and Dubois (1988), people systematically prefer and value internal explanations irrespective of their truthfulness.

Fundamental attribution error

According to the fundamental attribution error (Ross 1977), people underestimate the importance of situational factors in producing behaviors and have a tendency to make internal (dispositional) attributions for others' behaviors (see also TS7).

We have seen that people can accept their minority condition and the beliefs associated with it, or they can engage in strategies to change the situation. According to SIT (TS3), the choice of strategies will depend on the strength of identification with the minority group and the perception of the structural conditions that characterize the relationship between groups. Relative deprivation theory (TS8) has suggested that an important factor in determining the choice of strategies is the feeling of resentment that people have when they believe that they do not get what they deserve. Researchers (panel 1.9) have attempted to clarify when these factors lead to collective or individual strategies.

Panel 1.9   Strategies for Coping with Negative Social Identity: Predictions by Social Identity Theory and Relative Deprivation Theory (Mummendey et al. 1999)

Research question

The study aimed to investigate the power of the theories of social identity and relative deprivation to predict identity management strategies in the case of a negative social identity. A possible integration of the theories was also explored.

(Continues)

Panel 1.9   (*Continued*)

- For *social identity theory*, the authors hypothesized that identification with the ingroup will mediate the effect of sociostructural variables (i.e., legitimacy and stability of the status relationship between groups and perceptions regarding the permeability of boundaries) on identity management strategies.
- For *relative deprivation theory* it was hypothesized that feelings of resentment about one's group position and perceptions of group efficacy would mediate the effects of the outcome of comparison between what the group has and what it feels it deserves (referent outcome), the perceptions of the procedures leading to this outcome (referent instrumentality), and the perceptions of future amelioration on identity management strategies.

Six identity management strategies were identified: individual mobility and recategorization to a higher level corresponded to *individual* strategies; social and realistic competitions were considered as *social change* strategies; preference for temporal comparisons and the reevaluation of the material dimension were presented as *social creativity* strategies.

Theoretical framework

Social identity theory (SIT) (TS3) and relative deprivation theory (RDT) (TS8).

Method

Participants: 517 people born and living in different regions of East Germany, of both genders from 17 to 87 years old and of various educational levels and professional activities.
  Materials: Participants completed a questionnaire measuring:

- Independent variables: perceptions of stability and legitimacy of the status relations between East and West Germans, perceptions of permeability of boundaries between the two groups, perception of the material position of the East Germans in comparison to the West Germans (only for RDT test).
- Mediators: identification with the East Germans (for SIT test), feelings of resentment with regard to the relation between the two groups, expectation of ingroup efficacy to change the situation (for RDT test).
- Outcome variables: individual strategies, social change strategies, and social creativity strategies.

Results

Three models were tested using structural equation modeling techniques. The first model tested the predictions of SIT. In this model the sociostructural variables were considered as predictors of the strategies through the mediating effects of identification. From this analysis the authors conclude that:

- The model can reasonably predict individual strategies, whereas the prediction of social creativity strategies is rather weak.
- Legitimacy predicts only social competition strategies. (The more that intergroup relations are perceived to be unfair the more likely it is that people will engage in competitive strategies.)
- Stability predicts powerfully individual mobility, recategorization at a higher level, and realistic competition. (If people perceive the asymmetric relationships between groups to be stable, they will try individual mobility strategies or will compete for reversing the material conditions.)
- Permeability directly predicts individual mobility and social competition. (The more open the boundaries between groups are perceived to be the more people will choose individual mobility strategies and not engage in social competition.)
- Identification with the group predicts the use of strategies either directly or as a mediator of the effects of stability and permeability.

The second model tested the predictions of RDT. In this model the predictors were referent outcome, likelihood of amelioration (stability), and referent instrumentalities (legitimacy); mediators of these effects on identity strategies were perceptions of group efficacy and resentment about the group's situation. The test of this model indicated:

- This model is better than the SIT model in explaining strategies of competition.
- Group efficacy and fraternal resentment are better mediators of competitive strategies than identification to the group.
- Recategorization to a higher level was better predicted by SIT.
- Again, social creativity strategies were not explained satisfactorily.
- Group efficacy was predicted only by referent instrumentalities (legitimacy). This seems to indicate that perceptions of the group's status as illegitimate might afford considerations of group efficacy to change the situation. Group efficacy is important once illegitimacy is perceived to mobilize people towards change. Legitimacy of the group's status might be accompanied by feelings of helplessness and low efficacy.

A test of an integrative model that included predictors and mediators of both theories revealed that:

- Identification was directly related to individual strategies.
- Negative feelings of deprivation and resentment were connected to collective strategies.
- The relation between identification and collective strategies was mediated through resentment and group efficacy.
- The model could not explain social creativity strategies satisfactorily.

(*Continues*)

Panel 1.9   (*Continued*)

General discussion

This study has shown how perceptions of the structure of the relationships between groups can predict identification and feelings of resentment, as well as strategic responses to the situation. Each theory has its unique concepts (permeability for SIT and perceptions of status for RDT). Moreover, SIT emphasizes the cognitive aspect of identification, whereas RDT emphasizes the emotive response to status inequalities. The authors suggest that these different emphases relate to different strategy preferences: individual strategies relating to group identification and competition relating to resentment and group efficacy.

However, what is important to highlight is that collective action is likely when members of minority groups feel *discriminated* against. In chapter 2 we look at cultural diversity from the point of view of the members of cultural majorities and discuss the origins of discrimination and the prejudice that feeds and sustains it.

Receiving Immigrants, Perceiving the Other: Reactions of People Belonging to Dominant Cultural Groups

Plate 2   British tabloids.

Outline

Having discussed the issues that people face when they move and start living in new environments, it is time now to discuss multiculturalism from the point of view of those who are members of cultural majorities. While people from non-dominant cultural groups have to deal with the novelty of their environment, people from dominant cultural groups have to deal with the novelty that these people represent. People from cultural majorities have to adjust to the diversity that newcomers bring. They have to become accustomed to a diversity of beliefs and practices that might concern fundamental values and religious beliefs (see chapter 1 on individualism/collectivism and value systems), and ways of dressing, eating, and behaving. In these ways their environment also becomes "unfamiliar" and they have to deal with the changes. They construct their own commonsense theories or social representations (TS1) to manage this unfamiliarity. These theories vary in relation to the different beliefs people hold (psychological anchoring), their different memberships – age, gender, socioeconomic status, etc. – (sociological anchoring), and their understandings of social relationships, constructions of otherness, and perceptions of the nation (social psychological anchoring). These theories form representations of immigration that are used to respond to questions as to why these new people are here, whether and how they will acculturate, and what are the consequences of their presence for society. They include elements concerning "what our nation is" and particular perceptions of the Other.

In this chapter we explore these issues by discussing the social psychological explanations of the roots of prejudice, perceptions of other groups, stereotyping, racism as a particular form of prejudice, and perceptions of otherness. Further, we deal with intergroup anxiety and identity threats. This is not to imply that everybody in the receiving society is intolerant and prejudiced, nor that perceptions towards immigrants and immigration take the same form and content in each country.

The economists Bauer, Lofstrom, and Zimmermann (2000) analyzed data from twelve OECD countries and looked at the receiving population's attitudes towards immigrants. They suggest that, although it is difficult to say whether different immigration policies *determine* attitudes or vice versa, different attitudes towards immigration are certainly linked to different policies. These differences are also related to a country's history of immigration (whether it is a new or old immigrant country; whether it receives skilled immigrants, asylum seekers, or economic migrants). For example, in traditional immigration countries, people might wish a reduction in immigration rates mainly through fear of job losses. However, in countries that receive mainly refugees and asylum seekers, people seem to fear higher crime rates. Pettigrew (1998a) used the Eurobarometer Survey 30 to present data from different European countries and analyzed them within a social psychological framework. His study also suggests a variation in prejudiced attitudes in relation to the diversity of policies or country of origin of immigrant groups and their historical relationship with the receiving society. Such studies highlight the fact that different sociohistorical contexts organize people's representations of immigration differently. Our task, as social psychologists, is to look closely at the relationship between structural conditions and people's perceptions and to understand the social psychological processes that sustain these perceptions. However, if attitudes towards immigration vary so much between countries, are we able to say anything sensible about these processes?

In an important paper, Pettigrew et al. (1998) tested two hypotheses. First, they asked whether constructs and measures developed in the USA in relation to Black/White relationships hold in Western European countries in relation to immigration. Their analysis concludes that these constructs and measures behave in a similar way, at least in Western industrialized countries (research is needed in less developed countries) and across a variety of target groups. Second, they asked how psychological processes generalize, given the societal differences due to the diversity of sociohistorical conditions. In answer to this question they suggest that societal phenomena at a macro-level constitute "distal" causes of prejudice, whereas psychological phenomena operate at a meso- and micro-level and constitute "proximal" causes that mediate the effects of societal factors. For example, they found that political conservatism, group-relative deprivation, intergroup contact, and national pride mediated the effects of education in explaining poor White racism, and that prejudice and group-relative deprivation mediated the effects of age and education on attitudes towards immigration. They "posit that similar social processes pattern majority–minority relations in industrial countries. In turn, these processes shape similar intergroup situations, behavior, and attitudes. Mean levels of such political variables as attitudes towards immigration can vary sharply, yet their relationships with prejudice remain relatively stable" (ibid: 269). Our task will be to look at these proximal variables as they have been studied by social psychologists in different contexts and to discuss what their effects might be in relation to multicultural societies. Thus, in this chapter, discussing the perspective of culturally dominant groups, we begin this journey by briefly presenting the social psychological theories on prejudice. We then look at the social psychological processes linked to social perception and their impact on constructing otherness. These perceptions constitute part of more general commonsense theories and social representations about immigration, ethnicity, and culture that shape intergroup relations. We also discuss a particular form of prejudice – racism – not only to illustrate these representations, but also because of its importance in people's lives. Finally, the concept of threat is introduced as one of those proximal social psychological variables that can help us understand the reactions of dominant cultural groups.

Social Psychological Theories of Prejudice

At the end of World War II a question haunted humanity: "How was it possible?" Many social psychologists were among those who tried to understand how the Holocaust occurred. Solomon Asch (1951, 1952, 1956) (TS10) showed that, even when faced with

Prejudice

Ethnic prejudice is an antipathy based upon a faulty and inflexible generalization. It may be felt or expressed. It may be directed toward a group as a whole or toward an individual because he is a member of that group.

(Allport 1954: 10)

An unjustified negative attitude toward an individual based solely on that individual's membership in a group.

(Worchel, Cooper, and Goethals 1988: 449)

The holding of derogatory social attitudes or cognitive beliefs, the expression of negative affect, or the display of hostile or discriminatory behavior towards members of a group on account of their membership of that group.

(Brown 1995: 8)

Discrimination

Treating a person or a group of people unfairly or differently because of their membership of a particular social group.

a self-evident truth, people might refuse to spell it out in the presence of a group of people who unanimously give an obviously wrong answer. Stanley Milgram (1974) (TS10) showed that people who are part of a hierarchical structure are likely to consider themselves as the mere agents of the will of the authority. Under such circumstances, it is possible for them to carry out extreme actions. They act, perhaps against their beliefs, when they are ordered to do so and when they are cleared of the responsibility for their actions.

These studies highlight the existence of social psychological processes of social influence that intervene in and affect people's actions. What are the origins of extreme actions and conflict? In most social psychological explanations, **prejudice** is implicitly at the root of conflict. It is important, therefore, to understand what prejudice is and what are its determinants.

If we look at social psychological definitions of prejudice it is noticeable that prejudice seems to be both a negative belief/affect and a discriminatory action towards somebody on the basis of his or her social membership. In general, social psychologists assume that prejudice leads to **discrimination** (and as we saw in chapter 1, discrimination may result in intergroup conflict: see TS9).

Given this assumption, social psychologists have worked to understand why people are prejudiced. Three main explanations have been advanced. The first roots prejudice in the *type of personality* people have (TS11). This approach focuses on individual differences – in other words, understanding why some people are more susceptible to prejudice than others. Such personality and individual approaches to prejudice have been criticized. Apart from methodological criticisms (see Altemeyer 1988), the main objection relates to the core assumption that prejudice is linked to personality characteristics that are supposed to remain stable. Studies by Minard (1952) and Siegel and Siegel (1957) suggest that social context impacts on levels of authoritarianism. In Minard's study, white American miners who lived in a racially segregated town did not reproduce discrimination and segregation towards their black colleagues when they were in the pit. In the Siegel and Siegel study, young college women were influenced by the norms of their sorority and displayed more authoritarianism when living in a prejudiced ward than those girls who were exposed to more progressive norms.

One can also ask whether levels of authoritarianism are linked to prejudice at a wider societal level. Pettigrew (1958) studied such highly segregated societies as the American South and South Africa under apartheid. He found that although there was a link between prejudice and authoritarianism at an individual level (people that were more prejudiced also displayed higher levels of authoritarianism), there was no such link at a societal level. In other words, these societies did not have a greater distribution of authoritarian personalities in comparison to other, less prejudiced societies.

All these studies point to the importance of social norms in explaining prejudiced behaviors. Reynolds et al. (2001) ask whether it is even appropriate to try to understand prejudice at an individual level of analysis, instead of focusing on the psychological processes linked to group membership and the meanings associated with it. Drawing upon self-categorization theory (TS12), their experimental findings suggest "the salience of certain identities can affect the power of authoritarianism to predict prejudice" (p. 433). The importance of group memberships and **intergroup behavior** are the focus of two other social psychological approaches to prejudice.

The second approach to prejudice suggests that competition over scarce resources forms the origin of ethnocentrism and **ingroup** favoritism.

This approach draws on Campbell's (1965) realistic conflict theory and is linked to the work of Muzafer Sherif and colleagues (Sherif et al. 1954; Sherif 1966) and their famous summer camp studies (TS13). For Sherif, the nature of the relationships between functionally related groups that belong to an intergroup system is at the root of prejudiced behaviors. His concern is with situations where "the goals, policies and actions of each group have an impact on events within the others, for good or evil" (Sherif 1967: 465). Multicultural societies are just such a functionally related intergroup system and people are concerned about resource distribution between groups, and the goals and intentions of different groups. (The situations that arise from these functional relationships are discussed in detail in chapter 3.)

The third approach to prejudice advances a cognitive–motivational explanation and has its origins in the work of Henri Tajfel and his colleagues (TS14). Their studies, based initially on experimental groups, point out that the cognitive existence of two groups is sufficient to ignite feelings of **ethnocentrism** and **ingroup favoritism**.

Why is this so? Tajfel suggests a motivational explanation and proposed the theory of social identity (TS3). Because people derive a sense of identity from the groups to which they belong, they are motivated to attribute a higher status to these groups. One way of achieving this is to favor group members on perceptual, attitudinal, and behavioral dimensions and to make sure that a positive distinctiveness is established on important dimensions between their ingroup and other relevant groups. Initially it was thought that only members of groups that have a lower status would be motivated to discriminate in order to obtain this positive difference and enhance their self-esteem. However, it was soon noticed that ingroup favoritism is also a feature of high-status group members (Ellemers et al. 1992). Furthermore, the hypothesis that the enhancement of self-esteem is the powerful motivation behind ingroup favoritism has not been conclusively verified (Messick and Mackie 1989; Hogg and

Intergroup behavior

Whenever individuals belonging to a group interact collectively or individually with another group or its members in terms of their group identification, we have an instance of intergroup behavior.

(Sherif 1967: 62)

Ingroup favoritism

Describes any tendency to favor ingroup over outgroup members on perceptual, attitudinal, or behavioral dimensions.

(Turner and Giles 1981: 66)

Ethnocentrism

Defined as "the technical name for this view of things in which one's own group is the center of everything and that the others are scaled and rated with reference to it"

(Sumner 1906; in Tajfel 1981: 323)

Ingroup

Social psychological jargon qualifying the group or social category to which one belongs or with which one identifies. Similarly, "outgroup" qualifies the group or social category to which one does not belong or with which one does not identify.

Abrams, 1988, 1990). Other motivations, such as reducing uncertainty, have since been proposed (Mullin and Hogg 1999; Hogg 2000). The sources of these motivations might also be culturally bound (Vignoles, Chryssochoou, and Breakwell 2000, 2002a, 2002b).

In a nutshell, this highly influential social psychological theory suggests that members of receiving societies and dominant cultural groups will tend to be prejudiced against people belonging to different cultural groups, in an attempt to maintain their higher-status position at a symbolic level. Moreover, people belonging to non-dominant cultural groups will also favor their ingroup on different dimensions. Where one's group stands in the social hierarchy is an important factor in influencing perceptions and behaviors. However, status perceptions are linked to perceptions of social relationships in terms of how stable and legitimate they are perceived to be and whether it is possible to change group membership (TS3). Research by Echebarria-Echabe and Gonzalez-Castro (panel 2.1) indicates how important status perceptions are for the acceptance of immigrants and for the perceptions of intergroup relations.

Panel 2.1   Images of Immigrants: A Study on the Xenophobia and Permeability of Intergroup Boundaries (Echebarria-Echabe and Gonzales Castro 1996)

Research question

The study aimed to assess social–contextual factors of prejudice about immigrants. In particular, it focused on the permeability of boundaries between the ingroup (receiving society) and the outgroup. It also manipulated the status of the immigrants in an attempt to measure whether it moderated the effects of perceptions of permeability.

The authors hypothesized that a "closed frontier policy" (low intergroup permeability) will reduce the threat felt from the presence of immigrants; therefore, the receiving society's members will have a more positive representation of immigrants than they would have with an open frontier policy. There was also an alternative hypothesis. If negative representations of people serve to justify discriminatory policies, a closed frontier policy will induce more negative representations. In addition, the authors suggest that representations of immigrants depend on their status in relation to the ingroup. Thus, a more negative representation is expected in the case of immigrants from poorer, third world countries, in comparison to immigrants from more developed countries. Finally, it was hypothesized that the status of immigrants can moderate the impact of policies. Thus, an open frontier policy will be more threatening when immigrants are of lower status (third world countries) and induce more negative representations of immigrants. The same policy in relation to higher-status immigrants (from developed countries) will induce more positive representations.

Theoretical framework

Social identity theory (TS3, TS14).

Method

Participants: 393 Basque people from Spain of different professions, with a mean age of 36.64 years.

Materials and procedure

Participants completed one version of an experimental questionnaire that followed a 2 (open vs. closed frontier policy) × 2 (third world vs. European Union immigrants) design. At the beginning of the questionnaire participants read that the EU is discussing a policy project for its member states about the opening (or closing) of frontiers to all immigrants from third world (or EU) countries. They were then asked to complete different measures: stereotypes of immigrants and Basque people; attitudes towards immigrants; the feelings of natives and immigrants towards each other; acceptance of immigrants; perceived conflicts between immigrants and Basque people; responsibility for these conflicts and behavioral intentions towards immigrants.

Results

The effect of immigrants' status: third world immigrants are described as more friendly, generous, open, and good than Europeans, whereas Europeans are described as more intelligent, clean, and hard working.

- European immigration is explained to a higher degree than third world immigration because immigrants are attracted to the way of life, desire to make money easily, and have different skills.
- Third world immigrants are believed to fear, distrust, and envy Basque people and to feel rage towards them more than Europeans are expected to do. Basque people despise, envy, and feel rage more towards third world immigrants than towards Europeans.

The effect of the frontier policy: When a *closed* frontier policy was anticipated:

- Basque people felt more fear, distrust, contempt, and rage, and less sympathy and respect towards immigrants. Immigrants were thought to feel less sympathy and respect and be more despising of Basque people.

(*Continues*)

Panel 2.1   (*Continued*)
- Immigration is explained on the basis of lack of opportunities and political corruption in the countries of origin.

The opposite trend was found when an open frontier policy was anticipated. *Interaction effect between frontier policy and immigrant status:*

- The image of the third world immigrants remained stable irrespective of the policy.
- Under an open policy, more conflicts and more support for anti-immigration movements were observed when the immigrants were from third world countries.
- Under an open policy, European immigrants are better perceived and more accepted. There are more positive attitudes towards immigrants and a decrease in support for anti-immigration movements.

General discussion

As predicated by the second hypothesis, a closed frontier policy induced more negative representations of immigration (policy effect). However, this effect interacts with the status of immigrants, as expected. Higher-status immigrants are better perceived under an open frontier policy, perhaps because they will enhance the image of the whole group. Although people tend to anticipate more intergroup conflict between natives and immigrants when the latter come from third world countries, it is important to highlight that the frontier policy does not alter the image of these immigrants – it remains negative. The authors were surprised to find that third world immigrants in general were described in more positive terms than Europeans. However, this might be the effect of representations of group status (see the discussion about collection and aggregate groups in chapter 1; also Chryssochoou 2000b, 2000c).

Very early on in the development of social identity theory (SIT), it was noticed that an important factor contributing to the expression of prejudice and discrimination was the status and power of the groups that people consider important for self-definition (Sachdev and Bourhis 1984, 1985, 1987; Bourhis 1994; Zanna and Olson 1994). In addition, group status has an important role to play in the construction of the content and meaning of social categories that people use to define themselves and in the acceptance of new identities (Chryssochoou 2000b).

SIT's crucial point is that ingroup favoritism is an important part of the self: people need to identify with the category. The importance of social categories for self-definition is the focus of self-categorization theory (TS12), which attempts to understand the impact of the cognitive definition of the self – in terms of social categories – on behaviors and in particular on intergroup behavior. According to self-categorization theory, people's collective psychology as group members influences cognitions and behaviors. When the social context makes particular self-categorizations salient and people see themselves as interchangeable members of a particular group, it is likely that they will enact this identity. Under such circumstances intergroup behavior is likely.

In this section we have discussed three different explanations of prejudice. The first one roots prejudice in personality, the second in the functional relationships between groups, and the third in cognitive processes of categorization and motivational processes linked to identity and self-definition. Their presentation may give the impression that they are mutually exclusive. Indeed, those who adhere to the self-categorization approach will not embrace personality and individual differences approaches to prejudice. They rightly accuse these approaches of being reductionist and neglecting the social contextual factors that impact on prejudice. Others have criticized self-categorization theorists for neglecting how self-categories are constructed and represented (Deaux 1992, 2000, 2001) and what guides the individual's decision in favor of a particular identity (Huddy 2001). Further, competition between groups may be a sufficient condition, but not a necessary condition (as Sherif thought), for the development of prejudice.

Despite the criticisms, these theories have proposed important ideas to help us understand prejudice. Although I agree that restricting the explanation of prejudice to personality factors is reductionist, personality approaches (such as social dominance theory) make an important point in suggesting that there is a link between beliefs about the social system and psychological organization (i.e., personality). Maybe these beliefs are not linked to personality as such but to the organization of self-perception and self-definition. We cannot deny that there are individual differences in the endorsement of prejudiced views. Although we are not yet able to detail the factors that lead to some people having higher levels of prejudice than others, understanding the relationships between different beliefs about society and their impact on how people perceive themselves might move us a step forward.

Even if competition between groups is not a necessary and sufficient condition for prejudice, the important point made by Sherif's approach is that we need to take into account the functional relationships between groups, seen as part of an intergroup system. In multicultural societies, cultural groups are part of a system (the nation-state, the European Union, international organization, etc.) which defines rules of membership, entitlements, duties, and responsibilities, and which regulates resource distribution and intergroup relationships. We need to understand better under which conditions prejudice is more likely to be the consequence of these relationships, within culturally diverse societies.

The third approach contributes to our understanding of prejudice by highlighting the importance of social membership for intergroup relations. It is crucial to remember that people are not mere observers of the social world. They are active participants who view that world from their own position. Phenomena such as discrimination might be due to people's identification with particular social categories and the importance that these categories have for self-definition. Categorization, however, is not only important for auto-perception but also for hetero-perception. If we want to understand relationships between groups it is important to understand how these groups are represented. This is the topic of the next section.

Representations of Groups: Stereotypes and Social Categorization

Lippmann (1922) borrowed the word "stereotype" from the world of printing and introduced it to the social sciences. In printing, a stereotype is a metal cast that is used to make identical images of a character on paper repeatedly. The origins of the word are Greek, where *stereos* means "firm" and *typos* equals "print." Thus, Lippmann's stereotypes were firm, identical, "pictures in our heads."

Lippmann believed that these enduring cognitive pictures comprised a distorted image of the world. The fact that they were *inaccurate* pictures in our heads made the link with prejudice and discrimination possible and fueled research in this area.

The idea of stereotypes as distorted images persisted for a long time in social psychology, and stereotypes were (and still are in some traditions) considered the result of the limits of our cognitive abilities for information processing (i.e., biases). Researchers focused on understanding how much of a distortion a particular stereotype was, but other scholars suggested that there might be *a kernel of truth* in the stereotypes (Triandis and Vassiliou 1967). This argument occupied research on stereotypes for a long time (for an excellent review consult Oakes, Haslam, and Turner 1994), but it died slowly when it was observed that the values of researchers influenced what part of the stereotype was found to be accurate and the appropriateness of methods to investigate this accuracy. In addition, research moved away from the *content* of the stereotypes to investigate *how* stereotypes are formed, *why* they are formed, and *what* they do.

There is a long research tradition on how stereotypes are formed, which is closely related to different theoretical assumptions. Most of the research roots the formation of stereotypes in cognitive processes. Some theorists consider the formation of stereotypes to be linked to the operation of heuristics (cognitive strategies used to process information quickly and efficaciously) (Hamilton and Gifford 1976; TS15). Following research by Tajfel and Wilkes (1963) (TS 15), a link was made between processes of category formation (accentuation/contrast) and stereotyping. In conjunction with Sherif's (1936, 1966) work, which considered stereotypes as group products within a system of intergroup relations, this link led self-categorization theorists to consider stereotypes as outcomes of categorization processes operating to produce intergroup behavior. According to self-categorization theory (TS 12), social categories are formed on the basis of perceived similarities and differences between people within a context of intergroup relations. When people consider themselves as belonging to a particular category, a process of depersonalization occurs whereby they feel themselves to be interchangeable members of the category and they endorse its characteristics.

According to self-categorization theorists, this process of self-stereotyping is responsible for intergroup behavior. Thus, intergroup behavior between culturally dominant and non-dominant groups is likely to occur when people categorize themselves as members of their respective cultural groups and consider that the stereotype of the group also applies to themselves.

However, cognitive theorists have suggested that categories are not only formed on the basis of similarity (Murphy and Medin 1985; Medin and Wattenmaker 1987). Categorization presupposes a theory about the world that guides the process of category formation. For example, the division of the world into nations is not simply based on perceived similarities and differences between people. Perhaps it is based on naive theories about what it means to be a nation. Therefore, perceptions of similarity might not be the *criteria* of categorization and stereotyping but their *outcomes*. In other words, we do not form categories and stereotypes exclusively on the basis of how similar we perceive people to be. The inclusion of a person in a category depends on what we think this category is about. For instance, if nations and ethnic groups are formed around the idea of kinship, there will be an expectation of similarity between their members. However, modern multicultural nations violate these assumptions and require new commonsense theories to be formed.

There are different theoretical suggestions as to *why* stereotypes are formed. One suggestion is that stereotypes constitute a distortion of reality. They simplify the social environment by reducing social information; therefore they are considered the biased outcome of information processing (Fiske and Neuberg 1990; Hamilton 1981). Within this perspective, members of the receiving society might construct stereotypes about immigrants due to the limited ability of human cognitive systems to process individualized information. Other theorists, however, dispute the claim that stereotypes are due to shortcomings of our cognitive system and consider them instead as perceptual devices that make sense of reality in specific contexts from the standpoint of the perceiver (Oakes, Haslam, and Turner 1994; McGarty 1999). They are the outcome of an elaborative process that selectively uses information that fits the context and the goals of the perceiver. In this perspective, stereotypes are "group phenomena, determined by intergroup relations" (Oakes, Haslam, and Turner 1994: 114). Following this line of thought, members of a receiving society might construct a stereotype of immigrants that fit their goals in the specific context. This approach is close to the suggestion that stereotype formation responds to self-enhancement motivations (Tajfel 1981; Tajfel and Turner 1979). In other words, stereotypes are the outcome of attempts to present the ingroup, and hence oneself, in a better light. In this case, negative stereotypes about other cultural groups enable people to feel better about their own cultural group.

It is undeniable that expressing stereotypes can be a way of positively evaluating the ingroup and thus feeling better about it. Perhaps, as has been suggested, stereotypes are formed cognitively to justify existing social relationships (Leyens, Yzerbyt, and Schandron 1994; Tajfel 1981). This is of crucial importance for our discussion here because it implies that the formation of particular stereotypes regarding immigrants in

Stereotyping

The derivation of knowledge about categories that serves to explain similarities and differences on relevant dimensions at that time in ways which are shared.

(McGarty, Yzerbyt, and Spears 2002: 198)

The formation of social representations of groups that help people to transform an unfamiliar social context into a familiar one and to coordinate social behavior.

(My definition)

Psychological representations of the characteristics of people that belong to particular groups.

(McGarty, Spears, and Yzerbyt 2002: 2)

general, or specific ethnic groups in particular, justifies relationships between cultural groups and their status within a multicultural context. For example, the stereotype that immigrants are scroungers justifies the belief of some members of the receiving society that immigrants should not benefit from welfare provision.

Tajfel (1981) considered that stereotypes have four functions:

1 They help people understand and adapt to the social environment.
2 They help people defend and preserve their individual values.
3 They create and maintain group ideologies that are used to explain and justify actions.
4 They create and maintain positively valued differences.

In this respect, stereotypes are shared descriptions of social groups that, instead of matching reality, fit the particular social context and are formed to guide interactions. Thus, the stereotype of the immigrant or ethnic minority member is not an attempt to produce an accurate description of immigrants or ethnic minorities. It is an attempt to fulfill the purposes of encounters in the social context and to provide guidance on how to interact with these people.

It is important to keep in mind that **stereotypes** are not something we hold only about others. The self is implicated in many ways. We are all members of social groups. When we form stereotypes about others we do it from our own perspective and position: we stereotype ourselves and members of our own groups. Spears (2002), inspired by categorization and social identity traditions, has suggested four principles of stereotyping. Firstly, stereotypes are formed to make sense of the social environment. Hence, for their construction, people use the knowledge they have about social situations (the meaning principle). Secondly, to the extent that the self is implicated, people form stereotypes in order to distinguish between social groups (the distinctiveness principle). Thirdly, by distinguishing between social groups, people might follow identity motivations and aim to present their group in a better light (self-enhancement principle). Fourthly, stereotypes are about social groups and therefore their formation will be constrained by other processes taking place in the social world (the reality principle). These principles, of course, are distinguished for theoretical purposes in an effort to integrate different traditions. However, they operate together in the process of stereotype formation.

We have discussed *how* stereotypes are formed and *why* they are formed. The last question we need to ask ourselves is *what* they do. As group phenomena produced within a context of intergroup relations, stereotypes reflect relationships between groups. In this context they have two important features. Firstly, stereotypes are *shared* representations of groups (Haslam et al. 2002). This is actually a very important aspect of stereotypes: if stereotypes weren't shared we wouldn't bother understanding either their content or their formation, as they would only concern individual thoughts. The fact that stereotypes are shared helps people communicate and coordinate their behavior. It allows us to understand how prejudice becomes consensual and how we can explain its historical specificity. In order for stereotypes to become consensual knowledge about groups, their formation obeys processes of communication and social influence (Haslam et al. 2002; Moscovici and Doise 1992; Reicher, Hopkins, and Condor 1997).

Secondly, as we have already seen, stereotypes help people make sense of the social context. The meaning-making feature of stereotypes helps people make sense of the social world by expressing meaningful social entities in a specific context. Through social categorization and stereotyping, abstract social relations are translated into social categories, thus becoming "concrete" entities of meaning. "The outcome of categorization (the division of the social world into categories) is the objectification of the social relations and their associated values" (Chryssochoou 2000a: 348). Social categorization and stereotyping objectify these relationships. However, by making these relations concrete there is a danger of reifying and **essentializing** social categories; in other words, generating the idea that social categories have essences (Medin and Ortony 1989; Yzerbyt, Rocher, and Schandron 1997).

This is a very important issue for the student of culturally diverse societies, as categories such as ethnicity, nationality, and culture tend to be reified and differences between categories tend to be considered as natural. In this case, the social relationships and positions linked to these categories are considered also to be natural and immutable. For example, in the current social context, since September 11, 2001, there has been a social debate about civilization and the degree to which certain cultures are part of it. The consequence of the essentialization of cultures and the view that cultural differences are natural is to maintain beliefs about the natural superiority of certain cultures and people, and therefore sustain the social relationships that these beliefs entail. As we will see later, the construction of otherness can be a powerful expression of prejudice that throws groups of people outside the boundaries of humankind.

Categorical essentialism

Essentialism refers to the classical, Aristotelian view that each concept has a set of necessary "essential" features (Haslam, Rothschild, and Ernst 2000: 113).

Here I make reference to the concept of psychological essentialism described by Medin and Ortony (1989). *Psychological essentialism* is the lay belief that categories have essences. People have implicit theories from which categories draw their necessary characteristics or essences. Such theories may concern religion, nationhood, race, or ethnicity.

Prejudice Linked to Racial Differentiation

Racism has occupied social scientists for a long time. Many worked on racial division in order to combat it; unfortunately, many also did so to establish it. The division of people according to physical characteristics (e.g., skin color) gave rise to biological theories about the inferiority of some categories (races) and their exclusion from material and symbolic resources. For obvious historical reasons, due to the condition of black people in the United States, most of the social psychological research on racially based prejudice has been conducted in the US (Allport 1954;

Eberhardt and Fiske 1998; Fiske 1998; Philogène 1999). However, studies have been conducted in other places as well (Augoustinos and Reynolds 2001; Billig 1978, 1979, 1981; Wetherell and Potter 1992). In many respects prejudice has been equated with racism.

Since the Civil Rights movement in the US in the1960s and the abolition of apartheid in South Africa, interracial relationships have improved. However, has racism been eclipsed? It is still true that black people find themselves worse off in every statistic (employment, mortality, education, wealth, etc.) in all Western countries. If racism is defined as the negative situation of black people compared to their white counterparts, it is easy to see that racism is still a reality that greatly affects people's lives. The zeitgeist *has* changed, however: overt racism is met, in general, with outcry and rejection.

Social psychologists have claimed that nowadays overt, old-fashioned racism and bigotry are rejected by the majority of people, who are careful to protect themselves from appearing racist. More subtle forms of prejudice have replaced this expression of racism (panel 2.2). Thus, theorists advanced different conceptualizations of subtle racism (Pettigrew and Meertens 1995), modern or symbolic racism (McConahay 1982, 1986), ambivalent racism (Katz and Hass 1988), and aversive racism (Gaertner and Dovidio 1986), or talked about the existence of a dissociation between conscious and unconscious racist beliefs (Devine 1989).

In particular, Dovidio and Gaertner (1998) consider that most people are very keen

Panel 2.2 Theories of Subtle Racism

Theorists who have studied the evolution of racial attitudes as measured in surveys, suggest that a change in norms has made the expression of racist beliefs unacceptable. Instead, more subtle forms of racism exist which are just as powerful. Different theories of "subtle racism" have been advanced.

Modern or symbolic racism (Sears and McConahay 1973; McConahay 1982, 1986)

Modern or symbolic racism is not expressed through bigotry and support for segregation and white supremacy. It is anchored to values of egalitarianism, individualism, merit, and self-reliance. Modern racists are not likely to reject black people as a result of pure bigotry. They tend to believe that black people violate traditional values and they are more likely to oppose measures that would redress historical inequalities, such as affirmative action, based on arguments of meritocracy, egalitarianism, and individualism.

Ambivalent racism (Katz and Hass 1988)

This is based on the assumption that pro- and anti-black attitudes are linked to different sets of values. People realize that black people are in a disadvantaged position and hold pro-black attitudes that relate to humanitarian values of equality and social justice. However, competing values of individualism, self-reliance, meritocracy, and individual freedom lead to anti-black attitudes. The contradiction between these strong cultural values enables racism to persist, as people remain ambivalent towards racial outgroups.

Aversive racism (Gaertner and Dovidio 1977, 1986)

This is a type of ambivalent racism. Aversive racists do not believe they are prejudiced. When a situation is unambiguous (with a clear distinction between right and wrong) and where racial prejudice would be obvious they will behave in a tolerant way. However, when a situation is ambiguous or when explanations other than those based on race can be advanced to justify their behavior, it is likely that they will behave in a biased way.

Dissociation model (Devine 1989)

According to this model, subtle types of racism exist at an unconscious level and are in conflict with conscious individual efforts to overcome them. Unconscious forms of subtle racism are learned from cultural experience and socialization. Some people go on to develop personal beliefs that are contrary to cultural stereotypes. Those people with low prejudiced personal beliefs experience dissociation between their personal and cultural beliefs, which leads them to try to compensate when they realize that – unconsciously – they have behaved in a prejudiced way. Those people whose personal and cultural beliefs are congruent respond with more blatant forms of racism.

Subtle vs. blatant racism (Pettigrew and Meertens 1995)

Pettigrew and Meertens suggest that racism is multidimensional and that there are two separate but related forms of racism. Blatant racism is based on feelings of threat and rejection of minorities. Blatant racists will oppose close contact with racial outgroups. Subtle racism is more indirect and is expressed by overstating cultural differences, defending traditional values, and denying positive emotions to racial outgroups. The separation of these two dimensions allowed Pettigrew and Meertens to cross-refer and categorize people according to high or low scores on both measures. They were able to show that bigots (high on both dimensions), equalitarians (low on both), and subtle racists (low on blatant and high on subtle) supported different immigration policies. This research also established that blatant and subtle forms of prejudice can coexist, even in the same individual.

not to present themselves as racists and are convinced that they are not prejudiced although they still hold negative feelings about people from other races. They do not hate them, but feel an aversion for them. Researchers call these people *aversive* racists (Gaertner and Dovidio 1986). They suggest that when the situation of interaction is clear, aversive racists are able to act in a way that enables them to present themselves in a manner consistent with their belief that they are tolerant and open-minded. However, when the situation is ambivalent and where there is opportunity to justify their feelings and behavior in non-racial terms, their aversion will be expressed. Dovidio and Gaertner (1998) report a series of studies that they have conducted with their colleagues over the years. They show, for example, that people who displayed lower prejudice in self-reported measures were likely to help a black person in danger as much as a white person when they were the only bystanders. However, when other people were present the black victim was helped less. Dovidio and Gaertner conclude that if such an emergency was real the white person would have died 25 percent of the time whereas the black victim would have died 62 percent of the time. They also report another study (Faranda and Gaertner 1979) in which low authoritarian jurors ignored the judge's instructions and considered inadmissible evidence when the defendant was black, whereas they expressed doubts about the guilt of the defendant when inadmissible evidence was presented in the case of a white defendant. The authors suggest that aversive racists do not display an anti-outgroup feeling but a pro-ingroup one. In other words, they would say "blacks are good but whites are better." Furthermore, using response latency measures and subliminal primes, Dovidio and Gaertner (1991) show that more positive associations were made with whites and more negative with blacks when people were unaware that their racial attitudes were measured. Finally, they report another study which found that the higher the status of the black person, the higher the bias against this person was (Dovidio and Mullen 1992). Dovidio and Gaertner (1998) conclude by reminding us that although its expression might be subtle, the consequences of racism are certainly not, and they draw our attention to the responsibility that each person has for combating racism by fighting their own aversive feelings in everyday life.

All these theories have been tested in the United States (with the exception of Pettigrew and Meertens 1995); as Operario and Fiske (1998) observe, they might reflect the structure of American beliefs or the particular historical relationships between black and white people in that country (slavery, civil rights acts, etc.). Walker (2001), for example, has analyzed the evolution of Australian attitudes towards immigrants and Aborigines and suggests that blatant and subtle forms of racism have coexisted all along. Furthermore, some of these theories (aversive racism, dissociation model) seem to suggest that racism operates unconsciously and opens the way to assumptions that racism stems from normal psychological processes such as categorization and stereotyping (Fiske 1998). However, as Reicher (2001: 276) observes: "We should be wary of claims that there is something about human psychology that makes prejudice and racism inevitable." He suggests that in order to understand racism and in order to fight its terrible consequences we should focus on the *racialization* of our societies and ask how race became a meaningful categorization.

Most social psychologists nowadays consider that race is a socially constructed category. Membership of a particular race was socially defined according to criteria that matched sociohistorical requirements. For example, if at some point being black was defined by having a black mother, later "a drop of black blood" over generations was sufficient to define membership of this category (Fiske 1998). Adopting a social constructionist approach (TS16), Wetherell and Potter (1992) aim to "map the language of racism." They are interested in understanding how society gives voice to racism and how racism is constructed in talk through the activities of justification, rationalization, categorization, naming, blaming, identifying, and attributing. Using discourse analysis, they analyze interviews, parliamentary reports, newspaper articles, and television reports in order to investigate the rhetoric strategies of white Anglo-Saxons (Pakeha) in New Zealand about intergroup relations and especially about their relations with the Maori, the aboriginal population. Their research shows how the categories of Maori and Pakeha are constructed in terms of race, culture, or membership of one nation. They look at accounts of social conflict and practical politics, such as the use of language, affirmative action, and land ownership, as well as accounts of racism and prejudice. In their analysis it is interesting to see how Pakeha New Zealanders legitimize and justify colonial history and the current discrimination and disadvantage of the Maori. Their research sets the tone in social psychology for analyzing racism within a discourse analytic perspective and highlights the socially constructed nature of social categories. Similarly, Hopkins, Reicher, and Levine (1997) argue that racialized social categories are constructed in a strategic way in order to make evident specific understandings of social conflict. Reviewing discourse analytic perspectives on racism, LeCouteur and Augoustinos (2001: 230) remark that "discourses are used flexibly and inconsistently depending on the rhetorical purposes in which they are put."

A social representational theoretical framework (Philogène 2000, 2001) shows elegantly the impact of a new "name" for black people in the United States. By changing the label of the category from "Black" to "African American" a shift is produced from a racialized category to a cultural one. This shift marks the presence of an *anticipatory social representation* (Philogène 1999) where the group, distinctive by its culture, is nevertheless included in the broader social category of Americans. It is important to note that this new name was adopted primarily by those people within the black community who occupied higher socioeconomic positions and it quickly became the "politically correct" way of addressing all black Americans. The social construction of categories seems both to reflect historical and socio-economic changes and to impact on them, since social categories are strategically constructed.

The question, however, is how these categories become meaningful divisions of the social world. Operario and Fiske (1998: 48) observe that "racial prejudice follows from the social and historical forces that have rendered intergroup boundaries meaningful

Reification

The process by which abstract arbitrary notions (such as race) become unquestioned and even legitimate concepts. (Operario and Fiske 1998: 38; see also parallels with the process of objectification in social representations, TS1).

Racism

Discrimination based on the reification of race and the essentialization of racial differences.

and conflictual." Because of these sociohistorical conditions, race became a **reified** category. Its parallel process of essentialization led to discrimination towards people who were believed to be inferior, worthless. and undeserving.

Following the previous discussion, I define **racism** as discrimination based on the reification of race and the essentialization of racial differences.

This definition aims to highlight three things: (1) the behavioral and action-oriented aspect of racism (discrimination); (2) the fact that race constitutes a social construction that became a "real" categorical division; (3) the fact that the content (essence) of racial differences depends on the sociopolitical context. Racism is linked to social practices that maintain inequalities. It is based on an arbitrary categorical division that is believed to be real and its content depends on the social context. The essence of racism can be based on beliefs about the supremacy of one race over another, on biological differences, or on cultural differences (Reicher 2001). Whatever the so-called essence of race, racism is based on the assumption that racial differences exist, are real and justified.

It was *power* that ensured that race became a meaningful division of the social world and produced all three aspects of racism (reification, essentialization, and discrimination). Operario and Fiske (1998) define power as the ability to control the outcomes of others; they consider that racism equals power plus prejudice. Powerful groups succeeded in imposing a division based on physical differences, gave "real" status to these categories, and dressed them with beliefs that advantaged them in material and symbolic ways. These beliefs then became natural attributes of the category. Social inequalities were justified, implemented, and sustained by these beliefs. In turn, the same beliefs were fed by the social practices that upheld their logic. None of the processes that constitute racism precedes the others. Reification, essentialization, and discrimination work together to maintain a particular vision of the world, a world characterized by racial difference.

To study this phenomenon one needs to understand the belief system associated with this division at a particular time. Reicher (2001: 288) suggests looking at racial theories as "an interconnected set of postulates which serve to characterize and explain the nature of our social world. Such theories are racial in the sense that they suggest that people relate to each other in terms of their membership of racial groups." He suggests that the practice of racism depends on racialization and outgroup problematization and power. Furthermore, along with others (Hopkins, Reicher, and Levine 1997; Wetherell and Potter 1992), he notices that psychology has fed commonsense theories about racial divisions and contributed to the racialization process.

Accepting the above arguments, I suggest that these theories are in fact social representations (TS1). Fed by scientific theorizations and reflecting social relationships, these social representations are commonsense theories about the social world. Power relations are objectified into particular social categories (Chryssochoou 2000a) and are anchored in beliefs, memberships, and understandings of social inequalities. Due to particular sociohistorical conditions, race became a meaningful category for explaining the way resources were distributed. The outgroup was problematized in terms of racial differences. Although always powerful, this category lives in parallel with other categorical distinctions, such as nationality, ethnicity, culture, religion, gender, sexual orientation, ability, age, and class. We need to understand how the system of classification is integrated into people's theories about the world in order to be able to foresee which categories may be subject to prejudice and discriminatory practices. Research by Haslam, Rothschild, and Ernst (2000) suggests (panel 2.3) that two separate dimensions underline essentialist beliefs about social categories: beliefs about the naturalness of social categories and beliefs about their reification (entitativity).

Panel 2.3   Entitativity of Social Categories, Essentialist Beliefs, and Social Status

Campbell (1958) suggested that categories have more or less "fuzzy" boundaries. He labeled the attribute of a category to be perceived as forming an entity: *entitativity*. He suggested that entitativity had four sources. An aggregate will be perceived more as an entity if:

1 Its components are close together: *Proximity*.
2 Its components are perceptually similar: *Similarity*.
3 Its components move together towards the same direction: *Common fate*.
4 Its components constitute a well-formed figure: *Pregnance*.

More recently, the concept of entitativity has been used by social psychologists, who suggest that people have naive theories about groups from which they draw to search for commonalities between group members. The sources of entitativity are among the principles upon which people base their judgments. Extensive research has been conducted to investigate the links between beliefs about entitativity, stereotyping, and essentialism (Yzerbyt and Schandron 1994; Yzerbyt, Rocher, and Schandron 1997; Yzerbyt, Rogier, and Rocher 1998; Yzerbyt and Rogier 2001).

  Drawing upon this research, as well as upon philosophical and anthropological theoretical accounts, Haslam, Rothschild, and Ernst (2000) conducted an interesting study that looked for the organizing principles of essentialist beliefs. They supplied their American participants with ten different concepts related to essentialism and forty social categories. They then asked them to rate the degree to which each category was related to the essentialist concept and to evaluate the social status of each category. Their results indicate that essentialist beliefs are structured in two separate dimensions:

1 *Naturalness*, including concepts such as discreteness, naturalness, immutability, stability, necessity.

(Continues)

Panel 2.3   (*Continued*)
2 *Reification,* including concepts such as uniformity, informativeness, inherence, exclusivity.

Categories portrayed in the first dimension were presented as natural, whereas categories presented in the second dimension were presented as entitative. Natural categories were exemplified by gender, race (black/white), and ethnicity (Asian/Hispanic), whereas Jews, political groups, homosexuals, and AIDS patients exemplified entitative categories.

It was concluded that "people's representations of social categories are clearly embedded in explanatory theories – social ontologies – that are consequential for the evaluations of them" (ibid: 123). The researchers suggest that there are two distinct ways to essentialize categories, based on beliefs either about their naturalness or their entitativeness.

Haslam, Rothschild, and Ernst (panel 2.3) found that perceptions of social status are correlated with these dimensions. Natural non-reified categories (male, white, and cancer patients) are considered of higher status, whereas natural and reified categories (disabled people, Jews, ethnic minorities, women, blacks, and AIDS patients) are considered of low status. In a subsequent study (Haslam, Rothschild, and Ernst 2002) they suggest that the link between essentialist beliefs and prejudice might be more complex: "links between implicit theories and prejudice may differ across categories and be moderated by as yet unknown variables" (p. 98). If the relationship between essentialist beliefs and prejudice depends on the category, we probably need to look at the broader picture of social categorization and the relationships between categories in order to understand what make some categories meaningful in specific sociohistorical contexts and how outgroups are problematized.

At present, there is a powerful division between the Western and the non-Western world that has somehow become equated with religious belief (Christianity vs. Islam). Furthermore, immigrants, even in traditional migration countries of southern Europe, are viewed as the quintessential Other (Triandafyllidou 2000). Perhaps a social representational perspective will allow us to study commonsense theories in a broader way than if we associate them with particular categories. It might allow us to "problematize the outgroup" and understand the organizing principles of the construction of otherness.

Constructing "Otherness": Extreme Problematizations of the Outgroup

Constructing somebody as Other means that this person is considered as separate. If membership of social groups is such an important aspect of our social life, people construct boundaries that delimit the ingroup and exclude the Other, the foreigner, from it. Otherness is associated with exclusion from the inner circle. Social psychologists have attributed the existence of intergroup conflict to the psychological phenomenon of distinguishing between ingroups and outgroups (Tajfel and Turner 1979, 1986; Turner et al. 1987). In particular, self-categorization theorists (TS12) suggest that shifting from an intergroup level of categorization to a superordinate level, which makes reference to the whole human species, would enable people to include others in a common superordinate category and reduce prejudice and conflict. However, there remains the chance that people and groups are denied this inclusion in humankind. In that case, there is the distinct possibility that prejudice will actually intensify. Acts of extreme violence against groups of people have been perpetuated and justified because the victims were not considered to be fellow human beings. The process of dehumanizing the Other is our focus here.

Leyens and his colleagues thought that if people have a tendency to essentialize social categories they might do so not only at the level of cognitive abilities (inferiority in terms of intelligence, for example), but also in terms of the ability to feel certain emotions. They use the distinction between primary emotions (emotions in French) and secondary emotions (sentiments in French) and notice in pretests that if the former are considered common to humans and animals, the latter are considered social constructions and are attributed only to humans. They suggest that in a process of *infra-humanization of the outgroup*, ingroup members will describe the outgroup as "lesser human beings." One way in which this infra-humanization is achieved is to reserve secondary emotions such as affection, admiration, pride, conceit, nostalgia, remorse, and rancor to the ingroup, and attribute more primary emotions (joy, sadness, anger, fear, disgust, surprise) to the outgroup. In a series of experimental studies (Gaunt, Leyens, and Demoulin 2002; Leyens et al. 2000; Leyens et al. 2001; Paladino et al. 2002) they confirmed their hypotheses and found that people do indeed attribute secondary emotions more easily and spontaneously to the ingroup and more primary emotions to the outgroup. Outgroups are even denied the possibility of having secondary emotions. What pushes people to make these attributions? Maybe our implicit theories about emotions are organizing the social classification along the dimension of nature vs. culture.

Studying the Gypsies, a group that over the centuries has been the target of discrimination, exclusion, and attempted extermination, Moscovici, Pérez, and colleagues (Moscovici and Pérez 1997; Pérez, Chulvi, and Alonso 2001; Chulvi and Pérez 2003) suggest that minority groups may not be subject to devaluation from the majority, but to a semantic differentiation that excludes them from the community of human beings (panel 2.4). Gypsies, in their studies, were not evaluated negatively, but were associated with attributes that belonged to the semantic universe that described animals. Pérez, Moscovici, and Chulvi (2002) suggest that the dimension opposing nature to culture can be used as a basis for a social classification within which certain minorities are represented outside the social map (*ontologization*).

The ontologization of minorities, based not so much on establishing differences between groups but on denying similarities, is considered the outcome of failed attempts over history to assimilate them. These results have obvious consequences for culturally diverse societies, since the non-assimilation of minorities might throw them outside the boundaries of humanity. If minorities are associated with nature as

Panel 2.4   When a Majority Fails to Convert a Minority: The Case of Gypsies (Peréz, Chulvi, and Alonso 2001; Chulvi and Pérez 2003)

Research question

What happens when a majority uses a series of strategies over time to achieve the assimilation of a minority and fails?

Theoretical framework

Social representations theory (TS1), theories of social influence (TS17), self-categorization theory (TS12)

Ontologization concerns the representation of a group as isolated in a particular symbolic universe outside the human species. There is a theory at the level of the meta-system that organizes the content of stereotypes in a way that excludes a particular group from humanity.

Three hypotheses are derived:

- Not all groups are considered worthy of being included in the superordinate category of human species. There is a distinction between discrimination and ontologization. Discrimination is the evaluative difference between groups (intergroup level), whereas ontologization is the exclusion of a group from the category human species (superordinate level).
- Some groups, like the Gypsies, are not treated as outgroups but as negative reference groups in relation to attitudes and values (Newcomb 1943).
- Ontologization may be the outcome of a history of failed attempts at social influence, where a culturally dominant group strives to culturally convert another group.

Method

Several studies were conducted in Spain using experimental and survey techniques.

Study 1

Defining the characteristics of human beings and positioning the Gypsies and the Gadje (non-Gypsies) in relation to them.

Materials and procedure

Participants (39 Spanish students) were asked to list the characteristics that they felt defined and were specific to humankind. Then they were asked to indicate to what extent there was a difference between Gypsies and Gadje in each one of these characteristics.

Results

Characteristics were grouped in different categories. The most important differences between Gypsies and Gadje were not in terms of rationality, biology, or feelings, but on the level of sociability. This is an important finding, as refusing to assign the characteristic of sociability to someone places them somewhere between animal and human. Being asocial means refusing to live in society or not knowing how to live with others in a sociocultural environment. For example, Nazis evoked the argument of the asocial character of the Gypsies to promote their extermination. The researchers also found that there is no correlation between the evaluation of the characteristic and the fact that it was used to establish a difference between Gypsies and Gadje. This means that both negative and positive attributes were used to establish the difference between the two groups. Hence, the distinction is of a semantic and not of an evaluative order. To further investigate this finding another study was conducted.

Study 2

Does the content of the animal/human distinction constitute the principle that organizes the classification of social groups/categories?

Materials, procedure

Participants (144 Spanish university students) were asked to think about the characteristics shared by humans and animals, and then to write one characteristic that (depending on the experimental condition to which they were assigned):

- was positive vs. negative;
- was more present in human beings than animals vs. more present in animals than human beings.

Participants were then asked to note one group that possessed this characteristic.

Results

Both characteristics and groups were placed in different categories. The distribution of characteristics differed according to the experimental conditions. Rationality and values were positive characteristics of humans, whereas immorality and discrimination were negative. Sentiments/fidelity and naturalness described the positive aspects of animals, whereas irrationality, instincts, and viscerality negatively characterized them. Aggression was a negative feature of both animals and humans.

The distribution of the social groups also differed in relation to the experimental conditions. The important point for us here is that ethnic minorities and age groups

(Continues)

Panel 2.4   (*Continued*)
were mentioned by the majority as being in the universe of animals, albeit at the positive level. An ethnic minority could be positively evaluated and at the same time positioned in the semantic space of the animal.

Study 3

Does the failure of a majority to influence a minority towards their way of living lead to its ontologization?

Materials, procedure

Participants (80 Spanish university students) were presented with information regarding the assimilation or non-assimilation of Gypsies in Spain and about the strategies that the cultural majority had put in place over the centuries to convert them. Participants were then given a list of 20 attributes that were either positive or negative and that had natural or cultural connotations and had been used in previous piloting to describe Gypsies. They were asked to indicate all the attributes that the Gypsies possessed and the Gadje did not. Their attitudes towards Gypsies were measured.

Results

More stereotypic descriptions of the Gypsies were produced in the experimental condition where participants were told that despite the attempts over time to convert them the Gypsies still not had been assimilated. Although no differences were found between the experimental conditions in cultural adjectives, there were significant differences in natural adjectives. In the condition where Gypsies were described as having resisted assimilation despite continous efforts, they were described with more natural adjectives compared to the Gadje. The fact that Gypsies and Gadje were differentiated in the natural dimension indicates an attempt to naturalize the Gypsies.

General discussion

Prejudice can be based not only on evaluative differences between groups but also on semantic differences. These semantic differences have as a consequence the social exclusion of the group. It seems that ethnic minorities can be simultaneously positively evaluated and excluded. This effect is more pronounced when the ethnic minority does not demonstrate a willingness to assimilate. It would be helpful to confirm or disconfirm these findings with other minorities.

opposed to culture, they are also outside the boundaries of civilization. In a study where discourse analysis was used, Verkuyten (2001) (panel 2.5) analyzed the rhetorical strategies used by majority members in the Netherlands to construct the

behavior and the practices of immigrants and ethnic minorities as deviant
from the norm (i.e., abnormal).

It is important to emphasize that one of the strategies used was to
present extreme cases of behavior or violation of basic values to justify
judgments of abnormality and accuse the minority. More importantly,
Verkuyten observes that majority members rejected the argument of
cultural diversity to explain differences in the behavior of ethnic minorities. Such an argument would have placed the groups, cultural majorities
and cultural minorities, within the same framework, in an intergroup
perspective of evaluative differences. Instead, people aimed to present

Psychologization

The belief that there
is a psychological
determinism, a causal
relation, between a
social behavior or an
ideological position
and psychological
characteristics.

(Papastamou 1987,
1989)

Panel 2.5 Abnormalization of Ethnic Minorities in Conversation (Verkuyten 2001)

Research question

How is the behavior of ethnic minorities constructed as deviant from the norm
(abnormal) by Dutch people when they talk about their multicultural neighborhood?

Theoretical framework

Discourse and conversation analysis and rhetoric strategies (TS16). The research
aimed to understand how norms and categories are constructed and contested in
debate and argumentation.

Participants and procedure

Focus group discussions with ethnic Dutch people (22 people in total) were organized. Participants of both sexes and different ages met four times in small groups to
talk about governmental policies to revitalize their neighborhoods. Although it was
not the focus of their conversation, the behavior of ethnic minorities became part of
the discussion. The analysis concerned the rhetoric strategies used to construct this
behavior as deviant from the norm (abnormal).

Results

In order to construct the behavior of ethnic minorities as abnormal, participants
used four main strategies:

- *Making a contrast with what is supposed to be ordinary behavior.* In participants'
  talk there was an attempt to define normal behavior as Dutch behavior, which
  also constituted the standard against which ethnic behavior could be contrasted.

(Continues)

Panel 2.5   *(Continued)*

- *Presenting extreme cases as examples in order to justify judgments or to make accusations.* Ethnic minority members are presented as having extreme and often violent reactions to what are supposed to be ordinary events. Extremity of behaviors justifies the claim that these behaviors are beyond the norm. Events are presented as facts with a multitude of details that give the description the quality of "out-thereness." Further, to enhance their facticity, the speaker or others are presented as witnesses to the events described. During these descriptions other participants' acquiescence contributes to the consensual nature of the accounts. All these strategies transform the claims of personal opinion to "objective reflection of reality."

- *Making reference to basic human values.* Participants present normal behavior by referring to basic human values that are considered to be beyond cultural differences. The behavior of ethnic minorities is qualified as abnormal because it transgresses such values.

- *Managing cultural interpretations.* Cultural diversity can be considered as an explanation of ethnic minorities' differences in behavior. However, in order to construct ethnic behavior as transgressing normality, participants have to refute cultural interpretations of this behavior. They do so by arguing about the meaning of culture and present behaviors as beyond the "real culture." Thus, minorities are presented as not following the evolution of their own culture. Moreover, their behavior is presented as contradicting what their culture is supposed to be about. This strategy weakens cultural claims. In addition, in order to reconcile beliefs of cultural tolerance with the wish that ethnic minorities adopt the Dutch way of life, participants distinguish between the private and public spheres. The right to have a distinctive cultural identity is restricted to private life, whereas in public conformity to Dutch norms is required. However, what is considered public or private is a matter of debate. For example, constructions of abnormality are based on the way ethnic minorities raise their children – arguably, part of the private sphere. Furthermore, the same distinction is not applied to Dutch practices, which are considered the norm and thus cross both spheres.

General discussion

This study shows the active construction in talk of ethnic minorities as deviant from the norm. Rhetoric strategies are used to achieve the exclusion of a group by presenting it as abnormal.

ethnic minorities as abnormal. They put ethnic minorities outside the boundaries of what is considered to be civilization in order to **psychologize** them.

The conclusions of Verkuyten are echoed by Volpato and Durante (2002), who looked at the social construction of anti-Semitism in Italy during Fascism. They analyzed a magazine with the evocative title *La Difesa della Razza* (The Defence of

Race), which appeared every fortnight from August 1938 till June 1943. This magazine was an important voice for biological racism in Italy and aimed to construct consensus among the general population about anti-Semitism. Volpato and Durante borrow the concept of *delegitimization* from Bar Tal (1990b, 2000) (panel 2.6) to suggest that the strategies used in the magazine aimed to delegitimize the Jews and exclude them from humanity.

Their analysis suggests five more categories of beliefs which comprise delegitimization (absence of attributes, habits, and practices considered fundamental by the legitimizing group; use of the Jewish group to delegitimize others; numerousness of the Jews; segregation; affirmation of the delegitimization of the group as taken for granted). It is important to notice that segregation, the category that included mentions of the refusal of Jews to assimilate or suggestions of segregationist measures against the Jews, was the most frequent. A chronological analysis of the material indicated that in the first two years of publication the delegitimizing beliefs were based on issues of segregation, absence of attributes, habits, and practices that are valued by the majority, and mentions of the numerousness of the outgroup. The next three years were linked to trait characterization and claims of the delegitimization of the group as taken for

Panel 2.6   Societal Beliefs of Delegitimization (Bar Tal 1990b, 2000)

"Delegitimizing beliefs are extremely negative stereotypes with clearly defined affective and behavioral implications. The extremely negative characteristics are attributed to another group, with the purpose of excluding it from acceptable human groups and denying its humanity" (Bar Tal 2000: 121–2). Bar Tal identifies five categories of delegitimizing beliefs:

1 *Dehumanization:* excluding a group of people from humanity and associating it with "inferior" races, animals or negatively valued creatures (i.e. the devil).
2 *Outcasting:* suggesting that a group is violating crucial social norms.
3 *Trait characterization:* attribution to a group of extremely negative traits.
4 *Use of political labels:* attributing negative labels to a group ("Nazis," "imperialists," "colonialists," etc.).
5 *Group comparison:* comparing the group with other groups that in a given society personify evil (barbarians, Huns, etc.).

These beliefs function as explanations of why the outgroup poses a threat and also predict possible actions of the outgroup. This epistemic function serves to justify violence perpetuated against the outgroup. The beliefs also serve to differentiate between groups and to ascertain the superiority of the ingroup over the outgroup and thereby fulfill identity motivations. Finally, they serve to maintain a sense of uniformity within a society and to uphold beliefs that this uniformity is necessary for its continuity and survival.

granted. The final year of publication was mainly characterized by the use of the Jewish group to delegitimize other groups and by group comparisons to ascertain the superiority of the ingroup. The authors conclude that in the first instance the minority group is presented as being outside normality and as refusing to assimilate. After this period the propaganda reinforces the stereotypes; at the end there is a process of reaffirmation of social distance between majority and minority members and this group is used to delegitimize other outgroups.

Thus, in the first instance, there are attempts to ontologize/delegitimize the outgroup (the similarity between ontologization and Bar Tal's concept of dehumanization is remarkable) and perhaps to present it as abnormal ("outcasting," in Bar Tal's theorization). Once this is established, negative stereotypes are reinforced and sustained. Finally, evaluative differences with the ingroup are made evident and its superiority ascertained.

It is important to notice that the groups on which this research was established are the Jews and the Gypsies, both of which have suffered expulsions and exterminations over many years and in particular during World War II. If we consider the situation of immigrants and ethnic minorities under this light the emerging picture is frightening. What would happen if immigrants and ethnic minorities did not follow an assimilation path over the years? Would they be located outside the boundaries of humankind and civilization, as Verkuyten's research seems to suggest? Would they be negatively stereotyped and finally distanced completely from the majority and denied inclusion in the same state? There are striking similarities between the first step of delegitimization described by Volpato and Durante (2002) and current discourses on immigrants and asylum seekers. Immigrants and asylum seekers are accused of being unwilling or unable to assimilate. In Britain there are discussions about putting them in detention centers, where they will live separately from the general population until their case is decided. We can see here the segregation phenomenon. In addition, cultural minorities are considered as lacking in basic values (such as freedom of choice of partner) and some are accused of supporting terrorism. In general, they are believed to swamp the country (numerousness). I cannot help thinking that cultural majorities in Western countries are in the process of ontologizing/deligitimizing cultural minorities, in particular Muslims. This is a very frightening thought, as ontologization or delegitimization has been associated with the justification of atrocities.

Whatever term we use, we have evidence that majorities tend to exclude minorities from humanity, to infra-humanize, ontologize, delegitimize, or exclude them from the moral community (Opotow 1990). An implicit distinction that organizes social differentiation seems to be an opposition between nature and culture, animals and humans. The question we need to ask ourselves is what makes majorities behave that way? The answer may lie in the concept of threat.

Feeling Threatened: Identity, Change, and Resources

Threat has been studied in social psychology mainly within the context of identity. As we saw in chapter 1, identity threat occurs either when one cannot have positive self-feeling (Tajfel and Turner 1979) or when a change in situational circumstances forces the assimilation–accommodation of new identifications (Breakwell 1986). Branscombe et al. (1999) define four types of threat at the level of identity, linked with social memberships, and consider the possible responses of those who strongly identify with the group and those who do not. The first type of threat occurs when people are categorized against their will (categorization threat). The second type occurs when the group is prevented from being distinctive (threat to distinctiveness). The third type occurs when the value of the group is undermined (threat to the value of identity). The fourth type occurs when one's position in the group is undermined (acceptance threat). These threats, as we have seen, concern non-dominant cultural groups, but equally they concern dominant cultural groups. The presence of cultural minorities redefines the meaning of the categories and the parameters of social comparison that are necessary for self-evaluation. It is possible that dominant cultural groups feel threatened by the new meanings and values of their membership. Equally, they might feel that their own position is undermined and that their group has lost its distinctiveness.

Discrimination might be used to ascertain the superiority of the ingroup and therefore of the self. Identities need to be rethought, since cultural minorities – who often share the same citizenship – call for a reconstruction of collective identities. For example, what does it mean to be British, French, Australian, or European? Cultural majorities have to deal with the changes that the presence of minorities brings to the way they perceive themselves and their world; this might be very threatening.

Another type of threat can be felt when minorities (as we saw in social influence processes: TS17) propose alternative ways of seeing things and set up mechanisms of change. The fact that minorities challenge the majority's worldview makes them threatening. Stephan, Ybarra, and Bachman (1999) call this type of threat *symbolic*, and have found evidence that it is linked to prejudice toward immigrants. To avoid contamination and conversion, especially when they are consistent and refuse to assimilate, minorities have to be problematized in a way that excludes them from the community. They are ontologized and delegitimized, and their practices are described as violating normality.

The double aspect of threat in terms of identity and contamination is theorized beautifully in a monographic study by Denise Jodelet (1991). Jodelet observed the way mentally ill patients who were living as outpatients in the care of a small rural community in France were perceived and treated by their hosts. Jodelet shows that the system of segregation put in place to exclude the patients from the family space and the public space was driven by feelings of double threat: the threat of being contaminated and the threat of being associated with them, and therefore acquiring a negative identity. In research by Echebarria-Echabe and Gonzales Castro (1996) we also saw how ingroup-identity concerns impact on perceptions of immigrants.

Thus, although levels of threat can be the same, their origins can be different. Reicher (2001: 291) reports from the autobiography of Rudolf Hoess, the Commandant of Auschwitz from 1940–3. Hoess describes the Jewish and Gypsy prisoners in his camp in different ways. Jews are described as low and scheming and dangerous, whereas Gypsies are innocent and childlike and dangerous. The argument of Pérez and Moscovici – that Gypsies could be evaluated positively yet be ontologized semantically – appears well illustrated in this description. The common feature of the descriptions is that both groups are considered dangerous – thus threatening – and therefore, in the Nazi logic, to be exterminated. The threats of being taken over by malicious people or "contaminated" by childlike, wild savages are equally powerful. Although Hoess "regretted" the extermination of the Gypsies, nevertheless both groups were sent to the gas chambers.

Threat can also be felt because of feelings of uncertainty about the future and about change. For example, Guimond and Dambrun (2002) (panel 2.7) suggest that not only feelings of relative *deprivation*, but also feelings of relative *gratification*, are associated with prejudice. Their results seem to indicate that an anticipated change in one's condition, even in a positive direction, might produce discrimination.

The concept of threat is a difficult one to investigate and is usually inferred from its consequences. However, it seems to me that we should be more careful in understanding those feelings of people that could lead to extreme behaviors. It appears that cultural diversity in itself has become threatening for some reason. It could be that people see the changes that multicultural societies bring and they are frightened. They fear losing "who they are" (the value, distinctiveness, and meaning derived from their memberships). They fear losing their own position. Thus, they seem unwilling to

---

Panel 2.7   When Prosperity Breeds Intergroup Hostility: The Effects of Relative Deprivation and Relative Gratification (Guimond and Dambrun 2002)

Research question

Would both relative deprivation and relative gratification lead to more negative intergroup attitudes?

Theoretical framework

Theories of relative deprivation (TS8) and relative gratification (feelings of gratification resulting from comparisons between oneself and other individuals or groups, or temporal comparisons whose outcome is positive for oneself). It is assumed that the perceived change (negative or positive) in one's condition produces feelings of deprivation/gratification that in turn lead to negative attitudes towards the outgroup.

Method

Two experimental studies.

Study 1

Participants: 125 students at a French university who participated on a voluntary basis.

Procedure

Participants were told that they were participating in a social perception study and were randomly assigned in one of three experimental conditions. They were led to believe that, according to official statistics, either their job opportunities after graduation were expected to be very poor (relative deprivation) or quite high (relative gratification) in comparison with what they used to be for graduates in the past (temporal comparison). In the third, control condition, no information about job prospects was provided. Then they were asked to complete a question-naire that included three scales:

- A scale of generalized prejudice against immigrants and ethnic minorities (i.e., those immigrants that do not have immigration documents should be sent back to their countries).
- A version of Adorno et al.'s (1950) ethnocentrism scale (TS11).
- A scale that rated the extent to which they were favorable to their ingroup (French) and several outgroups (Arabs, Americans, Canadians, Russians, and Europeans).

Results

Contrary to the hypothesis, participants in the relative deprivation condition did not express more prejudice than those in the control condition on any of the scales. However, participants in the relative gratification condition displayed more preju-dice and ethnocentrism than participants in the control condition, and more inter-group bias against Arabs, Europeans, and Canadians than those in the control condition.

Discussion

Although temporal relative deprivation did not increase intergroup prejudice, placing people in a position of privilege may trigger the need to justify this position. This justification may have been expressed by displaying prejudice and by denigrating outgroups.

Study 2

The second experiment manipulated relative gratification at an intergroup level.

(*Continues*)

Panel 2.7   (*Continued*)

Method

Participants (120 French psychology students) were told that their job prospects would either be lower (relative deprivation) or higher (relative gratification) than the prospects of students of economics. A control condition where no information was provided was also included. Participants were asked to complete a series of scales:

- A measure of prejudice (as in study 1).
- A measure of intergroup bias (as in study 1) with new outgroups (Arabs, Americans, Poles, black Africans, and Asians).
- A measure dealing with attitudes towards immigration policy.
- A seven-item behavioral measure of willingness to support and enforce a fictitious immigration law proposing to send home all North African immigrants.
- A measure of social dominance orientation (TS 11).

Results

Participants in the relative deprivation condition showed higher levels of generalized prejudice than those in the control condition. There were no other significant differences in other measures between participants in the relative deprivation and control conditions.

   The results of the relative gratification condition generally replicate the results of the previous study. Participants in the relative gratification condition expressed greater generalized prejudice and greater intergroup bias against North Africans than those in the control condition. Furthermore, they displayed more support for immigration policies that aim to send immigrants back home and more willingness to support discriminatory governmental policies than did participants in the control condition. Finally, despite the fact that participants in the relative gratification condition displayed more social dominance orientation than those in the control condition, social dominance orientation did not mediate the effects of relative gratification on prejudice. This is an important result because by manipulating the levels of social dominance orientation in different contexts the authors challenge the assumption that this orientation is a stable personality characteristic (TS11). It also indicates that social dominance orientation does not fully explain the effects of relative gratification on prejudice.

Discussion

These results confirm the role of relative gratification in the expression of prejudice. It seems that when people perceive that their group will benefit in terms of job opportunities they justify this situation by expressing prejudice.

General discussion

The results of these studies indicate that not only fear of loss relative to others (relative deprivation) can create prejudiced attitudes towards immigrants and ethnic minorities, but also the perception of being in a better condition in the future or in comparison to other groups. Confronted with the striking result that both economic scarcity and economic prosperity are linked to prejudice against immigrants, the authors suggest that "to prevent destructive conflicts, the goal of equality rather than economic improvements has to be kept in mind."

change their categorization systems and the meanings and boundaries of categories. They act to protect their vision of the world as they know it. Social psychologists can contribute toward understanding these phenomena by looking more closely at the concept of threat, in particular by studying what representations of the world are challenged and what are the processes of social influence that take place and produce those challenges.

This chapter has discussed possible reactions of dominant cultural groups. I have chosen to emphasize issues of prejudice and discrimination although obviously not all members of cultural majorities discriminate or hold such beliefs. For example, there is evidence (Manganelli and Volpato 2001) that people who hold conservative political beliefs and people that hold left-wing political beliefs differ in their levels of subtle and manifest prejudice (the former displaying more prejudice). However, the consequences of these beliefs and practices are sufficiently important to deserve greater discussion. In addition, as Moscovici and Pérez (1997) remark, discrimination concerns the ingroup and has nothing to do with the properties of the victims. It is the theories of the cultural majorities about immigration and ethnicity that we need to look at.

After presenting the classic social psychological theories about prejudice we looked at how people represent others. Our discussion on representations of groups (stereotyping) led to the important issue of social categorization. Looking at racism, we discussed the social construction of categories and their essentialization. Finally, we discussed extreme problematizations of outgroups that result in a denial of their humanity. I conclude this chapter by endorsing the view of many social psychologists in suggesting that this world characterized by negative representations of minorities, prejudice, and discrimination, is driven by feelings of threat. Cultural majorities might feel threatened at a symbolic level by the change that multicultural societies bring to their worldviews and the way they see themselves, and by fears of insecurity and contamination. Their reaction might be to exclude the minority. This exclusion is obtained by throwing them outside common frameworks, even by denying them membership in the human category. Multicultural societies oblige people to consider cultural groups interdependently and thus observe *realistic* threats. Realistic threats arise from the coexistence of different cultural groups. Ways to reduce prejudice and promote harmonious intergroup relations are the topic of the next chapter.

Chapter 3

Living Together in Culturally Diverse Societies

Plate 3   Toronto Greek town: signs in two languages.

Outline

In the previous chapter we discussed how cultural majorities might react to the presence of cultural minorities. In this chapter our discussion concerns how culturally dominant and non-dominant groups can live together. It seems evident that prejudice and discrimination poison relationships between groups and can undermine the cohesiveness, peace, and prosperity of societies. It is important therefore, in the first instance, to see how prejudice can be reduced. Groups in society, however segregated they may appear, are in functional interdependence (Sherif 1967). Such a relationship generates a whole set of issues around realistic conflicts, distribution of resources, and perceptions of justice, and will be the second part of our discussion. We will conclude with the need to address issues that arise from the common membership of groups in more inclusive categories.

Reducing Prejudice: Contact and Categorization Issues

One of the first ideas about prejudice to be discussed was that people are prejudiced because of ignorance (recall the concept of stereotypes considered as erroneous pictures in our heads). People held erroneous beliefs about others because they didn't know them. If they were to meet them, interact with them, and become close to them their prejudice would reduce and perhaps disappear. This argument led to the *contact hypothesis*. However, it soon became evident that contact alone was not enough to reduce prejudice. Allport (1954) described four conditions that are necessary for contact to be an agent in the reduction of prejudice (panel 3.1).

Allport's conditions are of crucial importance and the contact hypothesis has been widely investigated, mainly (but not exclusively) in the context of interracial relationships. Pettigrew and Tropp (2000) reported the results of a **meta-analysis** of studies using the contact hypothesis.

Meta-analysis
The statistical analysis of results from a large number of individual research studies so as to integrate their findings.
(Wood 2000: 417)

They reviewed 200 studies published before December 1998, including in their analysis only those studies that understood contact as face-to-face interaction between members of clearly distinguishable groups. Two other important criteria were taken into consideration: (1) contact had to be considered in the studies as an independent variable affecting intergroup prejudice; (2) prejudice measures had to be collected at an individual level, and not at an aggregate level, in order to evaluate possible changes in people's attitudes. On the whole, Pettigrew and Tropp's analysis confirmed the premises of the contact hypothesis: face-to-face interaction between members of distinguishable

Panel 3.1   Reducing Prejudice: The Contact Hypothesis

Allport (1954) identified four preconditions that ought to be met in order to produce optimal conditions for intergroup contact. Only under these conditions could inter-group contact contribute to the reduction of prejudice. The preconditions are:

- *Equal status between the groups:* if the groups in contact are not perceived to be of equal status then negative stereotypes could be reinforced and sustained.
- *Social and institutional support:* for contact to be beneficial it has to be endorsed and supported by the legitimate authorities and promoted by social norms.
- *Cooperative interdependence:* insofar as the groups in contact are interdepend-ent, this relationship needs to be a cooperative one. If competition between groups occurs, then that contact will not be beneficial for the reduction of prejudice.
- *Acquaintance potential:* contact has to be of sufficient duration, frequency, and closeness to promote the development of close relationships. If contact is super-ficial and there are no close relationships between people belonging to different groups, then not only will prejudice *not* be reduced, but there is also a risk that it will increase.

According to Wilder (1986), two conditions have to be met for intergroup contact to be judged successful. Firstly the interaction has to be positive and relationships with members of the outgroup have to be established. Secondly, the positive attitudes towards the people with whom one has had contact need to be extended to the other members of the outgroup.

groups reduces prejudice, measured in a variety of ways. Furthermore, they suggest that there is evidence that the benefits of contact can be extended beyond the participants of particular interactions to the whole outgroup. Contact with some out-groups (e.g., homosexuals) produced a greater reduction of prejudice than contact with other outgroups (e.g., people with disabilities). Importantly, they found that group status (majority vs. minority) played an important role in the reduction of prejudice. Indeed, in those studies with majority members, the effects in prejudice reduction after contact were larger than in those studies with minority members. Pettigrew and Tropp (2000: 109) conclude: "we should regard the contact theory's specified optimal condi-tions not as intrinsic features of the situation itself, but rather as conditions that can be perceived in contrasting ways by members of the interacting groups." The authors suggest that members of some groups might not perceive, for example, that the groups involved in contact share an equal status.

It is important to remember that Pettigrew and Tropp's meta-analysis only included studies involving face-to-face interaction. The authors emphasize that contact is beneficial for the reduction of prejudice when it is supported by institutions and authorities in ways that allow people to have *sustained interactions and develop friendships* (acquaintance potential). Friendship has also been found by Pettigrew (1998b) to be a causal agent of prejudice reduction in multinational studies. The importance of different levels of contact has been highlighted in other studies (Hamberger and Hewstone 1997). Volpato and Manganelli Ratazzi (2000) measured the relationships between different types of contact with immigrants (friendship, contact in the neighborhood, and direct but occasional contact) that young Italians (residing in two towns in the north of Italy) had in relation to their levels of prejudice. In one of the towns there was a greater numerical presence of immigrants and the authors were interested to see whether this had an effect on opportunities for contact and conflict reduction. In general, it was found that those people who reported having friendships with immigrants displayed lower levels of prejudice – in particular, of manifest prejudice – and were open to policies advocating an extension of immigrants' rights. Having other types of contact also had beneficial effects in the reduction of prejudice. These results – plus the fact that those who reported having friends of other nationalities, races, or language-speakers displayed less prejudice – led the authors to suggest that there might be a relationship between openness to contact and lower levels of prejudice.

A noticeable finding of this study, however, was that people living in the city with more immigrants did not reveal higher levels of contact than those people living in the city with a smaller immigrant population. More importantly, manifest prejudice was higher among those who were living in the city with a greater immigrant population. This means that the opportunity to meet people from the outgroup is not enough to make people engage in contact. Certainly, the other conditions proposed by Allport (equality of status, institutional support, and cooperative relations) must also be actively present. The contact hypothesis is not about living in close vicinity with members of the outgroup, but about establishing contact through interpersonal and close interaction. The fact that the town with more immigrants showed higher levels of prejudice might be due to the effects of their presence on categorization in term of natives vs. immigrants, making it more salient, as social identity and self-categorization theorists would suggest.

If intergroup categorization is responsible for prejudice, contact might make things worse by rendering the categorical differentiation salient. Thus, researchers suggested that in order for contact to be successful, the salience of the intergroup categorization should change. In that respect different models were proposed. (panel 3.2)

The change in the boundaries of categories is also expected to remedy a possible weakness of the contact hypothesis, namely the generalization of positive attitudes beyond specific interactions. According to these models, if we see people as individuals and not as group members (decategorization), if common identities are strengthened, if intergroup identities are maintained in the context of cooperation, then contact between people is more likely to reduce prejudice and change people's attitudes. Thus, the contact hypothesis and the categorization hypothesis are not opposed but complementary ideas on how prejudice might be reduced. Both hypotheses attack the

Panel 3.2   Reducing Prejudice: The Categorization Hypothesis

In order for prejudice to be reduced the salience of the categorization in terms of ingroup/outgroup should be changed. Different ways of altering this categorization are proposed.

Decategorization (Brewer and Miller 1984, 1996)

This model suggests that because categorization depersonalizes people and generates intergroup bias (TS3, TS12), in order to reduce prejudice one should reduce the salience of the categorization. In this case, people are encouraged to interact as individuals and not as members of different groups. The individuation of others enables people to focus on the personal characteristics of others and to leave aside possible stereotypical descriptions of groups. Such favorable interactions should reduce prejudice. The question is whether the more positive attitudes can be generalized to other outgroup members or whether they are limited to those who were part of the interaction.

Recategorization: The common ingroup identity model (Gaertner et al. 1993, 1999, 2000)

According to this model, prejudice can be reduced if the ingroup–outgroup categorization can be shifted to a superordinate level and members of the two groups can be viewed as belonging to a common inclusive ingroup. This model proposes that the benefits of the recategorization in terms of reduction of prejudice and generalization of positive attitudes should be even greater if the boundaries of the subgroups are maintained within the more inclusive category.

Subcategorization (Hewstone and Brown 1986)

According to this model, in order to effectively generalize positive attitudes towards members of the outgroup, the best thing is to maintain the interaction at an intergroup level. However, the encounter needs to be under the conditions laid out by Allport. In particular, the interaction needs to be cooperative, so that groups with complementary roles work together towards common goals. Empirical evidence has supported this hypothesis (Deschamps and Brown 1983; Van Oudenhoven, Groenewoud, and Hewstone 1996; Wilder 1984). The issue that needs to be addressed is the risk of a generalization of negative attitudes if the outcome of the encounter is not positive. Furthermore, the fact that groups have complementary roles might undermine the condition of equal status between the groups that is crucial to the contact hypothesis.

> ## Cross-categorization (Deschamps 1977b; Deschamps and Doise 1978a, 1978b; Doise 1978)
>
> Deschamps and Doise observed that although sometimes people belong to different categories according to one dimension of categorization, they might belong to the same category according to another dimension. In that case, categorical boundaries cross each other and the processes of accentuation of similarities and differences between and within categories are conflicting. The authors suggest that intergroup bias would be reduced because the person could be perceived simultaneously as both an ingroup and an outgroup member. This hypothesis has been confirmed subsequently by other empirical evidence (Crisp and Hewstone 2000; Rehm, Waldemar, and Eimeren 1988; Vanbeselaere 1987).

cognitive aspect of prejudice by suggesting that more accurate information about others (through contact) and a change in the frames of categorization will reduce prejudice.

However, our discussion in chapter 2 led us to believe that negative attitudes and stereotypes are just the tip of the iceberg. People might be led to hold such cognitions about outgroups by the different types of threat they might feel from the outgroup's presence. Stephan and Stephan (2000) propose an integrated model of threat (panel 3.3), suggesting that attitudes towards outgroups are determined by two types of threat (symbolic and realistic), by feelings of intergroup anxiety, and by negative stereotyping.

> ## Panel 3.3   An Integrated Threat Theory of Prejudice (adapted from Stephan and Stephan 2000)
>
> | *Antecedents of threat* | *Types of threat and orientation towards the outgroup* | |
> |---|---|---|
> | | | |
> | Ingroup identification | Realistic threats | |
> | Relevance | Symbolic threats | |
> | Contact | $\rightarrow$ | $\rightarrow$ Attitudes towards the outgroup |
> | | | |
> | Intergroup conflict | Intergroup anxiety | |
> | Group status | Negative stereotyping | |
> | Knowledge | | |
> | | | *(Continues)* |

Panel 3.3   (*Continued*)

- *Ingroup identification:* threats will be more salient for those who identify with their ingroup.
- *Relevance:* the more personal relevance the issues or policies have for the self, the stronger the perception of threat.
- *Contact:* the frequency and quality of contact will affect feelings of threat.
- *Intergroup conflict:* people will feel more threatened if the two groups have a prior history of conflict.
- *Status of the groups:* high-status group members might feel more threatened by realistic threats and feelings of intergroup anxiety, whereas low-status group members might feel threatened at a symbolic level and hold negative stereotypes of the outgroup.
- *Knowledge:* the less people know about the outgroup the more threatened they will feel.
- *Realistic threats:* "threats to the very existence of the ingroup (e.g., through warfare), threats to the political and economic power of the ingroup, and threats to the physical or material well-being of the ingroup or its members (e.g., their health)" (Stephan and Stephan 2000: 25).
- *Symbolic threats:* "perceived group differences in morals, values, standards, beliefs, and attitudes. Symbolic threats are threats to the worldview of the ingroup" (ibid).
- *Intergroup anxiety:* feeling personally threatened in intergroup interactions due to concerns about being embarrassed, rejected, or ridiculed.
- *Negative stereotyping:* holding negative stereotypes about the outgroup creates negative expectations about interactions and therefore feelings of threat.

They suggest different antecedents of threat, in which they include the quality of contact and the status of the groups, knowledge about the outgroup, the personal relevance of the relationship, and also group identification. Those people for whom the ingroup matters a lot will be more susceptible to threat. In that respect, information and contact, perception of oneself and others in terms of group membership, are factors that would influence the levels of threat that one might experience from the presence of others. Close contact with members of other groups and shifting the levels of categorization would definitely change levels of prejudice, but perhaps only for those who do not feel very threatened by the presence of the outgroup. In order to reduce prejudice, we also need to address the types of threat identified in chapter 2. We need to look at the fear of "contamination," the fear of acquiring a negative identity by the inclusion of the outgroup, the threat to values, beliefs, and practices from the presence of new ones, and the threat of change in general. We need to see what makes people feel threatened by the presence of a different group. To do so, we need to consider people's perceptions about the relationships between groups.

Relationships Between Groups: Issues of Negative and Positive Interdependence and Power

Groups living together are in a system of functional **interdependence**.

Remember, in the robber's cave studies (TS13), Sherif first kept the groups of boys independent. Then he introduced a situation of negative interdependence in which the groups competed with each other. In order to reduce the prejudice that occurred, Sherif and his colleagues (Sherif et al. 1954; Sherif 1966, 1967) had to change the relationship between the groups by introducing superordinate goals. The goals of each group were contingent on the actions and cooperation of the other group. The outgroup was no longer perceived as an "enemy" whose gains were linked to the ingroup's losses, but as a possible contributor to achieving a common goal. From this work the idea flourished that competition produces prejudice and that cooperation contributes to its reduction.

However, what seems to be at stake here is the representation that people have of the relationships between groups. Multicultural societies, with the salience of different cultural groups, obviously generate such representations. Popular discourse states that immigrants and asylum seekers seek to benefit from welfare systems (a relation of dependency), that immigrants are taking jobs from the native population, or that affirmative action policies are benefiting minorities at the expense of the majority (a relation of **negative interdependence**). These representations reflect relationships between groups as a zero-sum game and generate what we call realistic threats. These threats are believed to be pivotal to intergroup conflict (Bobo 1999; Esses, Jackson, and Armstrong 1998; Sherif 1967).

In the context of immigration, Esses et al. (2001) investigated the threat generated by the belief that resources are scarce and their distribution occurs within a zero-sum framework (panel 3.4).

> **Interdependence**
>
> The outcomes of one person or group are dependent on the actions and outcomes of another person or group.

> **Negative interdependence**
>
> Negative interdependence exists when the goals of people or groups are incompatible and when the benefits of one person/group have negative effects on the outcomes of the other group.

Panel 3.4   The Immigration Dilemma: The Role of Perceived Group Competition, Ethnic Prejudice, and National Identity (Esses et al. 2001)

Research question

The study aimed to investigate the role of perceived group competition for resources, social dominance orientation, and zero-sum beliefs (beliefs that more resources for immigrants means less for people in the receiving society) on perceptions of immigrants and attitudes towards immigration in Canada and the United States. The authors remark that although both countries were originally founded by immigration and both have policies that regulate immigration on the basis of employment skills and family factors, they place different emphases on these factors. Canadian policies are based on high-skilled employment, whereas in the United States such a

(Continues)

Panel 3.4   (*Continued*)

preference is not so clearcut. The similarities and differences in immigration policies between these countries make them interesting targets for investigation.

The authors seek to investigate ways of changing negative attitudes towards immigrants and immigration.

Theoretical framework

The instrumental model of group conflict (Esses, Jackson, and Armstrong 1998), influenced by realistic conflict theories (TS13), suggests that perceptions of competition over resources between groups will provoke anxiety over resource distribution (resource stress). Resource stress is a function of perceptions of the economic situation and the availability of resources, and perceptions regarding the ability of the outgroup to obtain these resources. The combination of resource stress with the presence of a salient outgroup will lead to competition and will generate zero-sum beliefs (beliefs according to which the gains of one group are the losses of another). Attitudes and behaviors towards the competitor will reflect strategies to remove the stressful situation. Such strategies might include prejudice and discrimination.

To the extent that the social dominance orientation (TS11) concerns beliefs about the inevitability of social hierarchies and unequal distribution of resources, people with high levels of SDO will be more prone to zero-sum beliefs.

General hypothesis

"Attitudes towards immigrants and immigration will be significantly shaped by perceptions of resource stress and by individual and group factors relating to motivations for an unequal distribution of resources" (Esses et al. 2001: 394).

Method and procedure

Several experimental studies conducted in Canada and the United States are reported. Different fictitious journal editorials were proposed to participants. In these editorials the independent variables of each study were manipulated. Participants' attitudes towards immigrants and immigration and towards ethnic groups were also assessed, along with zero-sum beliefs. In addition, participants completed an SDO scale.

Results

For more details on these experiments see Esses, Jackson, and Armstrong 1998; Esses et al. 1999; Jackson and Esses 2000.

Resource stress and competition for resources

The independent variable manipulated in the editorials was resource stress, where half of the participants read about immigrants' successes in a difficult job market.

In these studies, participants were also asked about their support for policies that aimed to help immigrants adjust to Canada, either by providing direct assistance or by empowering them. The results indicate that those who read the editorial describing immigrant successes in a difficult job market were less favorable to immigrants and immigration in Canada and were less willing to support policies that will empower immigrants.

Social dominance orientation effects

Those people who scored high on SDO showed more negative attitudes towards immigrants and immigration and were less willing to support empowerment policies. SDO levels did not have an effect on willingness to support direct assistance to immigrants. However, levels of SDO did not interact with the manipulation of beliefs about resource stress.

Zero-sum beliefs and prejudice against ethnic groups

The relation between zero-sum beliefs, SDO, and attitudes towards immigrants and immigration was assessed in the Canadian studies. It was found that not only was there a positive relationship between SDO and zero-sum beliefs, but also the latter mediated the effects of SDO on negative attitudes towards immigration and the empowerment of immigrants. Thus, it seems that people scoring higher in SDO are biased against immigration because of their zero-sum beliefs.

The same study conducted in the United States differentiated the attitudinal target, asking specifically about attitudes towards either Asian or black immigrants. This study also included a measure of willingness for contact with these ethnic groups.

The results of the American study confirmed the previous ones, inasmuch as SDO was positively related to zero-sum beliefs that in turn predicted attitudes towards both ethnic groups and mediated the relationship between SDO and these attitudes. In addition, SDO was weakly related to ethnic prejudice towards these groups and ethnic prejudice did not predict attitudes towards immigration. Finally, high levels of SDO, ethnic prejudice, and zero-sum beliefs predicted unwillingness to engage in contact with these ethnic groups.

General discussion

The authors conclude that "perceived group competition, whether situationally induced or a function of chronic beliefs in zero-sum relations among groups, is strongly implicated in negative attitudes toward immigrants and immigration" (Esses et al. 2001: 402). Interestingly, they observed that general negative attitudes towards ethnic groups play a less direct role in predicting attitudes towards immigration. Thus, it seems that it is a more specific set of beliefs

(Continues)

Panel 3.4   (*Continued*)
concerning competition over scarce resources that plays a major role. They also remark that the findings are similar in Canada and the United States despite their different emphases on immigration policies.

Among other things, their research showed that people's beliefs about the distribution of resources in terms of negative interdependence mediate the relationship between beliefs about the hierarchical structure of society and attitudes towards immigration. More importantly, they found that ethnic prejudice does not have the same effects. The authors conclude that

> it is not just an unfavorable overall attitude toward an ethnic group that drives attitudes toward the immigration of the group, but the specific component of the ethnic attitude that focuses on instrumental beliefs about competition with the group (p. 402) They conclude that ethnicity may also have an important role to play in immigration attitudes as an indicator of who is and who is not part of the non-immigrant group (p. 403)....

Representations of group relationships in terms of hierarchy and negative interdependence interact with social categorization and generate beliefs about who is entitled to receive resources and who is included in the ingroup.

An issue that exemplifies the perception of a multicultural society as a zero-sum situation is the debate over **affirmative action** policies.

Affirmative action

The general designation of a wide range of programs to overcome the effects of past discrimination and to provide equal opportunity for historically discriminated against groups.

Most of the research concerning affirmative action has been undertaken in the United States and Canada, where such policies have been in place for a long time (United States Civil Rights Act 1964; Equal Opportunities Act 1972; Human Resources and Development Canada 1988). Affirmative action does not aim to stop discrimination by simply reducing prejudice, but seeks to actively encourage the representation of minority groups in sectors where they previously had limited access because of discriminatory practices (education, employment, etc.) and thus to compensate for such discrimination. As the US Commission on Civil Rights (1977) declared: "affirmative action concerns any measure beyond simple termination of discriminatory practice adopted to correct and compensate for past and present discrimination and to prevent discrimination from recurring in the future." To do so, these policies target specific groups and try to redistribute resources. If one of the tasks of the modern state is to regulate the distribution of resources among its citizens, the issue of affirmative action brought to the forefront justice considerations (Dovidio and Gaertner 1996) (TS18). To what extent is affirmative action perceived to be fair?

After the implementation of affirmative action policies, debates started concerning the fairness of such measures. In the 1990s some US states abolished them. Opposition to affirmative action has been put down to prejudiced attitudes towards specific groups (Williams et al. 1999). However, there are also claims that opposition to affirmative action in the United States is not restricted to uneducated and poor white people, but that educated and politically sophisticated white Americans are also opposed on the grounds that affirmative action policies violate egalitarianism (Federico and Sidanius 2002). According to the "egalitarian opposition" argument, if American values are represented by meritocracy and individual achievement, then the promotion of people based not only on their individual merits but *also* on group membership violates these norms. The proponents of these views claim to be colorblind and to oppose affirmative action on the basis of cherished American values. This position raises several problems, which will become clearer later.

There are two things that I would like to highlight here. First, opposition to a policy can be "justified" on the basis of positive values and different norms of justice (TS18). Opposition to affirmative action based on arguments about the unfairness of procedures might constitute a valid justification for aversive racists (Dovidio and Gaertner 1996; Murrell et al. 1994). As discussed in chapter 2, if these people can explain their behavior without making reference to race they feel "liberated" and able to express discriminatory feelings and behaviors.

The second point is that in order to understand actions and attitudes, one needs to be aware of the whole context of beliefs in society. In the case of Western societies, beliefs about meritocracy seem to constitute the context within which affirmative action debates are taking place. There is evidence, for example, that in Western societies meritocratic beliefs are so important that, even in situations where it is clear that promotion is unfairly restricted (tokenism), people will still aim to change the situation by using individual strategies and rejecting collective solutions (Wright, Taylor, and Moghaddam 1990; Wright and Taylor 1998; Wright 2001).

Tokenism

An intergroup context in which the boundaries between the advantaged and the disadvantaged groups are not entirely closed, but where there are severe restrictions on access to advantaged positions on the basis of group membership.

(Wright 2001: 224)

The power of meritocratic beliefs is also evident in an experimental study conducted by Chryssochoou and Sanchez-Mazas (2000), which aimed to establish how someone who was offered the opportunity to leave a low-status group and be promoted would be perceived by fellow group members. We found that people are better disposed towards this person when she is promoted on the basis of meritocratic criteria and, surprisingly, even more so when membership of the lower-status group is not based on merit. Participants' belief in meritocracy was such that they looked up to the promoted person as a model even when there was no link between their own abilities and membership in the low-status group (therefore they could hope for individual promotion themselves). In other words, the organization of society on the basis of individual merit is so powerful that these beliefs operate in many contexts. People did not resent the fact that somebody abandoned the group for a better fate if this promotion was justified by individual merit. Given that meritocratic beliefs are so pervasive, the way people make sense of the distribution of resources and the procedures attached to it has to be understood within the context of those beliefs.

Meritocracy is based on the belief that opportunities in society are distributed according to individual merit. Such beliefs disregard the influence of factors such as discrimination and seem incompatible with programs designed to distribute resources on a collective basis because they challenge ideas about distributive and procedural justice (TS18). In addition, meritocratic beliefs can lead people to overemphasize the role of the individual as a maker of his or her own fate (a fundamental attribution error) and attribute failure to internal causes. Following this line of thought is only a short step from believing in a hierarchical organization of society where disadvantaged groups deserve what they get (belief in a just world). In combination with a representation of relationships between groups as negatively interdependent (Esses et al. 2001), these beliefs would almost certainly lead to opposing programs such as affirmative action, aimed at redressing inequalities.

The debate about affirmative action is so widespread that a whole book can be written about it. The efficacy of such programs is also challenged by those researchers who suggest that they may have the reverse of the effect intended for members of minorities: affirmative action could reinforce stereotypes about the lower position of members of minority groups (Steele 1990), stigmatize the recipients and reduce their self-esteem (Major, Feinstein, and Crocker 1994), lead to self-fulfilling prophecies (Pratkanis and Turner 1996; Turner and Pratkanis 1994), and contribute to stereotype threat. Maio and Esses (1998) found that an unfamiliar, positively described outgroup who were supposed to immigrate to Canada due to natural disaster in their country of origin, were perceived by Canadian participants as less competent when it was mentioned that this group would benefit from Canadian affirmative action policies. However, the authors remark that this assumption "was more common among participants who were unfavorable towards affirmative action" (Maio and Esses 1998: 71) It seems that those who are negatively predisposed to such measures will be those who see beneficiaries as less competent. The existence of affirmative action might not create negative perceptions about outgroups, but it might reinforce these perceptions in those who already have them.

Dovidio and Gaertner (1996) remark that affirmative action policies, because they are oriented towards outcomes, go beyond good intentions that can easily be forgotten. They therefore offer a good opportunity to redress inequalities and create an anti-discrimination ethos. Because affirmative action policies are institutionalized practices they also offer good grounds for intergroup contact by meeting one of Allport's conditions: institutional support. Thus, abandoning them in the current situation would probably mean losing an excellent chance of redressing long-entrenched inequalities.

I brought affirmative action into our discussion because these programs involve perceptions about the distribution of resources and inevitably call upon people's norms of justice (TS18). These norms are not individual beliefs, but socially constructed and shared beliefs that are part of the social representations of resource entitlements. In addition, my interest in affirmative action is based on the fact that these policies make salient the power and status of the different groups and represent their relationship as negatively interdependent.

To understand opposition to it, affirmative action has to be seen within the wider context in which these policies are necessary. Their necessity derives from inequalities in the distribution of resources among groups. Those who oppose these actions feel threatened by the possibility of resource redistribution because they see society as a zero-sum game (Esses et al. 2001) and because any change in the way resources are distributed threatens their group interests and their group position (Bobo 1998). This threat might be exacerbated by racist beliefs, or disguised under the cover of fairness considerations and meritocratic beliefs. It would be nice not to need affirmative action policies. However, until then, as Bobo (1998: 989) remarks, "it is the understanding of group interests and what affects those understandings that is analytically and politically most important." In other words, as social psychologists, we need to understand the social psychological mechanisms that lead people to hold these beliefs and to view the relationships between groups as negatively interdependent. There is much work to be done in this area.

> **Positive interdependence**
>
> Positive interdependence exists when the goals between people or groups are compatible and whatever benefits one person/group will also benefit the other person/group.

Would changing the perception of the relationship between social groups into a **positively interdependent** one reduce negative perceptions of the outgroup?

The answer is not simple. First of all we need to be very sure about what we mean by positive interdependence. Early on in social psychology it was made clear that sharing a common fate with others, independently of how this common fate was inflicted upon people, was enough to trigger behaviors of ingroup favoritism (Rabbie and Horwitz 1969, 1982). Thus, when one shares a **common fate** with others, the likelihood is that one will favor these people on cognitive, evaluative, and behavioral dimensions.

> **Common fate**
>
> A coincidence of outcomes among two or more persons that arises because they have been subjected to the same external forces or decision rules.
>
> (Brewer 2000: 118)

Culturally diverse groups in multicultural societies can be subjected to common events. But do they really share a common fate? Power differentials between these groups shape their fate differently even if they share membership in a nation-state. Furthermore, do they *perceive* themselves as sharing the same fate? In other words, do they feel that they are part of the same moral community? We are dealing here with the chicken and egg argument: does common fate generate or strengthen feelings of belongingness to a group, or does common group membership need to preexist for feelings of common fate to be activated? If the latter is the case, common fate with a group that is perceived as an outgroup might trigger feelings of threat. Thus, minority groups, instead of being included in the broader community, might find themselves held responsible for negative events and become even more excluded. The economic crisis and rise in unemployment in France during the 1990s brought to the surface arguments about "job priority" for French people by the French National Front. Although economists argue that there are two separate and parallel labor markets – one for the native-born population and one for immigrants – people still regard the labor market as a zero-sum game and blame immigrants for unemployment. Thus, the common fate of economic recession did not have positive effects on the relationship between the French and immigrants.

Marilyn Brewer (2000: 119) warns us not to confuse common fate with interdependence. Interdependence means that the outcomes of a person or group can be "affected or determined by what another individual in the interdependent unit chooses to do."

The outcomes of one cultural group are affected by the actions of the other. This interdependence is negative when the goals are incompatible – therefore the outcomes of one group will suffer (zero-sum game). It is positive when the goals are compatible and both groups can benefit. In the first case, the outcomes of the groups are the product of independent actors competing against each other, whereas in the second case they could be the cumulative effect of independent actors or the product of coordinated actions aiming to achieve common goals.

It is important to grasp these nuances in order to understand how different groups live together. In the case of common fate the outcomes of the different groups are the result of external actions. If outcomes for a group are negative, then coexistence may become threatening and the other group might be blamed (e.g., immigrants blamed for unemployment). In the case of negative interdependence the crucial issue is the incompatibility of goals. Group members believe that the goals of their group are incompatible with the goals of the other group and that the actions of the outgroup will hinder the attainment of these goals. This can generate competition and distrust towards the outgroup.

Brewer (2000) proposes two models for positive interdependence. According to the first model, the existence of compatible goals (a positive reward structure) will lead to attraction, trust, and cooperation among the groups which, in turn, could give rise to a common identity. This model, I believe, is more likely when positive outcomes are the result of the actions of independent actors. When cultural groups have compatible goals and each tries to achieve them, their actions may lead to trust, attraction, and cooperation and ultimately perhaps to a common identity. The second model suggests that the compatibility of goals and a common identity between groups interact together and produce attraction, trust, and cooperation. In this model a common identity pre-dates cooperation. This model seems likely when coordinated actions between groups aim to achieve common goals. To give an example, according to the model, the fact that people from different European nations work together for mutual benefit and share a common European identity will lead to attraction, trust, and cooperation.

Brewer (2000: 121) remarks that if there is positive interdependence between groups but intergroup differentiation remains salient (lack of common identity) then "the presence of positive interdependence makes intergroup relations worse than when there is no interdependence at all." Having common goals and trying to achieve them with the cooperation of an outgroup might be detrimental to the development of positive feelings towards this group if, for example, the goals are not achieved. Following the patterns of the well-established **ultimate attribution error** (Pettigrew 1979; Taylor and Jaggi 1974; Hunter, Stringer, and Watson 1991), actions that contribute to failure might be attributed to the outgroup, whereas successful actions might be attributed to the ingroup.

As Deschamps and Brown (1983) have shown in a most enlightening study, anticipated cooperation between groups can have negative effects, depending on their degree of interdependence. In this experiment the

Ultimate attribution error

An extension of the fundamental attribution error according to which negative acts of the ingroup will be attributed to external causes, whereas negative actions of the outgroup will be attributed to internal causes. In addition, positive acts of the ingroup will be attributed to internal causes, whereas positive acts of the outgroup will be attributed to external causes.

(Pettigrew 1979)

researchers asked students to work in teams to produce a project in the knowledge that their work would be combined for a final evaluation. Half of the teams worked independently to produce the desired outcome in its totality (interdependence based on cumulative efforts to produce a joint outcome). In the other teams the roles were divided, one team working on a part of the project and another team working on another (interdependence based on coordinated actions to produce a joint outcome). Measures of ingroup bias were taken before the task and after its completion. The results are very interesting. Before the completion of the task, those participants who were in a relationship of positive interdependence based on coordinated actions (division of tasks) displayed more ingroup bias than the participants who were in an interdependent structure based on their independent cumulative efforts. The opposite was true for the ingroup bias after the completion of the task. Indeed, the level of ingroup bias of those who had complementary tasks in producing the project was reduced and they displayed significantly less bias than those who worked on the whole project and amalgamated their outcomes at the end. These results indicate that the *type* of positive interdependence has different effects on the reduction of ingroup bias. It seems that not having full control over actions contributing towards the outcome and having to share the work with an outgroup can be threatening to people. In this case, they display more ingroup bias than if they had the opportunity to control actions leading to the outcome. However, such division of work might significantly reduce their negative perceptions once the goals have been achieved (of course, in a satisfactory way). Brewer (2000) suggests that the ingroup bias reduction might be due to the development of a common identity.

Let's look at the implications of these ideas in the context of culturally diverse societies. Deschamps and Brown's (1983) results suggest that under conditions where their final outcomes are joined, groups living in culturally diverse environments will have higher levels of fear when the actions to achieve these goals are divided. However, if the outcomes are positive, such conditions will lead to more positive attitudes towards the members of the other group and ultimately perhaps to the construction of a common identity. This is a very promising idea, provided that the common outcomes are positive. However, if we want to be closer to the reality of social relationships, then we need to introduce another major issue to our discussion: power differentials.

Till now we have assumed that equal groups fought to achieve goals that might be compatible. A simple observation of our societies shows that this is not the case. Social groups have different material and symbolic power. Therefore, an interdependent relationship can be a relationship of exploitation and dependency. One group can benefit more from the relationship than the other, or the relationships between groups can be shaped in such a way that a group must depend on another for survival. In this case an interdependent relationship can constitute a major threat to the non-dominant group, since its outcomes or its survival depend on the actions of the dominant group.

Let's not forget that the relationships between groups depend enormously on people's perceptions of them. What one group perceives as a negative interdependent structure can be perceived by the other as a positive one. Where some groups perceive the situation as positive interdependence, others might see it as a relation of dependency from which they wish to escape. The division and distribution of tasks under conditions of positive interdependence might be made in such a way that they increase the dependency of one group on another (Glick and Fiske 2001).

Furthermore, interdependent relations might mean that some groups seek assistance from those who have the resources and opportunities to provide it. Nadler (2002: 489) discusses the role of power differentials and social inequalities in helping relations and suggests that "intergroup helping relations may both reflect and be affected by differentials between group power relations." He suggests that "groups can assert, affirm or challenge their power relations in the acts of giving, seeking, and receiving help" (p. 490). Powerful groups, through the act of giving, may assert their power; powerless groups, by accepting assistance, may be forced to acknowledge their dependency.

The fact that some researchers highlight the detrimental effects of affirmative action programs on the self-esteem of recipients points to the issue of power. If affirmative action programs are presented as a "help to people who otherwise cannot make it on their own" no wonder that it undermines their self-esteem. Portraying affirmative action in such a way not only emphasizes the continuing inferiority of the beneficiaries, but also frames the relationship between groups in a way that perpetuates dependency. As Beaton and Tougas (2001: 75) remark: "disadvantaged group members may not recognize the benefits of belonging to a greater moral community if it merely perpetuates the advantaged groups' control over the manner in which social benefits and rights are granted."

Dependency oriented help

Providing recipients with the full solution to the problem.

Autonomy oriented help

Providing recipients with the tools to solve their own problems.

(Nadler 2002: 491)

Nadler (2002) proposes a model of intergroup helping behaviors and suggests that the perceived legitimacy and stability of intergroup relations (TS3), the status of the groups, and the type of help given (**autonomy oriented vs. dependency oriented**) will influence the willingness of people to give or receive help.

Nadler reports a series of experiments with interesting results. For example, low-status group members who seek help are perceived as less able than high-status help-seekers. This finding raises the frightening possibility that low-status help-seekers, seen to be less able, will be given dependency-oriented help, whereas high-status help-seekers will be offered autonomy-oriented help. Furthermore, in other studies reported by Nadler, conducted in a clear intergroup context (Israeli Jews/Israeli Arabs), the influence of status on the helping behavior has been further consolidated. It was found that help provided to members of a low-status group by an outgroup member, without it being requested, reduced their feelings of self-worth and worthiness as an Arab and increased their negative affect (Halabi 1999). In addition, when low-status members had the opportunity to ask for help they sought less help from an outgroup member than from an ingroup member. In similar conditions the high-status group members were not affected by the category of the "helper" and sought help equally from the ingroup and outgroup member.

In light of this we can turn again to the Deschamps and Brown (1983) experiment. We could hypothesize that their results would be different if power differentials were introduced. People might resent receiving help from a less powerful outgroup in the "division of roles" condition because such help challenges the superiority of their own status. Equally, when they are in a less powerful position, people might resent being in a condition of undifferentiated roles because this condition reasserts the power of the powerful group. These are just speculations and merit experimental investigation. I use them here as an illustration of my point about the perceptions of the relationship between groups when power differentials exist. Different levels of interdependence might interact with power and status, as we have seen in helping intergroup relations. The point here is that even the best of intentions (providing assistance) can be used as a means for asserting group position and power. Members of high-status groups willing to provide dependency-oriented assistance may be surprised when their help is rejected or challenged. Reaction to help-providing may reflect a challenge to the status quo of social inequality.

Representations of the relationships between groups (interdependence) and power differentials are also reflected in the content of the stereotypes people hold for other groups. Fiske et al. (1999) and Glick and Fiske (2001) argue that the content of stereotypes is shaped by principles and can therefore be predicted. These researchers suggest that the content of stereotypes is rooted in the structural relationships between groups, which are shaped by interdependence and power. The position of a group in the hierarchy of power relations should predict how competent this group will be perceived to be and the type of interdependent relationship should predict how warm it will be thought to be (for the importance of warmth in person perception, see TS 19). Eagly (1987) has suggested that gender social roles have produced stereotypes that described men as "agentic" and women as "communal." We can explore how people perceive, on the one hand, industrialized and technologically developed countries and their inhabitants, and on the other hand, non-industrialized and non-technologically developed countries and their inhabitants. We can observe the same pattern of descriptions (Orpwood 2002). Industrialized countries are described with agentic characteristics and their inhabitants are perceived as competent but cold. Non-industrialized countries are described as more communal and with warm inhabitants. These findings show that the status of groups organizes representations about them.

According to Fiske et al. (1999) and Glick and Fiske (2001), groups tend to be highly evaluated on one or the other dimension (competence or warmth), but not on both. Fiske and colleagues consider that the characterization of a group as competent but cold or incompetent but warm expresses ambivalence towards the group and leads to different types of prejudice. Competent but cold groups are respected but envied (envious prejudice), whereas incompetent but warm groups are liked but patronized (paternalistic prejudice). With this in mind, research by Echebarria-Echabe and Gonzales Castro (1996) (presented in panel 2.1) studied the feelings of Basque people towards immigrants from European and third world countries. The first group was respected but envied, whereas the second group was liked but disrespected. Relationships with the competent but cold groups can be competitive or characterized by dependency, whereas relationships with the incompetent but warm groups can be cooperative or exploitative.

These studies suggest that although people may describe others with positive characteristics, in doing so they position them in a hierarchy of status. Their stereotypes reflect the type of relationship they have with these groups. I have found similar results while studying the content of the stereotype of the European in France and Greece (Chryssochoou 2000b, 2000c). Europeans were described as wealthy, organized, and civilized by both French and Greek participants, and the latter also described Europeans as cold. Greeks reserved the description of warm and hospitable for their group. In contrast, the French described their group with what seemed like negative characteristics, which reflected an agentic orientation. Moreover, interviews with Greek and French participants illustrated a relationship of envious dependency that Greeks had with Europeans. Greeks felt anxious to justify their inclusion in the European group. They felt that they might not be recognized as Europeans because they were not organized and economically competent. In contrast, the French positioned themselves as the prototype of the European. The status of the national groups organized their stereotypes about the Europeans and influenced people's identification patterns.

There are several points that need to be made here. First of all, it seems that through self-stereotyping, the groups accept, negotiate, or consolidate their position in the social system. Secondly, imposing a position on a group is not only a matter of evaluating the group negatively. Positive characteristics can also convey a position of inferiority. Chapter 2 presented the ideas of Moscovici and Peréz regarding the ontologization of the Gypsies. They suggested that there is a difference between discrimination and ontologization. The latter occurs when groups that are described positively are nevertheless positioned outside the boundaries of humanity. Ontologization could be an extreme form of the same pattern: the "negotiation" of one's group position within the framework characterized by the perception of the power relationships between groups. In this "negotiation" stereotypes – as representations of the relationships between groups – convey a vision of the world that aims to sustain power hierarchies or to challenge them. Groups, in fact, struggle for power and for position. Within this struggle they might be threatened, they might change their perceptions of interdependencies, they might display hostility.

Inspired by Blumer's (1955, 1958) group position theory, Bobo (1999: 447) claims that "prejudice involves more than negative stereotypes and negative feelings... it involves most centrally a commitment to a relative status positioning of groups in a racialized social order." Bobo is interested in racial relationships. An important point of his approach is that the acceptance and use of racial categories preexist prejudice. Remember the discussion in chapter 2 about the essentialization and reification of social categories. The theories people have about the world (in other words the categories they use to give meaning to their experience and protect their interests, to establish their position and to impose one on others) produce the framework in which relationships between groups are shaped.

We began this discussion by looking at the impact of relationships between groups on hostile feelings, on negative perceptions of outgroups, and on prejudice. We have come to the conclusion that relationships of interdependence (negative and positive) and power issues play a crucial role in the development of intergroup relationships (Fiske 2000). This is important for our discussion of multicultural societies that involve different cultural groups living together within the same political organization. It is necessary to take on board people's perceptions about these relationships and try to understand when it is they feel threatened by sharing membership with other groups. We therefore need to look at issues of inclusion and exclusion in multicultural groups.

Superordinate Memberships: The Battle for Group Beliefs

Historical and socioeconomic conditions have created culturally diverse societies. Cultural diversity is not new. Throughout history we can find examples of societies where people belonging to different groups lived together, sometimes peacefully, at other times in conflict. Diamond (1997) provides a historical and anthropological perspective on the paths that different societies followed in their development. The crucial thing to keep in mind is that there is nothing inherent in human nature that prevents people from living in societies where different social groups coexist. We all have different memberships; most of the time, we feel that these are not incompatible. Problems occur when we perceive an incompatibility between two memberships. This incompatibility at an individual level is something that we will discuss in the next chapter. Here, we still need to clarify the difficulty that we sometimes have in accepting that different groups can be part of the same entity, the same superordinate group. Multicultural societies ask us to do precisely that: consider the coexistence of different subgroups within the same superordinate group.

To do so, we need to enlarge our moral community, our scope of justice. We saw in chapter 2 how people can be thought of as being outside the boundaries of humanity. Believing that others are entitled to fair treatment is a first step towards including them in this moral community. Justice concerns (TS18) are essential in culturally diverse societies. Group position theory (Blumer 1955, 1958; Bobo 1999) holds that prejudice and discrimination occur when group members have feelings of superiority over other groups, when they believe that subordinate groups are intrinsically different and alien, when people have proprietary claims over certain rights and feel their position to be threatened. Extending the scope of justice means precisely that people do *not* feel superior towards others, do *not* regard them as alien, and most importantly do *not* have proprietary claims over resources or feel threatened. What is considered a fair outcome in relation to the distribution of resources (TS 18) is an indicator of whether the scope of justice is extended to outgroups.

In a series of experiments, Sanchez-Mazas and colleagues (Mugny et al. 1991; Sanchez-Mazas 1994; Sanchez-Mazas, Roux, and Mugny, 1994) manipulated perceptions of interdependence and asked people to allocate resources to Swiss nationals (the ingroup) and foreigners (the outgroup). They found some interesting results. Under conditions of positive interdependence, when the Swiss and foreigners formed a single recipient group, participants allocated more resources to this unique group than they allocated to the outgroup under conditions of negative interdependence (a zero-sum game between the two groups) or independence (when the distribution of resources was performed for each group separately). When the outgroup is included in a common group, the fact that the overall amount of distributed resources increases is an indication that the former outgroup under such conditions becomes part of the ingroup.

More xenophobic participants gave less to this common group than they gave to the ingroup under conditions of independence. Xenophobia was measured in this study as the level of acceptance of foreigners in the country. Those participants who wished the percentage of foreigners to be smaller than it was were considered xenophobic; those participants who accepted a higher percentage than the current one were considered xenophiles; those who opted for the status quo were labeled intermediates. Thus, initial tolerance towards the outgroup does play a role in their acceptance as part of a super-ordinate group. Inclusion in a common group does not mean that everybody will consider this new common group as an ingroup. Indeed, Mugny et al. (1991) found no difference in levels of ingroup favoritism displayed by the more xenophobic or the less xenophobic people when resources were allocated either in conditions of negative interdependence or in conditions of independence. In other words, independently of the framework in which resources were allocated, the more xenophobic participants displayed the same level of ingroup favoritism. Seemingly, there was an absence of ingroup bias in both conditions of resource allocation for people who were less xenophobic. However, those participants who had intermediate attitudes towards foreigners (the status quo) became more open and less discriminatory under conditions of independent allocation than when they were under conditions of negative interdependence; they also displayed the same levels of bias as the xenophiles (absence of ingroup favoritism). In addition, xenophobes found the requirement to make independent judgments more disturbing and disruptive and believed the condition of negative interdependence to be a more honest way of thinking about resources than did the two other groups.

These results highlight the fact that the distribution of resources is influenced by the initial attitudes people hold towards outgroups and the framework (independent/interdependent) in which the distribution takes place. In my own research (Chryssochoou 1996a) I have also found that the type of resource (material, power, or cultural) and the status of the outgroup with whom people are supposed to share play an equally important role in the way resources are distributed.

Distributing resources between groups also involves the authorities responsible for the distribution and the procedures governing it. The role of the authorities in the distribution of resources and their procedures has been highlighted in the group-value model (TS18). In judging the fairness of resource distribution, people not only focus on the outcome, but also on the procedures and principles by which this outcome is reached. In addition, according to the group-value model, people do not only have instrumental concerns when considering the fairness of resource distribution, but also relational concerns. In particular, they focus on the relationship with the authorities distributing the resources. Smith and Tyler's (1996) research (panel 3.5) shows that

Panel 3.5   Justice and Power: When Will Justice Concerns Encourage the Advantaged to Support Policies Which Redistribute Economic Resources and the Disadvantaged to Willingly Obey the Law? (Smith and Tyler 1996)

Research questions

A series of questions were investigated in two studies:

- What is more important for policy endorsement? Does the way economic policies are distributed and/or the recognition of unfair differences in the economic outcomes for different groups have an influence on policy endorsement?
- What is a better predictor of policy endorsement? Is the instrumental evaluation of the authorities or the relational evaluation of the authorities more important for policy endorsement?
- Does identification with the superordinate category influence the relative importance of relational and instrumental concerns?
- Does identification change the importance of different sources of information?
- Are evaluations of procedural and distributive justice related to feelings of obligation to obey the social rules?
- Which is the better predictor of feelings of obligation to obey the social rules: instrumental or relational evaluations of the authorities?
- Does identification with the superordinate category influence the relative importance of relational and instrumental concerns to feelings of obligation to obey the law?

Theoretical framework

Relational aspects of justice, group value model (TS18).

Method

Two telephone survey studies were conducted. The first study investigated attitudes towards affirmative action policies proposed by the federal government of the United States and targeted the advantaged group. The second study investigated feelings of obligation to obey social rules and targeted the disadvantaged group.

Participants

- *Study 1:* 352 white residents of San Francisco of different ages and socioeconomic and educational background.

(Continues)

Panel 3.5 (*Continued*)
- *Study 2:* 150 African Americans from the San Francisco area of different ages and socioeconomic and educational status.

Measures

- *Policy endorsement:* concerning the powers of the US Congress (as the authority) and concerning affirmative action policies (this measure concerned only Study 1).
- *Legitimacy and obligation:* feelings about the US Congress and Supreme Court, feelings of obligation to obey the federal authorities, even when people disagree, and situations where support of the authorities would be withdrawn (this measure concerned only only Study 2).
- *Distributive injustice:* feelings of collective relative deprivation in relation to economic resources and comparison of the position of white Americans in relation to African Americans on economic grounds.
- *Procedural justice:* measure of perceptions of the fairness of opportunities for workplace success.
- *Relational evaluation of Congress:* is Congress trustworthy, neutral, and concerned about all citizens' rights when it makes policy decisions?
- *Instrumental evaluations of Congress' policy:* did affirmative action policies and anti-discrimination laws increase or decrease the job opportunities of white Americans and African Americans (Study 1). Do the decisions of Congress generally favor people like the respondent or does Congress take on board the views of people like the respondent?
- *Identification with one's racial group and with Americans in general.*

Results

Study 1
White respondents considered that the economic situation of the African Americans is much less fair and satisfying than theirs, in the sense that African Americans do not have the same opportunities and equal chances to succeed and still face discrimination.

- Both procedural and distributive justice concerns explained policy endorsement with a slightly greater weight for procedural justice.
- Both instrumental and relational evaluations explained policy endorsement with a slightly greater weight for relational evaluations.
- For those people who identified more with Americans than with the advantaged group, relational concerns were more closely related to policy endorsement.
- For those who identified less with Americans, instrumental concerns were more closely related to policy endorsement.

- *Equal identification* with the advantaged group and with Americans: relational concerns were more closely related to policy endorsement than instrumental concerns.
- *More identification* with Americans than with their advantaged group: they gave more weight to relational concerns.
- *Less identification* with Americans: greater weight to instrumental concerns.

Study 2
- The respondents felt that the economic situation of their group is less fair and satisfactory, that they had fewer opportunities and less chances to succeed, and that they faced racial discrimination.
- 39.2 percent reported that it was OK to disobey the law and 58 percent said that there were situations in which they would stop supporting government policies.
- Only procedural justice judgments were significantly related to feelings of obligation to obey the law.
- Only relational evaluations of Congress appeared to be linked to feelings of obligation to obey the law.
- Feelings of obligation to obey the law were not influenced by instrumental concerns for those respondents who identified with the superordinate category "Americans."
- Instrumental concerns were important for those who did not identify with Americans.
- *Equal identification* with the disadvantaged group and with Americans: relational concerns were more closely related to feelings of obligation than instrumental concerns.
- *More identification* with Americans than with their disadvantaged group: relational concerns were related to feelings of obligation, whereas instrumental concerns were not.
- *Less identification* with Americans: relational and instrumental concerns were *equally* important.

General discussion

The authors observe that justice issues do not rely only on self-interest for resources. People may be ready to sacrifice self-gains to fulfill justice motives and societal harmony. Identification with the superordinate category reshapes the perception of interdependencies between groups, but also makes salient the relational aspects of justice. Relational considerations of authorities are linked to endorsement of policies and feelings of obligation to respect the law.

provided people identify with the superordinate group that includes both themselves and the authorities, advantaged group members are ready to accept policies contrary to their self-interest, and disadvantaged group members accept the legitimacy of the authorities' decisions.

Thus, when advantaged group members identify more with a superordinate group than with their subgroup, they enlarge their scope of justice. Equally, disadvantaged group members who identify with the superordinate group display a willingness to be part of the framework of its rules and institutions. This, of course, should not be understood as meaning that inasmuch as they have others' respect, people no longer care about the outcomes of resource distribution. Proper access to resources is the way to prevent inequalities. The importance placed on how people are treated should be understood as meaning that valuing people is a resource in itself, the importance of which should not be forgotten.

Because memberships are important for self-definition, the way group members are treated by the authorities has an effect on their immediate resources and also sends a clear message about where they stand in the societal structure. Being taken account of is vital in determining how, for example, minority members would develop loyalties to the superordinate group, respect the institutions, abide by the rules, participate in society, and be and feel included. Two events in Britain illustrate this point.

In the 1990s a young black British man, Stephen Lawrence, was a victim of a racial attack while waiting at a bus stop. He died of his wounds. The police did not manage to bring the alleged culprits to justice due to serious procedural mistakes and omissions, provoking the anger of the family, the black community, and many Britons. For years, the parents of Stephen Lawrence and other parties campaigned for a public enquiry into Stephen's death. When this enquiry finally took place in 1997 it concluded, among other things, that the Metropolitan Police were guilty of institutional racism. The previous refusal of the police to consider the possibility that racism had influenced its procedures or to question the way they had handled the enquiry into Stephen's murder, sent a clear message to the British black community. The "message" concerned how much the state, through its institutions, valued the members of this community. No wonder, therefore, that the loyalty of some people to the superordinate group could have been eroded. The police, as representatives of the state, appeared to be biased, untrustworthy, and to have failed to protect equally the rights of all citizens. Although, since the enquiry, there have been efforts to change the ethos and practice of the Metropolitan Police, and positive messages have been issued by official authorities (the parents of Stephen received an OBE in the Queen's Honours in 2003), a second event shows that much more is needed.

On new year's day, 2003, two young black women, out to celebrate at a party, were shot dead when they were caught in the crossfire of a dispute between rival gangs in Birmingham. This horrible event occupied the British media because of the growth in gun crime. For days, the media presented the event in terms of an association between the black community and gun culture. The police urged possible witnesses to come forward, without success. People were afraid to disclose information partly through fear of reprisals. The media emphasized that the community seemed unable to trust the police and were disaffected with the procedures of justice.

This lack of trust could be the result of the "messages" the authorities had sent to this community over the years. The fact that they did not feel part of the superordinate group was exemplified during the inquest into the deaths. Addressing the audience, the coroner of the inquest (a white British man) said: "It is time for *your* community to *pay back* and to *conform* with *our belief*, which is that everybody has a duty to cooperate with the police" (Coroner A. Cotter, reported in the *Daily Telegraph*; my emphasis). Of course, his words caused distress to the family and disbelief in the whole black British community. He later apologized, saying that he did not mean to offend anybody.

We should have no doubts about the damage that this kind of statement can inflict on intergroup relations and superordinate identities. Categorizations are made salient ("your community") and conformity to the majority's beliefs is expected. Furthermore, it is implied that *this* community, presented as an outgroup, does not share these beliefs (an abnormalization of ethnic minorities). Finally, it reminds everybody that minorities should "pay back" for something (the privilege of living in the UK? assistance received? – one wonders what they have to "pay back") by conforming (recall also the ontologization of the gypsies who over the years failed to conform). That this statement was made by a person in his official capacity as a member of the judiciary further aggravates matters. Institutional support is one of the crucial conditions outlined by Allport for intergroup contact to be an agent in the reduction of prejudice. In the absence of such support it is difficult to expect peaceful intergroup relations, let alone the development of superordinate identities.

The coroner's statement also highlights another issue about the superordinate group: its values and beliefs. Shared beliefs serve as the basis of group identity, group formation, and group cohesion. They give meaning to the group and justify its actions (Bar Tal 1990a, 2000; Chryssochoou 1996b). When people ask, "What does it mean to be British?" they are asking about the **group beliefs** that provide an identity for this membership.

When groups are diverse, as in the case of multicultural societies, the battle for group beliefs starts. It is important, therefore, to identify the several aspects of this "war."

As we saw in the introduction, beliefs about acculturation are crucial in culturally diverse societies. The pattern of acculturation will condition the superordinate group in the future. If assimilation prevails, the superordinate group will be more or less uniform. If integration prevails, the superordinate group will be a colorful patchwork quilt. If separation or marginalization is dominant, neither uniformity nor a patchwork can emerge, and the coexistence of the different parts is made tenuous. Decisions about acculturation strategies are the outcome of interaction between the wishes of the culturally dominant and the culturally non-dominant groups, the history of intergroup relations, and the policies of the receiving society. These expectations are linked to the vision about the superordinate group and fears of losing one's identity or having its core values "contaminated."

Group beliefs

Defined as convictions that group members are aware that they share and consider as defining their "groupness."

(BarTal 1990a: 36)

A discrepancy between the expectations of the culturally dominant groups and the desires of the culturally non-dominant groups also influences intergroup relations (Bourhis et al. 1997). In particular, the interactive acculturation model considers that relationships between immigrants and the receiving society can be predicted by the relative "fit" between immigrant acculturation strategy preference and receiving-society preferences. If both immigrants and receiving society prefer either assimilation or integration, the type of fit is *consensual*. This will result in lower acculturative stress, more positive intergroup and interethnic relationships, few negative stereotypes and, as a consequence, low levels of discrimination. An intermediate situation labeled *problematic* fit occurs when either of the groups prefers assimilation and the other prefers integration. It also occurs when the receiving society favors assimilation or integration and the immigrant group opts for marginalization. This intermediate situation leads to more negative intergroup relations. Finally, *conflictual* fit exists when the immigrant group opts for separation or when the receiving society promotes segregation and exclusion. According to the model, when the fit is conflictual, more negative intergroup relations occur. Zagefka and Brown (2002) (panel 3.6) tested this model in Germany and found that the quality of intergroup relations increased when the fit was better between the acculturation attitudes of the receiving society and the immigrants.

Panel 3.6 The Relationship Between Acculturation Strategies, Relative Fit, and Intergroup Relations: Immigrant–Majority Relations in Germany (Zagefka and Brown 2002)

Research question

Does a good fit between preferred and perceived acculturation strategies lead to better intergroup relations? The consistency or discrepancy between immigrants and the receiving society's expectations about acculturation strategies will have an impact on intergroup relations. The study was designed to examine:

- the preferred and perceived acculturation strategies in Germany;
- the relationship between acculturation strategy preference and intergroup relations;
- the relationship between relative fit of immigrant and receiving society's preferences for acculturation strategies and intergroup relations.

Theoretical framework

The interactive acculturation model (Bourhis et al. 1997), which suggests that relationships between immigrants and receiving society will be *consensual* when both groups choose the same acculturation strategies that promote contact with the receiving society (both "choose" integration or both "choose" assimilation). If either of the groups refuses contact (separation or marginalization), the relationships will be *conflictual*. Finally, some cases are predicted in which the relationships are *problematic*. These cases are the following: (a) when immigrants wish to integrate and the receiving society expects them to assimilate, or vice versa; (b) when the receiving society promotes integration or assimilation but the immigrant groups "choose" to marginalize.

Method

- *Participants:* 321 school students in Germany: 193 Germans and 128 immigrants, most of whom were Turkish or Aussiedler (ethnic Germans from Russia and East European countries).
- *Materials/procedure:* questionnaires (one for Germans and one for immigrants) included measures of attitudes towards cultural maintenance and contact with the outgroup, and perceptions of the outgroup's attitude towards cultural maintenance and contact. The questionnaires included scales that aimed to measure the quality of intergroup relations (ingroup bias, perceptions of favorable intergroup relations, and perceptions of discrimination).

Results

Acculturation strategy preference

The results indicate that integration is the preferred strategy for both groups, although assimilation is also favored highly. What is noticeable, however, is that the desire of immigrants to assimilate is not reflected in how the German participants imagine the preference of immigrants. On the contrary, the German participants think that immigrants seek separation. In addition, quite a high percentage of receiving society members (19 percent) favor marginalization and a high percentage (12 percent) think that this is also the preferred immigrant strategy. Thus, although there is a high level of agreement between receiving society members' preference and immigrants' desires, there are also instances of misunderstandings. Finally, although the majority of Turks prefer integration, Aussiedler are split between integration and assimilation.

Acculturation strategy preference and quality of intergroup relations

In general, integration was associated with more favorable intergroup relations. The relationship between strategy preference and quality of intergroup relations was further investigated in the German sample. Again, a preference for integration was associated with favorable intergroup relations. Furthermore, it was found that the higher the tolerance for culture maintenance and the desire for contact, the lower the ingroup bias of the participants. In particular, those who advocated a marginalization strategy displayed higher levels of bias than all the other participants. Again, tolerance for culture maintenance and desire for contact predicted

(Continues)

Panel 3.6   (*Continued*)
favorable intergroup relations. However, no effects on discrimination were observed.

Relative fit between receiving society and immigrant strategy preference and quality of intergroup relations
The authors used different ways of measuring the fit between perceived and preferred strategies. In general, they found that a better fit is associated with a better quality of intergroup relations and a weakening of ingroup bias. However, we should be careful not to assume a causal relationship between relative fit and quality of intergroup relationships from these data.

General discussion

This study has the benefit of testing the effect of the desires and expectations of both immigrants and receiving society members on intergroup relations. Its findings suggest that when immigrants and receiving society agree on acculturation patterns ingroup bias is weakened and intergroup relationships are perceived to be more favorable.

Analyzing the history of German attitudes to immigration, Zick et al. (2001) report results showing that German citizens expect immigrants either to assimilate or to segregate (if immigrants want to stay long-term they should assimilate; otherwise they should segregate and return home after a while). The acculturation preferences of members of the receiving society and ethnic prejudice are highly correlated. Zick et al. also report on the acculturation strategies of minority members and their levels of prejudice. In general, respondents demonstrated greater antipathy towards other minority groups than towards Germans but, interestingly, those minority group members who were less supportive of integration held more negative attitudes towards both other minority groups and Germans. Thus, it seems that expectations and preferences about the acculturation of minority group members potentially influence relationships between all the different groups that coexist under a superordinate group.

Discrepancies between acculturation strategies might occur because majority members see the issues of adaptation and cultural maintenance as mutually exclusive, whereas minority members do not necessarily see it that way. Verkuyten and Thijs (2002) report data from the Netherlands, where they observed that Dutch and Turkish adolescents find cultural adaptation to be equally important, but differ in their levels of cultural maintenance, with the Turks rating this as more important than the Dutch. Furthermore, the more the Dutch participants identified with their ethnic group, the more they favored adaptation and the less they supported cultural maintenance. A similar link was not found between ethnic identification and adaptation among the Turks. However, ethnic identification for the Turks was related to cultural maintenance and, in addition, when their ethnic identification was low, Turkish attitudes towards cultural maintenance were influenced by perceptions of discrimination. Furthermore, those Turkish adolescents who highly identified with their ethnic group and perceived high levels of discrimination against it, were also less favorable towards adaptation. A key finding, among others, is that if, for Dutch adolescents, the issues of adaptation and cultural maintenance are mutually exclusive, this might not be the case for the ethnic minority group, provided that they do not feel discriminated against. We can see here that the relationships between groups within the boundaries of a superordinate group depend not only on group members' mutual expectations, their identification with their ingroup, and perceptions of threat, but also on whether they consider adaptation and cultural maintenance as mutually exclusive options.

Verkuyten and Thijs (2002) point out that our concerns about acculturation are unidimensional. We are concerned about the cultural maintenance and adaptation of ethnic minorities, but forget how majority group members feel about their own cultural maintenance. In the development of superordinate groups we should also be considering the way the majorities think about their own cultural maintenance and adaptation. The fact that the focus is on cultural minorities may be evidence that even the academic community is not immune from the tendency to focus on minorities when trying to explain differences between groups (Hegarty and Pratto 2001). For example, we talk about *black* British, whereas the white community is referred to only as British. In some respects the dominant position is taken for granted. Furthermore, Zick et al. (2001: 555) remark that the important precondition for social psychological interventions to change acculturation attitudes "is a political change in the nation's self-definition…as soon as Germany is seen as an immigrant state, both by its inhabitants and politicians, the debate about the future of ethnic intergroup relations can be opened – for the majority as well as for the minorities." Changing the nation's definition from a culturally homogeneous group to a culturally diverse one that includes different subgroups is not an easy task, but it is a crucial one if conflict is to be avoided.

The battle for group beliefs in superordinate groups does not relate only to expectations concerning acculturation strategies and the future image of the group as culturally homogeneous or culturally diverse. It also concerns which beliefs are the beliefs of the superordinate group. This issue is surely connected with strategies of acculturation. Obviously, when assimilation is promoted there is the implicit assumption that there is a dominant culture that prevails and which all groups should embrace and use for self-evaluation. The "struggle" here concerns the establishment of one's group as the prototype of the subgroup. Codol (1975) talks about the asymmetry that governs self-comparisons. He observed that people believed that others are more similar to them than they were similar to others, and that people tend to consider themselves as the point of reference for comparison. Naming this phenomenon *Primus inter pares* ("first among equals"), Codol explained that people tend to believe that they are more prototypical of their group. If this phenomenon also exists at a group level, we could reasonably expect that each subgroup would wish to present itself as the prototype of the superordinate group. This is the argument advanced by Mummendey and Wenzel (1999). Within a social identity (TS3) and self-categorization (TS12) tradition, they suggest that groups will project their attributes on the inclusive category and as a consequence they will claim to be more prototypical and therefore superior to the other groups. The importance of positioning oneself as the prototype and therefore obtaining a powerful position has been observed in other areas of research. For example, Sani and Reicher (1998) observed that each of the new parties that emerged from the split of the Italian Communist Party considered themselves as prototypical and claimed to represent the essence of the party. Hogg (2001), looking at the phenomenon of leadership, suggests that the most prototypical member of a group appears to have more influence and obtains the position of the leader. Simon and colleagues (Simon et al. 1998; Simon 1998) have found that participation in social movements is the outcome of people's identification with an activist group that seems to represent the aims of the large social category. We observed a similar phenomenon (Chryssochoou and Volpato 2002) when we looked at the rhetorical strategies used in the Communist Manifesto (Marx and Engels 1848), whereby in order to exert influence and provoke collective action, the communists position themselves as prototypical of the proletariat.

Thus, the battle for establishing the group beliefs and characteristics of the superordinate group is a battle for power. Achieving the power to present one's group as the prototype of the inclusive category means obtaining a higher position in the social hierarchy. At the same time, the groups that succeed to the dominant position hold the power to determine who is included in the superordinate category: those who are most similar to them. As Deschamps, Lorenzi-Cioldi, and Meyer (1982) observed, the dominants provide the model in relation to which the non-dominants have to compare themselves for self-evaluation. At the same time, dominants prevent the non-dominants from using the material and symbolic tools to reach this model. In the case of multicultural societies, as we have seen, non-dominant cultural groups may reject the dominant cultural model altogether, in the belief that they need to maintain their group attributes, beliefs, and culture. Sometimes this attachment results from the experience of discrimination and the realization that whatever they do they will never be accepted in the larger community. At other times, attachment to cultural beliefs and practices is part of the desire for these values to be given equal consideration in the making of the new superordinate group. Seemingly, dominant cultural groups might feel threatened by the presence of the beliefs and values of others. The battle for the group beliefs of the superordinate group is fought on the grounds of representations, identity, and social influence within particular sociohistorical contexts. This is discussed in the next chapter.

Chapter 4

Towards Cultural Diversity: Representations, Identity, and Social Influence

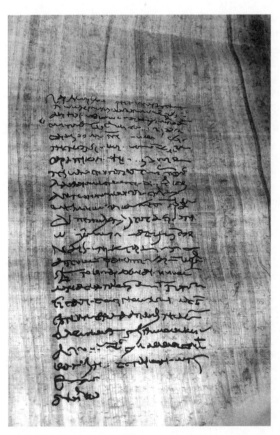

Plate 4 Papyrus, ca. 300 BC. A Greek citizen writes in half-Greek and half-Latin and demands his naturalization as a Roman citizen.

Outline

This book is about the social psychological issues raised by the movement of people and the existence of culturally diverse societies. In chapter 1 we discussed the perspective of the immigrants and culturally non-dominant groups and the issues they face. In chapter 2 we discussed the reaction of the receiving societies to cultural diversity. In chapter 3 we looked at issues that emerge when people live together in culturally diverse environments. It is time now to bring together all these elements and discuss the social psychological journey towards cultural diversity and multiculturalism.

Discussion about immigrants and culturally non-dominant groups revolved around three issues: (1) the necessity to deal with change and the unfamiliarity of the environment; (2) perceptions of the world, and challenges to values and practices from competing influences; (3) identity and status in the face of prejudice and discrimination. Reactions of people belonging to dominant cultural groups revolve around issues of prejudice, discrimination, and racism: how people represent other groups (stereotyping) and what leads to the extreme problematization of some groups and their exclusion from the moral community and humanity. We suggested that experiencing the presence of others as threatening could lead to such extreme reactions. The receiving society has to adapt itself to change. Its worldview is challenged and its identity shaken; thus, members of cultural majorities can feel fearful and insecure. When different cultural groups live together it is important that there is no prejudice. Justice concerns – justice of outcomes and justice of procedures – become salient. Intergroup relations are shaped by perceptions of interdependence and power. A "battle" begins to define group beliefs and the characteristics of the "new" superordinate group.

In all our discussions three issues have been prominent. Firstly, we were interested in how people deal with unfamiliarity, accommodate and construct new knowledge about their environment and about others. Secondly, we discussed how they perceive and position themselves within this environment and what are the consequences when these perceptions and positions are challenged. Thirdly, we looked at how people negotiate their understandings, convince each other, communicate and produce cultural artifacts.

All these issues are clearly linked to major concerns of social psychologists: the social construction of knowledge, how the shared nature of that construction helps people deal with unfamiliar events (representations), identity, and social influence. Together, these form the pillars of social psychology because they address the relationship between the individual and the social that the discipline has set out to understand.

The following discussion concerns what multicultural societies mean for people's self-knowledge and self-definition, what are the challenges people face in changing their worldviews, and how power issues intervene with the process of knowledge construction when societies change. It is perhaps worth stating now that I am unable to separate identity from representations and social influence. People's representations about the world feed the knowledge they have about themselves. At the same time these representations are shaped by self-positions and the processes of influence that take place when identities are enacted. This brings us back to an earlier point: how people see the world influences their perception of their place in it and how they see other people. These representations about the world and people's identities open new debates, impact on actions and behaviors, and contribute to societal reproduction and/or change. It is the interplay between representations, identity, and social influence that this book has aimed to present in the context of culturally diverse societies. This needs to be grounded in the context of the nation and its transformation from a political entity perceived as homogeneous (e.g., individual European nations) to one perceived as culturally diverse (e.g., multicultural countries, immigration-founded countries, the European Union).

The Nation-State: A Powerful Ingroup

We have seen how people can be categorized along different dimensions such as gender, age, nationality, religion, sexual orientation, class, ethnicity, and race. These dimensions seem to us to be "normal" divisions that structure our everyday life and make our interactions meaningful. However, all these categories are products of the interaction between sociohistorical factors and the way we think about our environment. The content and boundaries of categories change as sociohistorical factors evolve and the way we think about and experience our environment develops. The meaning of these categories and their relationships is our representation of the social relations at a given sociohistorical moment (Chryssochoou 2000a). These categories make concrete the existing social relationships and at the same time they shape social organization and social institutions.

Around the middle of the nineteenth century, sociohistorical factors in Europe brought into existence a sociopolitical organization: the nation-state (Gellner 1997; Hobsbawm 1990). The existence of the nation-state has been associated with the symbolic existence of the nation as an entity that assembled people around the idea that they shared common origins, a common culture, and common goals (panel 4.1).

As Ernest Gellner (1997: 95) observes, "cultures became a political principle." As a consequence, the nation-state as a political organization has been equated with the symbolic aspect of the nation, a culturally homogeneous entity. The symbolic existence of the nation has been a powerful provider of identity for its members. The nation-state as a sociopolitical organization, and the nation as a symbolic group for membership, developed on the basis of the construction of a common past, the establishment of a common present, and the guarantee of a common future for its members. Powerful bonds of interdependence and common fate have been developed among people who belong to the same nation-state. The development of common bonds between people living in the same physical environment occurred in parallel with the development of an internal organization (administration and government) that regulated relationships within the nation-state. At the same time, the nation-state established boundaries to distinguish itself from those that were not supposed to

Panel 4.1   Defining the Nation: A Difficult Task

One might think that defining the nation would be easy. When we talk about a nation we all seem to know what we are talking about. A nation is part of our everyday discourse – when we listen to the media, when we plan our holidays, when we learn history and geography at school, when we ask people where they come from, when we follow sporting events. But although we all seem to understand what a nation is, we get into trouble when we try to define it. What makes a community of people a nation and how does one belong to it?

There is a great debate in the social and human sciences about the definition of the nation. Some theorists look for objective criteria (e.g., common language, religion, culture, territory), while others use subjective criteria (e.g., the mutual recognition of belonging to the same national community). Definitions of the nation using subjective criteria regard nations as "imagined communities" (Anderson 1983). This is close to the social psychological definition of a psychological group (Turner and Giles 1981) and is related to the idea that belonging to a nation is an important aspect of who we think we are. The way lay people understand and define the nation is an important aspect of social psychological research. These understandings are related to the theoretical debates in the human and social sciences.

Irrespective of whether nations are defined on the basis of objective or subjective criteria, some theorists argue that nations have always existed throughout history, but they were "asleep" and were awakened at a particular time (Smith 1986, 1991). Other theorists believe that nations are the outcome of the particular sociohistorical and economic conditions that characterized modernity (Gellner 1997; Hobsbawm 1990). The first approach involves the implicit assumption that what characterizes a nation is the existence of a common culture and heritage. In the second approach, however, what seems to be of importance is that common interest and socio-economic conditions created a new political organization. The first approach is linked to ethnicity, culture, and ideas, and is believed to be related to emotional aspects, whereas the second approach is linked to interests, rights, and duties, and is believed to be connected to more rational aspects. The first approach constitutes an *ethnic* conception of the nation, whereas the second approach is a *civic* conception. Both are nothing more than theories about a specific organization of the world. In both, the nation is linked to political organization – it should exist as a state. Thus, the nation is a political project with great importance for the present. Billig (1995: 65) remarks: "in the contemporary world, the issue 'what is a nation?' is not merely an interesting topic for academic seminars. It touches upon issues which contemporary people think worthy of sacrifice." Therefore, what matters is "to reveal the different purposes served by nationalism" (Wicker 1997: 29), and to understand how "any version of national past and national identity serves contemporary interests" (Reicher and Hopkins 2001: 20).

be part of it. As we have seen (Tajfel and Wilkes 1963; TS15), criteria of national categorization became important and the perceived differences among people within the nation-state have been attenuated, whereas the perceived differences between nation-states have been accentuated. Within the boundaries of the nation, the processes of homogenization that took place produced feelings of similarity among people. This perceived similarity was based mostly on the idea that people belonging to the same nation shared common roots and culture. In fact, in many places, the different conceptions (civic and ethnic) became blurred in favor of a homogeneous conception of the nation. Membership of the nation-state was delimited not by the position/status of people, as was the case in traditional societies, but by culture. As Gellner (1997: 95) puts it, "culture (in this society) is the precondition of political, economic and social citizenship". People that satisfy this condition can benefit from the rights of citizens. Gellner remarks: "this membership or set of qualifications becomes a person's most valuable possession, for it is virtually the precondition of the enjoyment of or access to all other goals" (p. 75). The formation of the nation-state resulted in the psychological creation of an ingroup, where similarities among its members and difference to outsiders have been accentuated. The boundaries (physical and symbolic) of this ingroup defined entitlement to resources. Thus, membership of the national group and issues of justice (TS18) have been closely linked in the minds of people. Justice is conferred only on those who share the same membership.

One of the consequences of the idea that people had rights derived from membership of a certain community defined by common culture was the development of feelings and beliefs that each culture should be organized as a political entity; namely, as a state. These feelings and beliefs remain very powerful and give rise to nationalistic movements for whom a desire for independent political organization constitutes a fundamental drive (Scottish and Basque nationalism, for example, or ethnic Albanians in Kosovo).

Another consequence of the idea that people have rights if they belong to a community sharing the same culture is the belief that political organizations should be built on culturally homogeneous societies because only such societies are cohesive and viable. This belief motivated homogenization within specific territories. This often took peaceful forms through a common education system, as in France (although in Brittany and the Basque country people still resent and sometimes violently resist this trend). Homogenization can also take very extreme and violent forms, such as the "ethnic cleansing" in the former Yugoslavia.

Parallel to the homogenization process within the nation-state was a process of differentiation between nation-states, based on physical boundaries and borders, outside which people were believed to be different. Thus, the nation was not only grounded in a territory, but was also constituted as a bounded place that acquired psychological significance (Dixon 2001). These boundaries, very often, were established by means of conflict and war. One of the major functions of the nation-state, therefore, became the guaranteed protection of these boundaries, to maintain the differentiation from outsiders and to negotiate relationships between them and the nation. Inside the boundaries the function of the nation-state was to ensure the welfare and prosperity of its members and to regulate relationships between citizens.

However, all these functions of the nation-state are progressively challenged in an era of globalization. With economic activity transferred to global markets, the European model of the nation-state is increasingly unable alone to guarantee economic development. Nation-states need to be allied to other nation-states and to open their financial borders at the very least. Further, by the very existence of supranational regulatory bodies such as the European Commission, the European Parliament, and the European Court of Justice, the nation-state is no longer the sole decision-maker concerning the welfare of its members. Finally, the increasing movement of people around the globe and the new technological developments in communication impinge on the perceived cultural homogeneity within the nation.

All these factors challenge the belief that the nation-state, as we know it, is the only guarantor of the welfare of its members or that it has the power to be so. Increasingly, we are witnessing trends that confer on supranational organizations the responsibility for economic activities and perhaps more general concerns (i.e., the environment) and confer on local communities the autonomy to deal with the welfare of their people (e.g., devolution in the UK). The fact that the limits of entitlements, rights, and welfare are changing (for example, EU nationals when living in an EU country other than their own have entitlements which are similar to those of nationals) may contribute to changing the definition of the ingroup. Perhaps this will eventually challenge the idea that only culturally homogeneous entities can be viable political organizations.

It should be noted, however, that the European model of the nation-state based on cultural homogeneity and civic allegiance had already been challenged. Other countries, such as the US, Australia, and Canada, were founded by people from different European countries who emigrated and prospered, often at the expense of indigenous populations. In this context, criteria such as the color of skin became powerful means of categorization. People's skin color fed beliefs about the existence of different races. As we have seen, these racial categories were associated with internal psychological characteristics and abilities and were used to explain people's behavior. More importantly, race was used to legitimize the slavery and colonization that characterized socioeconomic relationships. Unfortunately, science and psychology have been used to legitimize these categories and the beliefs associated with them (Gould 1981). Nowadays, as we saw in chapter 2, social scientists accept that race is nothing more than a social construction that reflects people's understanding of the world at a particular sociohistorical moment (Reicher 2001; Wicker 1997). Nevertheless, the impact of beliefs about race remains powerful today in shaping relationships among people all around the world. Martin, Deaux, and Bikmen (2001) researched new trends of immigration in the United States and conclude that power inequalities along racial divisions are maintained in both native and immigrant populations. Although non-white immigrant populations promote multicultural beliefs in the United States, racial segregation still persists, as non-white immigrants prefer to interact with native people from their own racial background. Thus, these authors note the existence of a "color line" with respect to immigration in the US. Racial divisions are still operating all around the world and are used to justify acts of discrimination and mass killing.

After the abolishment of slavery and the recognition of black people and native populations in the US, Canada, and Australia as part of the national group, it was clear that cultural homogeneity could not be the basis of nationhood in the same way that it was in Europe. These countries, however, are still struggling to build a model of nationhood that includes people of different origins. In particular, they are struggling to reconcile the idea that they form a nation with the idea that this nation is composed by people of different origins. The implicit belief behind these debates is that a nation ought to be culturally homogeneous. There is an assumption that some group memberships are incompatible with the national group and that ethnic, racial, or religious group memberships, for example, will take precedence over the national and thus threaten the cohesion of the nation.

Belonging to a group and expressing loyalty to it are ideas that are closely linked. Throughout history the nation has asked its members for the ultimate sacrifice – life itself – to prove loyalty to the national group. Patriotism is a powerful feeling that national institutions still keep alive. We live in a world of nations where the presence of the nation unobtrusively characterizes our ways of living (Billig 1995) and constitutes the basis of our entitlements. Thus, there is the implicit assumption that the national group is entitled to our complete loyalty, as measured by our readiness to give our life for it. There is another implicit assumption that we can only be a "true" member of one group and be loyal to one group alone. In Britain, the Conservative politician Norman Tebbit rejected the idea of multiculturalism, suggesting that the fact that respective ethnic minorities support the West Indian, Pakistani, or Indian cricket teams, rather than the English team, showed that they did not identify with Britain. This meant that multicultural States are impossible because of divided loyalties. This "cricket test" idea says a lot about beliefs about acculturation. It implies that if assimilation is not the dominant strategy, then the national ingroup will be weakened by incompatibilities between people's loyalties.

Given this structural importance of nations it would be ludicrous to deny their significance for people's self-definitions and actions. Any sporting event reminds us, perhaps in a less painful way than a war, of the attachment that people feel to their nation. The strategic potential of these feelings should not be underestimated. Politicians and elites use them to promote particular projects. To dismiss such feelings or characterize them as altogether bad will not serve the purpose of reducing prejudice; indeed, it may lead to its increase if people feel threatened in what seems to be a crucial aspect of their world. National memberships and their symbols are important to people. It is a counter productive strategy, for example, to try to dismiss the feelings of Israelis and Palestinians towards their respective memberships. I believe it is important for those who work towards international peace to understand the roots and consequences of these beliefs, feelings, and loyalties and to use social influence strategies (TS17) to promote their own project.

Social psychologists who observed this loyalty to the national group developed the idea that there might be two different forms of loyalty and attachment to the nation. They suggested that there is a "good" form of attachment that is critical to the nation (Schatz, Staub, and Lavine 1999) and focused on how the nation stands in relation to its past (Mummendey, Klink, and Brown 2001a, 2001b). This form of attachment is called constructive patriotism, or simply patriotism. The other form of attachment constitutes a staunch allegiance to the national group, refuses criticism, and is focused on intergroup comparisons and outgroup derogation. This form of attachment is called blind patriotism or nationalism (panel 4.2).

Panel 4.2   Being Loyal to the Ingroup

Loyalty to the ingroup has attracted the attention of social psychologists studying various domains. For example, Tajfel suggested a form of ingroup loyalty when he discussed how members of devalued groups could stick with their group and choose collective actions to change their situation. Another form of loyalty was described by Irving Janis (1972) when he talked about *groupthink*. Janis – who studied decision-making – concluded that poor collective decisions are made under the following conditions:

- Complicity between members of committees and excessive group cohesiveness (pressures to maintain cohesiveness by avoiding conflict; conformity pressures and self-censorship).
- Belief in the moral and intellectual infallibility of the committee.
- Failure to contemplate possible alternatives.
- Desire to reach a unanimous decision, under the illusion that unanimous decisions conform to the majority opinion.

These conditions generate *groupthink:* a mode of thinking where the desire to satisfy their *esprit de corps* leads people to avoid conflict. Thus, people will be ready to censor themselves and avoid contradictory opinions to guarantee the cohesion of the group. Their decisions will not necessarily depend on the knowledge of individual members but on the relationships between members.

Similar types of loyalty might occur in terms of the national group. In this respect, authors have distinguished between nationalism and patriotism (Bar Tal and Staub 1997). For example:

Nationalism is an ideology that provides a justification for the existence or the creation of a state defining a particular population, and that prescribes the relationship between the individual and the state. Patriotism is an ideology – or a set of attitudes and beliefs – that refers to individuals' attachment and loyalty to their nation and country.

(Kelman 1997: 166)

Nationalism is an attachment to a nation characterized by a desire to enhance the nation's superiority or power *vis-à-vis* other nations. Patriotism consists of acts and beliefs based on securing the identity and welfare of the group without regard to either self-identity or self-benefit.

(Worchel and Coutant 1997: 191–3)

According to Kelman (1997: 173–5), two sources of attachment determine the strength of people's patriotism:

Sentimental: "People's attachment to a group based on perception of that group as representative of their personal identity" (attachment based on similarity).

Instrumental: "People's attachment to a group based on perception of that group as meeting their personal needs and interests and those of the other members of the social category encompassed by the group" (attachment based on interdependence).

This commitment will be expressed differently depending on people's orientation to the group:

- *Rule orientation:* compliance with group rules.
- *Role orientation:* identification with group roles.
- *Value orientation:* internalization of group values.

Staub and colleagues (Staub 1997; Schatz, Staub, and Lavine 1999) differentiate between two forms of patriotism:

- *Blind patriotism:* "requires uncritical loyalty to an entity like the nation or state and to a conception, vision, or ideology and related practices that purport to serve that entity. It also requires the absence or the willingness to disregard moral values that demand consideration for the welfare of human beings not included in the entity or the group that is the object of one's patriotic attachment" (Staub 1997: 215).
- *Constructive patriotism:* is the outcome of the interaction between *critical consciousness* – "the capacity to independently evaluate information, rather than simply adopt a 'group' (authority) perspective on events" – and *critical loyalty* – "commitment to the group's ultimate welfare and to universal human ideals and values, rather than to a policy or course of action adopted by the group at any particular time; it also means the willingness and capacity to deviate from – not support, but resist and attempt to change – the current direction of one's group" (ibid: 221–2).

Thus, "Blind patriotism is defined as an attachment to a country characterized by unquestioning positive evaluation, staunch allegiance, and intolerance to criticism. Constructive patriotism is defined as an attachment to country characterized by support for questioning and criticism of current group practices that are intended to result in positive change. (Schatz, Staub, and Lavine 1999: 151).

However, other social psychologists have criticized this distinction. As Kashti (1997: 159) observes, "all patriotism is potentially capable of spreading as a comprehensive social, cultural, and political schema and endangering the rights or even the life of a person labeled as a foreigner or as unpatriotic." Perhaps the distinction between "good" and "bad" patriotism is an attempt to legitimize the positions of those minorities that criticize the official policies of the nation-state – criticisms that would otherwise be regarded as unpatriotic and therefore dismissed. The work of Kelman (1997), Staub (1997), Schatz, Staub, and Lavine (1999), and Worchel and Coutant (1997) has been inspired by cultures (the USA and Israel) where being a patriot is of particular significance. Billig (1995) has shown how being patriotic is part of American ideology. Furthermore, in the aftermath of September 11, 2001, such patriotism in the US stifled dissent towards the war in Afghanistan.

Bar Tal (1993) discusses patriotism in terms of group beliefs. Where patriotism is the normative representation, it is possible to imagine that in order to influence the politics of the group one should avoid being characterized as unpatriotic. If one's social influence is to be strengthened by appearing "patriotic", then one might consider the attachment to the national group as something normal that can take positive as well as negative forms. A banner in an antiwar demonstration in Washington in January 2003 read: "Think! It is patriotic." The distinction, however, between patriotism and nationalism remains ideological (Billig 1995) and justifies the salience of the nation as a category that guarantees social solidarity and self-definition in comparison to any other possible categories (Hopkins 2001).

Furthermore, it is difficult to understand what it means to be patriotic/nationalist in terms of psychological phenomena without making reference to the concept and content of the nation, as both Hopkins (2001) and Condor (2001) remark in relation to the arguments of Mummendey, Klink, and Brown (2001a, 2001b). We need also to bear in mind that some people might reject an association with the nation and what it stands for if the image of the nation is associated with prejudice and intolerance. Condor (2000) (panel 4.3) has produced evidence from an analysis of interviews with English people of their uneasiness to talk in an explicit way about "this country" for fear of being seen as endorsing beliefs about the superiority of the national group or as justifying its colonial past.

Panel 4.3   Pride and Prejudice: Identity Management in English People's Talk About "This Country" (Condor 1996, 2000)

Research question

In a series of studies (mainly through interviews) Condor investigates how English people talk about their country (referred to as "this country") or their national identity. Condor looked at both the content of people's talk and the way this content was expressed.

Theoretical framework

Discourse analysis (Condor 2000) (TS16).

Method

Series of interviews with people living in England, from both genders and different ages and socioeconomic backgrounds.

Results

What is apparent in these studies is a hesitancy on the part of respondents to talk about their national identity, and the country in which they live, when they are asked to do so. In the 1996 studies the respondents hesitate and qualify their answer when asked about their self-definition, and confuse being English and being British. In the 2000 study the respondents treat the subject as a delicate topic and feel uncomfortable talking about it, rather as if they were talking about race. In particular, respondents:

- treated national categorization as prejudice and refused to use it;
- avoided the topic by using banal national references such as "we," "they," "here," "other people," all taken-for-granted categorical distinctions;
- put themselves in the role of a relayer (other people say/think ...) to externalize opinions about "this country";
- disavowed national identity.

In addition, respondents felt that expressing national pride was equivalent to expressing intolerance and prejudice and distanced themselves from this. In particular, they:

- expressed a normative ethos against voicing the superiority of "this country";
- took a relayer role to say positive things about "this country," fearing that they might be seen as a "closet nationalist" (as one respondent put it).

General discussion

The respondents in these studies seem to have a difficulty perceiving themselves in terms of national identity and displaying national pride. It is possible that this is a context-dependent finding and that in other situations the same respondents would have been more at ease in expressing such feelings. Condor (1996) raises the question as to whether social psychologists should take these accounts at face value or consider them as forms of strategic self-presentation. In addition, "boasting" about one's identity might counter social norms and thus prevent people from expressing such feelings. Condor (2000) believes that the issue of impression management in research should be treated as a research topic in itself and not merely as an inconvenient bias.

Condor also suggests that the context in which the nation-state has historically developed in the UK, along with its colonial past and multicultural present, might explain the difficulties in using such self-definitions as "English" or "British" and more generally in accepting these identities as part of oneself. There is also the possibility that English people, as the dominant group, simply take their identity for granted.

The content of nationhood and national identity can be contested and used strategically to promote specific projects (Hopkins and Reicher 1996; Reicher and Hopkins 2001). The nationalist project traditionally is based on the idea that a cultural entity needs to find political expression: in other words, a nation ought to become a nation-state. But equally there are other projects that one could claim under the banner of nationalism. There have been calls for national unity (to unite people of the same nationhood under the same political organization) or national purity ("cleansing" the nation of those who are not worthy of it or who are alien). Being patriotic is to be attached to and abides with the nationalist project whatever its content might be.

In an early paper, Tajfel (1969: 163) discussed the formation of national attitudes. He suggested that the focus of a social psychological enquiry should be "the steps which make the transition between national integration and its psychological counterparts in the individual." In a tone familiar to us from his subsequent work, he suggests that

> for nationalism to come into being as a wide-scale social phenomenon, it is necessary that a large proportion of the individuals who are members of a nation: (1) perceive that nation as some form of an entity, however various individuals may define that entity to themselves; (2) feel to some extent emotionally identified with that entity; (3) consequently share an involvement in the events affecting it ... there can be obviously no uniformity in the population with regard to these three aspects of nationalism. The private definitions of the nation will vary from individual to individual or from group to group; emotional involvement will vary in its intensity; and the involvement in the events affecting the nation can take many forms. *(Tajfel 1969: 157)*

Thus, the nation is not experienced in the same way by all people belonging to the group. For Tajfel (1969), the existence of these aspects of nationalism depends on the existence of channels of communication. These channels, following properties of social influence, are able to "build up a cognitive structure which will be capable of coexisting with or dominating the competing views of the world in which classifications of human groups in terms other than national are not seen as more salient and more important." According to Tajfel, these messages also need to be congruent with individual motives. Social-influence processes promote a project that produces a cognitive structure and a system of classification that dominates the way people see the world and themselves. Following this logic, I would say that **nationalism** is a particular social representation (TS1) that translates specific social relationships between people and groups to cognitive organizations (national categories) and regulates the relationships within these groups by promoting specific forms of social solidarity.

National affiliation is the attachment to this project and to this form of social solidarity. National identity is constructed in relation to this project and represents it. As Reicher and Hopkins (2001) show, the content of national identity might differ and might be contested and argued. It is

Nationalism (1)

Nationalism is a particular social representation that translates specific social relationships between people and groups to cognitive organizations (national categories) and regulates the relationships within these groups by promoting specific forms of social solidarity. (My definition)

used, though, strategically to serve particular political projects and promote particular definitions of the world.

Since the nation objectifies social relations at a given sociohistorical moment, it loses its socially constructed origins and becomes a natural category in people's minds. It becomes essentialized and reified and is given a natural, ontological priority (Moscovici 1988a). In other words, people "forget" that national categorizations are constructed to reflect particular socioeconomic conditions at a specific historical period and consider them as part of the natural way of existence. Hence, national categories are viewed as unchangeable and sacred, with inflexible boundaries. People within the national boundaries acquire "natural" properties that define the national character and differentiate them from other nationals. These attributes can subsequently be used to promote political projects. The essentialization of the nation is part of the process of promotion of political projects. As Reicher and Hopkins (2001: 222) assert, "national identity is always a project, the success of which depends upon being seen as an essence." We can see here that the essentialization of a category is not only something that other groups do in order to justify discrimination, but also a process that concerns one's own group and identity.

To give an example of how national identity and character are constructed and essentialized to promote a political project, let me quote from President George W. Bush's State of the Union Address to the American Congress on January 28, 2003:

> Americans are a resolute people who have risen to every test of our time. Adversity has revealed the character of our country...Americans are a free people, who know that freedom is the right of every person and the future of every nation. The liberty we prize is not America's gift to the world, it is God's gift to humanity.

Preparing his nation for war with Iraq, the American president conjures an essentialized image of American people as resolute, fearless of adversity and freedom-loving. Freedom is presented not as a human-made value, but as natural, "provided by God" to humanity.

We could give here a second definition of nationalism, similar to the one we gave of racism in chapter 2. **Nationalism** is a particular political project based on the reification of the nation and the essentialization of the national character.

Nationalism (2)

Nationalism is a political project based on the reification of the nation and the essentialization of the national character. (My definition)

As with racism, I aim here to highlight (a) the behavior and action-oriented aspect of nationalism (political project); (b) the fact that the nation constitutes a social construction that became a "real" categorical division; (c) the fact that the content (essence) of the national character and of the national project depends on the historical context in which the nation was built and the sociopolitical context in which it thrives.

If nationalism is a political project, it is based on the socially constructed and shared theories (social representations) people have which constitute the founding myths (group beliefs) of the national group. What it is that constitutes the group beliefs of a particular nation can vary. Although there is a common understanding of what it is to be Greek, French, British, or American, people anchor these understandings differently and produce different accounts about the nation depending on their other memberships and beliefs. Jacobson (1997), for example, discusses "boundaries of Britishness," which operate in the popular understandings of what it means to be British and are shared both by majority and minority members. In her research, young British Pakistanis identify three interrelated boundaries of Britishness that impact on their life: the civic boundary, the racial boundary, and the cultural boundary. The respondents seem to anchor Britishness to these boundaries and therefore give a different meaning to the concept and to their identity.

The nation is an imagined and argued community. One should regard any attempt to present it as if it were speaking with a single voice as an attempt to promote a particular political project and to present itself as *the* voice of the nation. As already discussed, individuals and groups will try to present their position as prototypical of the group's position in order to obtain power, exert influence, and convince others to follow them.

Social representations of nationhood also guide the criteria for membership of the national group. As we have seen (panel 4.1), there are two main founding myths concerning the nation: ethnic origins and civic origins. In the ethnic conception there is a correspondence between nationality and ethnicity: only people for whom this correspondence exists are deemed worthy of inclusion. In the civic conception there is no such correspondence: national membership is independent of other memberships and religion or ethnicity should not be taken into account when judging people's membership of a nation.

Gellner (1997) claims that what characterizes the modern nation is the fact that people's participation in it is unmediated by any significant subgroupings. In other words, membership of a modern nation is an "individual property," a qualification that characterizes each individual. If we accept the civic conception of nationhood this argument holds: each of us is a citizen of a nation. Citizenship is a membership that qualifies a political relationship with the group, a relationship that confers rights and presupposes duties. However, if we hold an ethnic conception of nationhood we are faced, in modern multicultural societies, with a "problem," because only people for whom there is a correspondence between nationality and ethnicity are considered to be part of the national group. In this case, the relationship between the individual and the nation is a cultural one and nationality is no longer an individual property. What is considered now as an individual property is ethnicity. This ethnic membership impacts on the membership of the national political group. Ethnicity is closely linked with culture. It means belonging by birth to a community that shares the same culture. Thus, culture becomes a concept that defines membership (at the ethnic level) and impacts on membership (at a national level).

Ethnicity also becomes essentialized and is presented as a "minimal self-definition" that requires preservation and protection. Ethnicity can be presented as an identity that satisfies all principles in Breakwell's identity process theory (TS4). It provides beliefs about continuity, self-esteem (in terms of pride), distinctiveness, and self-efficacy (the ethnic group's survival over the years). The essentialization of ethnicity can coincide with attempts to build a nation-state (on the basis of shared ethnicity), but also to acquire rights or fight discrimination within existing nation-states. Its close links with culture provide ethnicity with a "naturalness." Socialization processes in ethnic culture provide people with beliefs and practices and constitute the lenses through which they see the world. Ethnicity is taken for granted and constitutes the point of reference for evaluations and judgments. Thus, a threat to ethnicity (whatever ethnicity might mean for people) would probably constitute a major attack on their world, as Sumner (1906) suggested. How ethnic identities develop, their content and meaning for people and communities, should be one of our areas of study as social psychologists. However, such a study should be careful not to further essentialize these identities by looking at how attributes, practices, and beliefs considered inherent to particular groups are acquired. The acquisition of ethnic knowledge and practices is an important domain and should be studied within the wider context in which it takes place. This context might be, for example, a nation-state that sees itself as homogeneous or multicultural. Ethnic membership in these cases might be related to immigration or relations of dominance (slavery, colonialism). Another context where ethnic identity might develop could be a wider framework where other memberships (such as religion, or the European Union) are more salient. Equally, ethnic identities might develop in the absence of a political organization and therefore their development could be tied to the construction of a political organization. Finally, the development of ethnic identities can occur in contexts of disintegration of superordinate political organizations (e.g., the former Soviet Union and former Yugoslavia).

In an EU-funded international program (INTAS-NERID 2001), Barrett, Lyons, and colleagues (Barrett, Lyons and del Valle in press; Barrett in press) looked at the development of national, European, and religious identities of different groups of children living in the new independent states of Russia, Ukraine, Georgia, and Azerbaijan. They also compared their findings with data from a previous project (CHOONGE 1997-Britain (England and Scotland), and Spain (Catalonia, Andalusia, Basque Country). Looking at data from the new independent states, they observed differences in the identity development of children belonging to the same ethnonational group but growing up in different geographical locations in the same country. In addition, differences were found in the identities of children of a different ethnonational group but growing up in the same geographical location. Furthermore, differences in identity development were observed when children of the same ethnonational background attended schools using different languages of education. The data confirmed previous findings from the Western countries, were differences in identity development were observed in relation to the different contexts. Interestingly, they also found differences between children growing up in new independent states and children growing up in Western countries. Of particular interest is that national pride increased from childhood to adolescence for the Western European countries, whereas it decreased in adolescence for children growing up in new independent states. This finding suggests that the development of national pride is not an inherent characteristic of human beings.

Different contexts entail different meanings of ethnicity, different contents associated with it, and different levels of intensity of identification, because ethnicity will incarnate different projects. Furthermore, ethnicity might not be a salient identity when there is no project attached to it or when the group is in a powerful position. For example, the ethnicity of the members of culturally dominant groups is rarely explicitly acknowledged, even in research papers (for an exception see Verkuyten 2001), whereas it is mentioned in the case of minorities referred to as ethnic. The ethnicity of powerful groups becomes a personal characteristic and not a collective identity: even if it is problematic (see panel 4.3), it is not problematized. The reason for the absence of problematization is that there is not likely to be a project associated with it at the moment. It constitutes the "norm." However, multicultural soci-

Possible selves

Possible selves represent individuals' ideas of what they might become, what they would like to become, and what they are afraid of becoming. Possible selves derive from representations of the self in the past and they include representations of the self in the future.

(Markus and Nurius 1986: 954)

eties that necessitate changes in our representations of groups as homogeneous might alter this status quo. Attached to a project of redefinition of the norms of the superordinate group, majority ethnic identities might reconstruct themselves to emphasize their difference from others that are beyond these norms. This is a message that we can take from Verkuyten's (2001) research, presented in panel 2.5. Differences in the behavior and practices of ethnic minorities are not constructed on the basis of cultural differences, but on the basis of a deviation from the norm that the majority constitutes. In the next section we will discuss the issue of identity in the context of founding myths of superordinate groups.

Supranational Groups, Multiple Identities, and Founding Myths: Developing New Projects

Optimal distinctiveness theory

A model in which social identity is viewed as a reconciliation of opposing needs for assimilation and differentiation from others.

(Brewer 1991: 475)

One of the consequences of living in culturally diverse societies is that people need to negotiate different identities. Inclusion in supranational groups provides people with the opportunity to joggle between different identities and construct several **possible selves** (Markus and Nurius 1986, 1987). Furthermore, according to **optimal distinctiveness theory** (Brewer 1991), people strive through their identifications to reconcile opposing needs of assimilation and differentiation.

Thus, they will define themselves in a way that gives them inclusiveness in a category and at the same time maintains their individuality.

Inclusion in superordinate groups might disturb this equilibrium and urge them to reestablish it by changing their self-definitions.

The possession of multiple identities is not something new. We belong to different groups and we attribute different characteristics to ourselves and others. However, the identities we adopt and the characteristics we attribute are not random. Our identities correspond with particular projects and our attributions arise from particular theories about personality (TS19), representations of groups, or cultural norms. Similarly, there might be a shared aspect in the way people perceive the relationships between their different identities (Chryssochoou 2003). Freeman (2001), for example, looked at the internalization of different identities in a particular social structure, Sri Lanka. He makes several hypotheses as to the salience of 11 different identities in relation to status, numerical minority position, urban–industrialization processes, and intergroup contact. Thus, he links culture-level variables to the salience of identities. Although his findings attest to within-culture variability in the salience of identities, there are also important consistencies. He notes, for example, the importance of nation, race, and religion across the sample. "The ongoing civil war, ruefully described as the mother of all problems in this developing country, continues to fuel and to be fueled by the salience of these identities at the individual level" (p. 303). There is therefore a dual traffic between identity importance and social context. What I argue here is the possibility that a shared understanding exists in the way identities are perceived to relate to each other.

This is a crucial issue for the existence of new superordinate groups in which, as Hornsey and Hogg (2000) have advocated, subgroup identities should be maintained within the context of a superordinate identity. The aim of the dual categorization model that they propose is to acknowledge and promote simultaneously both identities. Imagine that these identities are perceived to be incompatible. In order to follow Hornsey and Hogg's suggestion, it is important that an ethos is created within superordinate groups in which there is *no* perceived incompatibility between identities: in the same way that one can be a woman and a surgeon, one could be of Pakistani descent and a British citizen, a Catholic and a Greek citizen, black and a European citizen, a Moroccan and an Italian or French citizen. None of these examples has been chosen lightly. There was a time when being a woman was seen as incompatible with being a surgeon. Today, somebody claiming to be Greek-Catholic may be looked at with curiosity by other Greeks; a black person with a European passport may be delayed in passport control; a Moroccan born in France or Italy may be denied citizenship; a British Pakistani may have his allegiances called into question. Reactions to perceived incompatibility of identities may range from surprise, to restricted access to an identity and discrimination. The identities one is allowed to claim constitute part of one's representation of the self (Chryssochoou 2003).

Roccas and Brewer (2002) (panel 4.4) propose the concept of social identity complexity to refer to an individual's subjective representation of the interrelationships between his or her multiple identities.

This approach is useful in understanding which groups might constitute an ingroup or an outgroup for a particular person in a given situation. According to this model, the type of subjective representation of the social identity complexity will impact on the reaction towards other people with whom one might seem to share a membership. An interesting addition would be to look at the meaning attached to these memberships and whether particular identities lead to the construction of a particular type of identity representation within a culture. For example, it would be interesting to look at whether ethnic, national, supranational, and religious identifications are represented systematically as intersections, compartmentalized, merge, or in a relation of domin-

Panel 4.4   Social Identity Complexity

Social identity complexity (Roccas and Brewer 2002) refers to the nature of the subjective representation of multiple ingroup identities. Four models of social identity complexity are proposed, each with implications for the inclusion and exclusion of others from what is considered to be the ingroup:

- *Intersection:* the formation of a single ingroup identity defined by the intersection of multiple group memberships. Only people who fall into the category defined at this intersection are considered part of the ingroup.
- *Dominance:* the adoption of one primary ingroup that dominates all other memberships. Only people who share membership of the primary ingroup are considered part of the ingroup.
- *Compartmentalization:* multiple identities are differentiated and separate from each other. In this case identities are context specific. People are evaluated positively and considered as ingroup members at different levels to the extent that they share either some or all these identities.
- *Merger:* social identity is the outcome of the combination of one's multiple identifications. The ingroup in this case is highly inclusive and diverse.

In relation to multiculturalism Roccas and Brewer suggest:

- *Hyphenated identities* correspond with a representation of *intersection*.
- *Assimilation or separation* strategies correspond with a representation of *dominance* (one identity overrides the others).
- *Cultural ambidextrousness* (the ability to mobilize different cultural identities) corresponds with a representation of *compartmentalization*.
- *Integrated biculturalism* corresponds with a representation of *merger*.

ance in a given sociohistorical context. In other words, I argue for the possibility that self-knowledge is socially constructed and to a certain extent shared.

As we have seen, the need to negotiate old identities and create new ones is one of the requirements of multicultural societies (Chryssochoou 2000a). Those who move have to adjust to new environments; those for whom their ethnic or other identity is salient because of its minority status have to negotiate these identities within the wider social context. Equally, those who are in a dominant position are forced to rethink themselves and their societies to include the cultural diversity of their environment. As Ethier and Deaux (1994) suggest (panel 4.5), these readjustments do not necessarily mean changing the intensity of identification with particular identities or reducing their importance. Rather, it requires changing the meaning of these identities by *remooring* them to elements of support existing in the new context. Such remooring might even preserve these identities and strengthen them.

Panel 4.5   Negotiating Social Identity When Contexts Change: Maintaining Identification and Responding to Threat (Ethier and Deaux 1994)

Research question

What happens when the context that supports a particular identity changes dramatically and for a long period or ceases to exist? The study aimed to investigate the relationships between threat, efforts to maintain ethnic identity, and changes to that identity among Hispanic students at a primarily Anglo college in the US. The study examined these trends longitudinally and followed students during their first year at college.

Theoretical framework

During transitions and periods of change in the life span individuals need to adapt. Sometimes this adaptation is not just a situational change, but also involves more central changes in the meaning and significance of identities. The meaning and values associated with identity can be brought into question and identity can be threatened.

Hypotheses

The authors hypothesized that in situations where support for a particular identity is no longer present, people need to develop new bases of support and "remoor" their identity to new social supports. They expected Hispanic students to do the following:

- Change the way they supported their ethnic identity (different trends of remooring).
- Make efforts to maintain stability: those who identified strongly with their ethnic identity would get involved in activities with Hispanic groups. These efforts will be positively related to the changes in identity.
- React differently to the change in relation to their previous identification and background; feelings of threat, involvement, and self-esteem will be influenced by these factors.

Method

- *Participants:* students of two Ivy League colleges were interviewed three times during their first year at college. They were all of Hispanic background but of different nationalities (mostly Mexican and Puerto Rican). Of the 45 students who took part in the first interview, 36 participated in all three interviews.

(Continues)

Panel 4.5   (*Continued*)

- *Measures:* the interview included questions on identity, self-esteem associated with ethnic membership, perceptions of threat, ethnic involvement, and about the past and present context of ethnic identity.

Results

The number of identities that the students mentioned, the importance of their ethnic identity, and the self-esteem associated with it did not change during the course of the year. However, levels of threat increased at time 2 (after returning from a break) and stayed almost at that level at time 3.

The majority of students mentioned Hispanic identity as an important one; however, all students mentioned the identity of being a student and a friend and rated these identities as higher in importance. Hispanic identity was significantly related to collective self-esteem. The authors observed qualitative changes in the meaning of this identity over time. This finding supports their idea that its level of importance may remain stable over time but its meaning might change.

Although at the beginning of the year the strength of Hispanic identity was significantly related to family background, this link was no longer significant by the time of the second and third interviews. Instead, involvement in Hispanic activities on campus showed a positive link with the strength of ethnic identification at times 2 and 3.

The stronger the ethnic background of the students prior to college, the more likely they were to become involved with ethnic activities on campus, and this involvement predicted the changes in their ethnic identity between times 2 and 3. The more they got involved, the stronger their ethnic identification became. However, for those who had a weaker ethnic background prior to college the opposite was true. They felt more threat during their first year, expressed lower levels of self-esteem associated with this identity, and showed more negative changes in identification.

General discussion

It is important to stress the ecological validity of these findings, which were obtained longitudinally. The authors suggest that what enables identities to remain stable is a process of remooring to new elements of support. The students in this study who wished to maintain their strong ethnic identification replaced the elements of cultural background that they had prior to college with new ones. The study also highlighted that the strength of prior identification is important in determining how people will negotiate their identity in the new environment. Perceptions of threat from the environment and ambivalence about their ethnic identity led students to move away from it.

Thus, people choose one of two paths to negotiate their identity under conditions of change: stick with it and strengthen it through a process of remooring, or move away from it.

Thus, a process of reconstruction of self-knowledge is taking place in situations of life change. In the case of superordinate group development this process can take the form of a collective construction of shared meanings. In the development of these new meanings, issues of power are inevitably present. As we saw in chapter 3, there is a battle for establishing oneself or one's group as prototypical of the superordinate group and thus obtaining the power to define the beliefs of the new group, the project of the new identity.

We have seen that multiple identities – their perceived incompatibilities, the way they interrelate, and the meaning they have for people – are at the center of discussions regarding superordinate or culturally diverse groups. Perhaps it is time to ground these issues within the context of real culturally diverse groups, such as the US, Canada, and Australia as countries founded on immigration, and the European Union. Labeling all these groups as supranational is quite problematic. Their cultural diversity has different roots and refers to different issues, and it would be inappropriate to tackle the issues they raise in only a few lines. Just as diversity in national groups in Europe has existed all along, and just as multiculturalism is understood and enacted differently, so too the issues concerning these groups are different and it would be reductionist to consider them simply as categories at a higher level of abstraction. This is precisely the terrain where social psychologists would be foolish to venture without the torches lit by sociologists, historians, and political scientists.

The formation of the European Union (EU) has attracted the attention of many researchers, including myself (Chryssochoou 1996a). A first point of interest was to look at attitudes and representations towards the EU and the unification process (Hewstone 1986; Hilton et al. 1996; De Rosa 1996), either by collecting new data or analyzing Eurobarometers (Deflem and Pampel 1996). The idea was to understand how people within the EU perceived the unification process and whether they would construct an identity that indicates their attachment to it (Barrett 1996; Chryssochoou 1996b). The EU brought to the forefront a perceived incompatibility between identities. European unification was viewed as asking people to consider their national identity as being nested within the European identity; as a consequence, the latter identity was resisted (Cinnirella 1997; Huici et al. 1997; Mlicki and Ellemers 1996). The belief that European identity is incompatible with national identity has its roots, in my opinion, in the very construction of the EU. It rests on the fact that in order to be able to claim an EU identity, the national ingroup has to be a member of the Union. EU identity is not something conferred on people as individuals but as nationals of a member state (I could claim an EU identity because Greece is a member of the EU). Thus, the members of the EU are nations, not individuals. European identity is resisted because – it is claimed – it will homogenize the cultural differences of national groups. Here we see the belief that *belonging* to a group means being *similar* to other members; therefore, unification equates with homogenization. This belief makes identities to be perceived as incompatible.

In addition, the EU is seen as a new political organization that seeks to transfer power from the nation and thus threatens the status of the nation-state. The presence of the EU redefines the meaning of the national project and therefore the national identity (Brewer 1999; Chryssochoou 2000b). At the same time, it is anchored in national representations and other identities; thus the representation of the EU is not unique around the continent (Chryssochoou 1996a; Echebarria-Echabe et al. 1992; Tapia 1997). Furthermore, European unification calls for a new conceptualization of the relationship between the individual and the political organization (citizenship) (Licata 2001) and makes salient issues of political participation and the accountability of governing bodies. The enlargement of Europe calls for a rebalance of power and resource distribution and will inevitably make salient those issues of justice presented in chapter 3. These are all issues that social psychologists can investigate (Breakwell and Lyons 1996; for a review see Doise and Devos 1999).

It is possible that people in Europe, particularly those from powerful European countries, do not perceive a Europe-wide project as any different to a national project. For example, some French respondents in my studies (Chryssochoou 1996a, 2000b) did not see a difference between being French and being European and therefore seemed quite indifferent to the second identity. Perhaps European identity will be problematized due to the presence of immigrants from non-European countries and the political trend in Europe to restrict the movement of non-EU members within its boundaries (Licata and Klein 2002). Others might resist the idea of a "cultural" European identity that they fear would homogenize them. In particular, people from smaller and less powerful countries are keen to maintain their specificity. The battle for prototypicality for European identity and beliefs is very much open and in this battle the economic power of countries plays a crucial role. For example, Greek participants use the dimension of competence to describe Europeans and the dimension of warmth to describe themselves (Chryssochoou 2000c), falling into the stereotyping ambivalence presented by Glick and Fiske described in chapter 3. At the same time Greeks showed high levels of identification with Europe measured quantitatively. Positive response to these measures might in this case denote that Europe is seen as a reference group and not yet as a group that contributes to self-definition. In light of such findings, we need, as social psychologists, to bear in mind that a high level of identification on a scale might have different meanings for different people and groups. Thus, we would need to investigate more qualitatively the content of people's attachment to a group, not just ask them to quantify how much this group is important for their self-definition. We can see here how some of the social psychological issues we have discussed throughout this book – identity, representations, power, and social influence – relate to the project of European unification.

Countries founded on immigration raise quite another set of questions. Such countries were built around multicultural beliefs, although these beliefs might have been different from country to country (panel 4.6). Furthermore, there is an awareness of this diversity and often this awareness is built into their state policies. These policies are differently implemented in each case and relate to the history of each of these countries.

The US was founded on a civic conception based on the idea that all residents of a territory are subjects of a state and thus (at least potentially) citizens (Plotke 1999). One

Panel 4.6 Types of Cultural Diversity

According to Moghaddam (1998) there are different types of cultural diversity:

- *Assimilation:* minorities abandon their heritage cultures in an attempt to melt into mainstream society.
- *Multiculturalism:* heritage cultures are retained and developed in an attempt to achieve a cultural mosaic.

There are two types of assimilation:

- *Minority assimilation:* minorities abandon their heritage cultures and adopt the majority way of life.
- *Melting-pot assimilation:* majority and minority groups contribute to the formation of a new common culture.

There are two types of multiculturalism:

- *Active multiculturalism:* a policy of intentionally supporting the cultural heritage of people.
- *Laissez-faire multiculturalism:* cultural diversity is neither protected nor suppressed.

Multiculturalism can be also distinguished in the following ways:

- *Collective multiculturalism:* equal and respectful treatment of the heritage culture of groups.
- *Individual multiculturalism:* equal and respectful treatment of each individual as the carrier of a unique culture.

of the founding myths of America is the famous "melting-pot." This expression was popularized by Israel Zangwill, author of *The Melting-Pot* (1909), in which one of the characters says: "America is God's Crucible, the great Melting-Pot where all the faces of Europe are melting and reforming!" This became one of the most cited ideas about cultural diversity in America and it expresses some of the issues we have examined. It presents the issue of acculturation with a double face. The melting pot can mean that all differences are supposed to melt towards one norm and reform; therefore it provides grounds for support for an assimilation strategy. However, it can also mean that as differences melt they form a new common culture. That this founding myth can be interpreted in different ways brings us back to our discussion about how socially shared knowledge is constructed. The American founding myth, as Gerstle (1999) suggests, consists of four different claims: (1) European immigrants wanted to abandon their old world ways and become American; (2) Americanization was an easy process without any obstacles; (3) this process "melted" people into a single race and nation, erasing old categorizations; (4) Americanization was experienced as emancipation from poverty, servitude, and deference: it was the path to freedom. Gerstle (1999: 291) contests these claims and concludes "coercion, as much as liberty, has been intrinsic to our history and to the process of becoming American."

Becoming American inevitably leads us to issues of power. Zangwill only mentions one category – "Europeans" – that are melting and reforming. Are they the only ones participating in the construction of this culture? America's battle for group beliefs had started. In this battle for prototypicality the racial divide is very salient. America is still a racialized community trying to move from a racial to a cultural division (Philogene 2001). From a social psychological point of view the claim of hyphenated identities (X-American) is of great interest in understanding how people assert their diversity within a context of participation in a common culture. Moreover, the bipolar racial divide along the black–white dimension brings other issues to the forefront. Sanchez (1999: 376) talks about a racialized nativism, which is an intense opposition to an internal minority on the ground of its foreign "un-American" connections. The 1992 Los Angeles riots and the violent events preceding them attest to the rise of racialized nativism directed towards recent immigrants. Furthermore, long-established Asian and Latino communities were portrayed as recent immigrants. In this context, Plotke (1999) remarks that to make sense of immigration requires attention to normative issues and processes; in other words, to what people are supposed to do to become American: "contemporary immigration highlights the tension between more open and more closed notions of membership in the United States" (p. 300). It raises the questions of what citizenship means and the relationship between the individual and the group. What types of bonds might one have with the group? Which are the practices that sustain these bonds and what are the consequences of this membership? These questions interest the social scientist and also lay people. Commonsense theories and representations about these issues guide practices and behavior and shape policies. This is where social psychology ought to step in to understand better the processes of lay knowledge construction, the contents of this knowledge, and their links with expert knowledge.

Canada and Australia are in some respects similar to the US, for example in relation to nativism and to reactions towards recent immigrants (Augoustinos and Quinn 2003). However, these countries acknowledge diversity as an essential part of who they are (group beliefs) and incorporate active protection of this diversity in their policies. For Canada, multiculturalism was considered as a national property and symbol that contributed to the construction of a distinctive identity (Esses and Gardner 1996). In 1971 multiculturalism became an official Canadian government policy and in 1977 the Canadian Human Rights Act was passed. In 1988 the Canadian Multiculturalism Act was designed to "encourage and assist the social, cultural, economic, and political institutions of Canada to be both respectful and inclusive of Canada's multicultural character" (Canada Fact Sheets). Seemingly in Australia multiculturalism is part of the national identity project. The governmental site on Australian immigration talks about Australian Multiculturalism as a term that "summarizes the way we address the challenges and opportunities of our cultural diversity." In 1999 the Australian government set a New Agenda for Multicultural Australia that aims to achieve "enhanced community harmony, and maximum benefits from our diversity in the national interest." Australian Multiculturalism is defined as "accepting and respecting the right of all Australians to express and share their individual cultural heritage within the overriding commitment to Australia and the basic structures and values of Australian Democracy." Multiculturalism is based on four principles of civic duty, cultural respect, social equity, and productive diversity. We can see here the idea, discussed previously, that cultural identities are expected to be nested within an overriding (Australian) identity. Loyalty is expected to be shown towards the superordinate group. This highlights again the issue of the definition of values and principles with which one ought to abide. It also presents cultural identity and ethnicity as individual properties that are perhaps to be enacted in the private sphere, while at the same time it encourages the view of ethnicity as a set of attributes and characteristics that define the individual, thus reifying ethnic categories. The balance between respect for ethnic and cultural rights and reification of ethnicity is a delicate one. It is something that social psychologists need to investigate further. Multiculturalism as a national ideology and project makes salient another way of categorizing the world: the ethnic division.

The battle for power continues in these societies in which cultural tolerance is part of the national credo. In Canada, for example, the French community has brought the issue of respect, cultural equality, and identity to the forefront of political debate in its struggle for bilingualism, autonomy, and independence.

The USA, Canada, and Australia have to deal with the issue of indigenous populations and rights. These groups of people have been neglected and are at a severe disadvantage according to all major socioeconomic indicators. Their presence raises questions about resource distribution and the theories that underlie it, as well as nationhood and citizenship. For example, land claims are a key issue in indigenous politics. The deservedness of particular rights for people who claim that they were the first to inhabit a territory raises questions about the important connection between people and land/ territory in the definition of nationhood and citizenship. We will visit the issues of citizenship and rights in a little more detail in the final section of this book.

In the Name of Identity: Self-Knowledge and the Politics of Rights, Claims, and Recognition in Culturally Diverse Societies

I have presented a brief overview of the issues raised by real superordinate groups. The discussion has highlighted one issue emphasized by many theorists and researchers: citizenship. The issue of citizenship is vast and requires the contribution of historians, sociologists, and political scientists in order to grasp its implications. That endeavor is beyond the scope of the present book. (Interested readers should consult Isin and Turner (2002) for a detailed overview.) I have described how the changes within states and the ways in which people and states conceptualize cultural diversity have an impact on what citizenship means and how it is enacted. I will focus now on aspects of the citizenship debate that seem of crucial importance in our societies and to which previous sections of this book implicitly referred: respect, dignity, trust, and social recognition.

According to Janoski and Gran (2002: 13), "citizenship is grounded in the guarantee of legal and political protections from raw coercive power." They define citizenship "as passive and active membership of individuals in a nation-state with universalistic rights and obligations at a specified level of equality." Thus, citizenship in this definition is linked to membership of a political organization and is conceptualized as active (ability to influence politics) and passive (rights of existence within a legal system). This definition of citizenship contains the idea of rights and protections. These rights can be legal (personal security, access to justice, conscience, and freedom of choice), political (voting, protest, forming of political parties, collective rights, immigration, naturalization, asylum and cultural rights), social (enabling rights welfare, opportunity rights education, redistributive and compensatory rights), and participative (labor rights, advisory rights). The existence of these rights highlights the necessity to protect people and groups from the exercise of power. The expression of these rights constitutes a regulation of the relationship between the individual and the state and among individuals and groups.

Trust/distrust is an inherent part of these relationships. It is important to consider whether relationships allow attributions of trustworthiness to be made towards the other party in order to enable the reduction of uncertainty inherent in any relationship. Trust is a crucial element of social relationships (Simmel 1950). It has been studied in different areas of psychology (Deutsch 1958; Kramer 1999; Luhmann 1979; Rempel, Holmes, and Zanna 1985; Rotter 1971; Slovic 1993) and recently renewed calls have been made to investigate its role in intergroup relations (Brewer 2000). The oppositional pair trust/distrust is also an important **thema**, organizing our representations of social relationships (Marková 2000).

In order to communicate with others and engage in action with them we need to have a common understanding of the contracts that regulate our relationships. In an era of globalization and in accordance with the previous definition of citizenship that qualified rights as universalistic, Doise and his colleagues advanced the hypothesis that what regulates relationships is a normative social representation attached to the Universal Declaration of Human Rights (panel 4.7). They set out to investigate whether there are common grounds in lay understandings of these rights, whether these understandings are close to expert definitions and classifications, what could explain variations in the position-taking concerning those rights, and who is considered responsible for their implementation and respect.

Themata

Source ideas, image-concepts that are culturally shared and transmitted through collective memory and from which notions emerge.

(Moscovici and Vignaux 2000)

Oppositional categories that historically, at a particular time, become problematized because for whatever reason they became the focus of attention as a source of tension and conflict.

(Marková 1999: 63; my translation)

Panel 4.7   Human Rights as Normative Social Representations

In a large research program Doise and colleagues set out to investigate human rights as a normative social representation (TS1) (see Doise 2001; Doise and Herrera 1994; Doise et al. 1994; Doise, Spini, and Clemence 1999; Spini 1997; Spini and Doise 1998; Staerklé 1999; Staerklé, Clemence, and Doise 1998). Three tasks underline this work:

- If there are common grounds in the social representation of human rights, one needs to find their components and describe the way that they are organized.
- Differences in individual positions regarding human rights should be investigated so that systematic variations are brought to light.
- One needs to examine how positions about human rights are anchored in collective reality by studying the three distinct types of such anchoring (Doise 1992; Doise, Clemence, and Lorenzi-Cioldi 1993; TS1). In other words, one must seek to understand how people's positions vary in relation to their anchoring to other beliefs and values (psychological anchoring), in relation to people's understanding of social relations (social psychological anchoring), and in relation to people's memberships and social positions (sociological anchoring).

This vast program, using different populations and methodologies, cannot be described here. I will merely highlight some issues of relevance to our discussion (for further information see Doise (2001) or the papers cited above):

- The Universal Declaration of Human Rights constitutes a common reference for people. This reference increases with age.
- However, the existence of a common reference does not mean an absence of variation in positions. For example, a dimension that opposes an individualistic and juridical view of human rights to a socioeconomic perspective seems to organize people's evocations of human rights.
- Differences in the dimensions that organize perceptions of human rights exist between adults and young people, professionals and others. These differences are linked to understandings of sociopolitical and economic issues (for example, the issue of asylum and immigration).
- In general, people seem to agree strongly with the principles of human rights. However, this agreement is moderated by the context. People agree strongly with the principles of human rights presented in *abstract* terms, but when these rights are put in *specific* contexts this agreement is weakened.
- When people are faced with a specific case, the normative general principle is weakened and other social regulations organize perceptions. For example, a human rights violation is tolerated if the victim is deviant or outside social norms.

(*Continues*)

> Panel 4.7   *(Continued)*
> • There is an ethnocentric vision of human rights violations. Some violations of human rights are judged less serious when the national ingroup is the perpetrator.
>
> Crosscultural research involving 35 countries has indicated the following:
>
> • Respondents in these countries use the same classification as Cassin (an expert and co-author of the UN Declaration) to categorize different rights. There appears to be a common understanding of human rights across countries.
> • However, there is variation in position-taking both within and between countries. This variation concerns the role attributed to individuals and governments in relation to the respect and protection of human rights. People (and countries) can be categorized in relation to their investment in human rights and the importance they attribute to them in: sympathizers, activists, skeptics, and governmentalists (the responsibility for human rights lies with governments). Examples of this analysis at a cultural level are: sympathizers (Argentina, Basque Country, Canada, Greece, Mexico, Romania, Spain), activists (Brazil, Cameroon, Indonesia, Ivory Coast, Philippines, Tunisia, Zaire), skeptics (Albania, India, Japan, UK, Zimbabwe), and governmentalists (Austria, Czech Republic, Germany, Hong Kong, Russia, Yugoslavia).
> • Positions about human rights are anchored in values, perceptions, and personal experiences of conflict and discrimination.

Their research suggest that there might be a consensus (TS17) built around respect for human rights as a way of regulating relations. However, people take different positions in relation to this respect according to their memberships, beliefs, and values, and their experience of conflict and power issues. Furthermore, there is a difference between agreement with the abstract principles of human rights and respect in specific cases. And responsibility for respecting human rights is variably attributed to governments or individuals.

Human rights as regulators of social relations acquires a crucial significance in a globalized era.

> Individual rights, expansively redefined as human rights on a universalistic basis and legitimized at the transnational level, undercut the import of national citizenship by disrupting the territorial closure of nations. The same human rights that came to be secured over the centuries in national constitutions as the rights and privileges of a proper citizenry have now attained a new meaning and have become globally sanctioned norms and components of a supranational discourse.   *(Soysal 1994: 164)*

Following Soysal's thesis, identity has been dissociated from rights within a scheme where membership is multiple, spanning the local, the regional, and the global. Immigrants are a good example of membership where rights, duties, and loyalties interact. According to Soysal, what makes them rightful members of their new environment is not common blood and lineage, or their allegiance and loyalty to a state. It is migrants' sharing of a social public space, the practices associated with it, and a set of abstract rules and principles called human rights. This is not to deny, of course, that there is still in place a dichotomy between national citizen and foreigner, or that rights are still conferred on the basis of national citizenship. On the contrary, these distinctions remain powerful and shape the representations of communities. However, there might be other ways of establishing the rights of individuals without relying on the nation-state. The post-national path might include other issues that one needs to take on board. How, for example, can one avoid a war or embargo launched in the name of human rights against a nation-state in which the victims of the intervention would be those whom it was meant to protect? Who is in fact responsible for the implementation for and respect of human rights and who would legitimately "police" them? To which legitimate authority could individuals appeal and claim their rights when these are violated by the state? How will these authorities be democratically accountable and to whom?

All these questions have to do with our understanding of power and its use. Perhaps, strictly speaking, these are not questions for social psychological enquiry. Not only social scientists but also lay people are asking them. Their answers depend on their memberships, positions, power, status, beliefs, and values. They may come to question the universality of these rights and the ways in which they are implemented. Thus, they may become disaffected and withdraw from political participation in the construction of regulations that organize social relationships. Feelings of helplessness and feelings of threat have never been good counsellors for social relationships.

Thus, citizenship, trust, and human rights are the ingredients of social relationships in our societies. Modern societies have been problematized around the notion of human rights and the concept of dignity (Markovà 1999). The concept of dignity marks the transition from a premodern society based on honor to a modern society where individuals independently of their class, race, gender, beliefs, and sexuality are part of the same category of humanity. We have seen the importance of the process of ontologization whereby humanity is denied to those who are seen as unwilling to conform.

Identity in modern times is not ascribed and regulated by codes of honor, but rests on individuals who are increasingly conscious of their positions and identities. Thus, the Hegelian concept of social recognition appears. Social recognition constitutes a thema that has been problematized in modern times where "the quest and the battle for social recognition become essential for the development of the self" (Markovà 1999: 68; Markovà 2000). It is the opposition between recognition/non-recognition that drives the claims in terms of rights and identities in our societies. "Lacking social recognition is like having the feeling of being incapable to function like a human being" (Markovà 1999: 68).

Identity and the self-concept have been at the heart of numerous theoretical accounts and publications in social psychology (Ashmore and Jussim 1997; Breakwell 1986; Brown 2000; Capozza and Brown 2000; Harré 1987, 1998; Mead 1934; Neisser and Jopling 1997; Sedikides and Brewer 2001; Stryker 1980, 1992; Stryker and Burke

2000; Tajfel 1974, 1981; Tajfel and Turner 1986). Different aspects of identity have surfaced in our discussion about our culturally diverse societies. We have seen identity as a threatened position and we have discussed identity as attached to a particular project.

I have argued elsewhere (Chryssochoou 2003) that identity expresses a relationship between the individual and the world and can be seen as having three elements: (1) an element of cognition (self-knowledge) answering the question "what do I know about me?"; (2) an element of self-action pertaining to the claims I want and can make about myself; (3) an element of Others' actions that recognize me and allow me to make these claims. Thus, identity is a threefold concept constituted by cognition–claims–recognition. Our answers to the questions attached to these processes (who am I? who are they? what is our relationship?) constitute the lenses through which we see the world. We decide who is good and who is evil, who is allowed to become a citizen, what type of acculturation strategy we will follow, and what rights are violated and when.

We acquire the elements of self-cognition through processes of socialization within a culture, where the actions of others (recognition) enable us to develop knowledge about ourselves that we are supposed to transform in culturally appropriate claims. We communicate our identity claims and seek social recognition. We fight for this recognition through processes of social influence. This is when identity is used strategically to promote particular projects (Reicher and Hopkins 1996). Claims constructed and argued in a strategic way draw upon existing knowledge and aim to influence recognition and alter existing categorical boundaries.

Thus identity, as a threefold concept of self-knowledge claims and recognition, presents a particular representation of the world from the vantage point of the speaker. So when identity is threatened it is in a sense people's vision of the world that is shaken. We have seen that people will act to restore a devalued identity, or to protect their privileged position. We have seen that under changing social conditions the content of memberships, the beliefs associated with groups, the boundaries of the groups, will also change. Self-knowledge needs to be reconstructed and unfamiliarity domesticated. In their effort to accommodate novelty, people might react in order to protect the already-there: their vision of the world, their identity. They might also act in the name of identity to produce change. Claims are actions upon the world. They include, exclude, impose, or accept different versions of the world. Challenging claims means to challenge people's position in the world and all the symbolic and material power that this position means. When we discussed justice issues we saw the importance of messages of respect (Lind and Tyler 1988). The absence of social recognition equates to a loss of humanity (Marková 1999, 2000).

To conclude, my argument is that people act to protect themselves from, to accommodate themselves with, to provoke and respond to, change. Social changes are problematizing cultural diversity nowadays in a way that made it the focus of attention as a source of tension. The dichotomy of Us–Them takes new forms following familiar paths. If we are to achieve "enhanced community harmony and maximum benefits from our diversity" we need to work to ease feelings of threat. We need to find ways to deal with the unfamiliarity that diversity brings, to understand and calm the fears of "contamination," to change the ethos towards those who we feel failed to convert. We need to acknowledge the role of power and the battles for group beliefs. Finally, we need to do all this by actively participating in political and social debates and by influencing decisions and policies. Early social psychological research (TS20) has shown that attitudes are not causally linked to behavior and that actions can provoke change in attitudes. Thus, change in attitudes and prejudiced beliefs can be achieved by changes in practices and behavior. The task is tremendous because our whole system of social categorizations and the world as we know it are shaken. We have no choice, however, because it is our own actions, communications, and games of influence that change the world.

We must learn to develop other ways of establishing associative relationships with others than the ones based on similarity. "The possibility of living in close association with other people or groups – families and communities are good examples – without losing one's identity is one of the biggest difficulties of personal and social relationships but equally the fundamental necessity for their survival" (Moscovici 1996: 231). Respect and mutual recognition are the ingredients for this recipe. For my part, I leave you here. I hope you have enjoyed our social psychological discussion and that it will help you in your journey within our culturally diverse societies.

Theoretical Snapshots

Snapshot 1: Social Representations Theory

The concept of social representations originates from Serge Moscovici's work. He expanded the concept of collective representations used by Durkheim (1898) to understand the production and elaboration of knowledge.

In his seminal work on psychoanalysis, Moscovici (1961/1976) studied what happens when scientific knowledge becomes part of commonsense: the process involved and its outcomes. In particular, he asked what happens to the conceptual theoretical framework of psychoanalysis when it becomes the object of everyday communication and influence. In very simple terms, for Moscovici, science and commonsense belong to two different universes of thinking. The former is based on experience, validation, and the seeking of a "correct" answer; the latter is based on beliefs. When a conceptual scientific framework becomes an object of communication and influence in the broader society then it is transformed into a representation.

Such representations are "social" in the sense that they are not individual mental activities but collective elaborations of knowledge. The attribute "social" qualifies these representations not only because they are shared among members of different groups, but essentially because they are also the outcomes of a collective production of meaning about an object. This collective production is the result of processes of communication and social influence that characterize the arena of public debate. The fact that they are shared does not necessarily mean that each individual holds exactly the same views. It means that the organization of individual knowledge is influenced by common principles that are shared by people. It is important to have a common basis of knowledge if we want to be able to communicate with each other. This is one of the functions social representations serve: they allow communication to take place.

Moscovici suggested that when people are faced with complex theoretical frameworks and novelty, they try to make sense of them by transforming abstract ideas into concrete images and by trying to incorporate the new knowledge into already familiar frameworks. Social representations are formed as the result of two processes.

1 Through the process of *objectification* abstract concepts are transformed into concrete images.
2 Through the process of *anchoring* new knowledge is named and classified into familiar frameworks.

Making the unfamiliar familiar and helping people to deal with novelty is another of the functions that social representations serve.

Social representations theory places emphasis both on the processes that produce knowledge and the content of this knowledge. Another function of social representations is that they constitute the framework of people's worldviews that help them give meaning to their environment and that guide their practices.

Social representations also have a symbolic function. Not everybody holds exactly the same representation. People position themselves differently in relation to this common knowledge. According to Doise (1992), people can anchor new knowledge to their previous beliefs and values (psychological anchoring). In addition, new knowledge might be understood in similar ways by people who belong to the same groups (sociological anchoring). The way new knowledge is anchored might depend on the ways people have to understand social regulations and power asymmetries between people and groups (social psychological anchoring). Thus, the expression of social representations helps "locate" people within a social system.

How does our thinking become social? Moscovici suggested that when we think, two systems intervene. The first (the *operational*) performs basic cognitive operations (i.e., categorizations, associations, inclusions, discriminations, deductions, etc.), whereas the second (the *meta-system*) guides these operations by controlling, verifying, and selecting according to rules (logical or not) the informational material. This system is characterized by the social regulations of the society/culture in which we live and the groups in whose life we participate. Processes of objectification and anchoring are working within the meta-system to translate these social regulations and guide cognitive operations (Lorenzi-Cioldi and Clemence 2001). Thus, social relations and regulations are intrinsically linked with our cognitive elaborations and the social knowledge we produce.

For example, in his work on psychoanalysis Moscovici observed that different social institutions, such as the Catholic Church, the communist party, and broadsheet newspapers, had different ways of relating to their audiences and different ways of communicating with them. Broadsheet journalists were like their readers: recipients of information about psychoanalysis. Their aim was to *diffuse* the information they collected and create a common base of knowledge. The Catholic Church, on the other hand, is a group with a specific vision of the world, and has a different relationship with its audience. This group has a vision to *propagate*. However, it tries to accommodate other knowledge in this framework. Finally, the communist party aimed to make salient a clear antagonism between their worldview and an opposite one. Its communication style was characterized by *propaganda*. These modes of communication (diffusion, propagation, propaganda) originate from the different relations between the source and the recipient of a message, and imply different social regulations. It is these regulations that constitute the material of the meta-system and that guide the operations of the cognitive–operational system, producing different cognitive organizations. Moscovici suggested that diffusion leads to the elaboration of *opinions*, propagation to the genesis of *attitudes*, and propaganda to the production of *stereotypes*.

Social representations theory has attracted many researchers who have emphasized different aspects of the theory. Some focus on the content of representations and how they guide everyday practices (Jodelet 1991, 1993); others focus more on communication and language (Bangerter 2000; Elejabarrieta 1994; Markovà 2000; Markovà and Foppa 1990; Markovà, Graumann, and Foppa 1995; Rouquette 1996). Another approach investigates the structure of social representations to examine whether some elements of their content are more central than others and therefore less easy to change (Abric 1993, 2001; Guimelli 1994, 1998). Others focus more on the factors that produce variation within social representations and the positioning of individuals and groups (Clemence 2001; Doise 1990, 1992), or on the way in which people are socialized and transform representations in the course of their development (Duveen 1997; Duveen and Lloyd 1990). The link between social representations, ideology beliefs, and attitudes has been also investigated (Augoustinos 1998).

Many issues have been the targets of social representational research. Examples include health, sexuality, and AIDS (Apostolidis 2001; Campbell and Jovchelovitch 2000; Herzlich 1973; Jodelet 1991; Jovchelovitch and Gervais 1999; Markovà and Farr 1995; Morin and Apostolidis 2002), new technologies such as biogenetics (Bauer and Gaskell 1999; Wagner and Kronberger 2001), perceptions of risk (Joffe 1999; Joffe and Haarhoff 2002), the development of essentialized social categories such as nation, gender, and race (Lorenzi-Cioldi 1988; Lloyd and Duveen 1990, 1992; Philogène 1994, 1999), the development of concepts such as intelligence and identity (Breakwell 1993, 2001; Chryssochoou 2003; Doise 1998; Doise and Lorenzi-Cioldi 1991; Doise and Mugny 1981; Duveen 2001; Elejabarrieta 1994; Lorenzi-Cioldi and Doise 1994), and perceptions of different professions (Palmonari and Zani 1989). In chapter 4 we discuss research concerning the normative understanding of political issues such as human rights, democracy and citizenship (Doise 2001; Doise, Spini, and Clemence 1999; Markovà et al. 1998; Spini and Doise 1998; Staerklé, Clemence, and Doise 1998).

An important function of social representations is to help people deal with unfamiliar environments. This is a crucial issue for the discussion on acculturation.

Snapshot 2: Self-Evaluation and Social Comparison Theory

In 1954 Leon Festinger proposed nine hypotheses that established a theory of social comparison that influenced subsequent research. His main premise was that in order to evaluate themselves people will seek to compare themselves with similar others. These were his nine hypotheses:

1 People have a motivation to evaluate their opinions and abilities.
2 When there are no objective (non-social) means to evaluate their abilities and/or opinions, people will make an evaluation by comparing their abilities/opinions with those of others.
3 People will avoid comparing themselves with very dissimilar others.
4 When evaluating abilities, people (at least in Western cultures) are motivated to establish who is better, whereas the value of opinions comes from the subjective feeling that the opinion is correct.
5 Non-social restraints make it difficult to change one's abilities, but there are no such restraints on opinions. When there is a discrepancy between self and others, people will try to modify their position or else modify others' positions to bring them closer to their own. However, when there is a big discrepancy there will be a tendency to cease comparison with those people who are too different.
6 Comparing oneself with others is accompanied by hostility and derogation if continued comparison has unpleasant consequences for oneself. The fact that others are made incomparable is linked to *status stratification* because it equals the acknowledgment that others are far better or far worse. Thus, people and groups are ranked hierarchically in comparison to one another.
7 When a particular group becomes an important point of comparison for a specific ability/opinion there will be pressure towards uniformity among its members in relation to this particular ability/opinion.
8 People will avoid comparing themselves to those who are very different from them, especially when they are also perceived to be different in other attributes associated with the opinion/ability under evaluation.
9 Within a group, those people who are closer to the mode (the medium point) will have stronger tendencies to change the opinions of others, relatively weaker tendencies to avoid the comparison, and much weaker tendencies to change their own opinion.

Snapshot 3: Social Identity Theory

In seeking to understand the origins of discrimination and ethnocentrism, Henri Tajfel considered that membership in a social group and perception of oneself as a group member are the minimum required for such behaviors to take place. Social identity theory (Tajfel 1974, 1981, 1982) became a major theoretical framework in current social psychology (Brown 2000; Capozza and Brown 2000; Ellemers, Spears, and Doosje 1999; Abrams and Hogg 1999).

The theory starts from the premise that society is a collection of social categories of different social status and power. Social categories are defined by the opposition between them and their dynamics depend on economic and historical forces. People's identity is derived in large part from the social categories to which they belong. Social identity theorists believe that intergroup relations and behavior are due to a cognitive redefinition of the self in terms of group memberships. SIT suggests that there is a distinction between the self as an individual (personal identity) and the self as a group member (social identity). When social identity is salient, group behavior is possible because people accept a group membership as part of the self and define themselves in terms of group memberships, and because these identities are shared.

The psychological structure that establishes the links between the individual and the group and allows intergroup behavior is *social identity*: "that part of an individual's self-concept which derives from one's knowledge from one's membership of a social group (or groups) together with the value and emotional significance attached to that membership" (Tajfel 1981: 255).

According to SIT, two processes are responsible for intergroup behavior:

- Social categorization
- Social comparison

"Social identity treats categorization and social comparison as psychological processes which provide the parameters within which sociohistorical factors, or more accurately, subjective understandings of those factors, operate" (Hogg and Abrams 1988: 54).

Social categorization

SIT asserts that categorization has two functions: a *cognitive function* and an *identity function*. The cognitive function helps people to simplify perception. This is fundamental, as it contributes to people's adaptation in the world and which helps them to organize and order their environment. Two processes are involved in this organization of the environment: *accentuation* and *contrast*. Accentuation means minimizing the differences between stimuli belonging to the same category, whereas contrast means maximizing the differences between categories.

The identity function: in a social system, social categories are associated to specific values. The value of the category reflects upon its members. Ingroup membership has consequences for people's self-esteem. Individuals will try to maintain or obtain a positive self-esteem. Therefore, they will try to establish a positive difference between their ingroup and relevant outgroups. In other words, group members discriminate in order to maintain a positive self-esteem.

Social comparison

The evaluation of a category depends on its frame of reference and it is established by social comparisons. For social identity theory, knowledge is a social product and individuals need to compare in order to know themselves better, validate their beliefs, and understand better the surrounding world. When it comes to evaluating the ingroup, individuals need to ensure that the outcome of the comparison is positive. In other words, the evaluation of the position of the individual in the social structure is relative; it is established in relation to another individual (member of the same or different group) or in relation to an outgroup. As we know from social comparison theory (TS2), the outcome of the comparison depends on the point of reference used – other members of the ingroup, other members of the outgroup, another group, past situations, future expectations – and the dimensions of the comparison

Social categorization and social comparison work together to produce intergroup behavior. Categorization leads to a stereotypic perception of group members and to a differentiation between ingroup and outgroup. Social comparison regulates the differences between groups by selecting the dimensions of comparison and monitoring the frame of the comparison.

SIT bases its explanation of intergroup behavior on a cognitive/motivational hypothesis: the understanding of the world in terms of social categories and the perception of oneself as part of them (cognition) and the motivation for a positive social identity are responsible for intergroup behavior. In the early stages of the theory emphasis was placed on the role of self-esteem as a fundamental motivation guiding intergroup behavior. Subsequent research revealed inconsistent findings (Hogg and Abrams 1988), suggesting that feeling positive about one's social identity may be more than an issue of self-esteem. In any case, SIT is a theory of group behavior. Tajfel's major concern was to understand when the fundamental motivation for positive social identity leads to individual behavior (acting for one's own advantage) and when to collective behavior (seeing oneself as part of a group and acting for the advantage of the whole group).

SIT suggests that the shift between individual and collective behavior depends on the belief systems individuals hold. It identified two major belief systems:

- Social mobility
- Social change

The social mobility belief system holds that the boundaries between groups are permeable and thus it is possible to change one's memberships. The social change belief system holds that the boundaries between groups are impermeable, and thus the only possibility one has is to try to ameliorate the position of the entire group. These belief systems promote different behaviors (individual/collective) when the outcome of the comparison between groups is negative for the ingroup.

Snapshot 4: Identity Process Theory (Breakwell 1986, 1993, 2001)

Identity is a psychological process manifested through action, thought, and affect. People are "self-constructors," building, changing, and monitoring their identity. This involves two processes:

1 The *assimilation–accommodation process* deals with how identity absorbs new information and how this information is accommodated within the structure of identity.
2 The *evaluation process* occurs continuously and confers value on the contents of identity.

The theory holds that these are universal psychological processes that interact to determine the content and the value of identity over time. They are guided by four motivational principles:

1 *Continuity:* the sense that despite changes, the self is the same over time.
2 *Distinctiveness:* feeling unique, separate, and distinctive in relation to others.
3 *Self-efficacy:* a sense of agency, competence, and control.
4 *Self-esteem:* a sense of self-worth.

The importance of these principles may be culturally and historically determined. If they are satisfied appropriately, the processes of assimilation–accommodation and evaluation can resume their work satisfactorily and people feel at ease with "who they are." However, when these principles, for whatever reason, are obstructed (when one cannot obtain or maintain appropriate levels of self-efficacy, self-esteem, distinctiveness, or continuity), identity is *threatened*. Changes in the conditions of one's life, or new identities, are potential threats to one's identity.

When a threat occurs, people engage in *coping strategies* to restore appropriate levels of continuity, distinctiveness, self-efficacy, and self-esteem. Coping strategies aim to:

• change those aspects of the social context that produced the threat;
• move the individual into a new, less threatening social position;
• amend the content and value of identity in order to enable the identity processes to operate in accordance with the principles.

The strategies can operate at three levels: intrapsychic (strategies within the individual), interpersonal (strategies involving other people), and intergroup (strategies concerning one's group).

Intrapsychic

- Deflection strategies (involving denial of the situation, generating unreal selves, etc.).
- Acceptance strategies (reconstructing the self, accepting changes only in one area of one's life or in a more fundamental way),
- Reevaluation of the current and future contents of identity.

Interpersonal

- Isolation (isolating oneself from others in order to minimize the effect of the threatening position).
- Negativism (engaging in conflict with anyone or anything that challenges one's identity).
- Passing (abandoning the position that is threatening).
- Compliance (with the expectations of the new position and behaving accordingly).

Intergroup

- Membership of multiple groups (attempting to satisfy identity principles through different memberships).
- Group support (seeking support through social networks or through processes of consciousness raising or self-help).
- Group action (joining pressure groups and social movements to fight for the value of one's memberships)

Thus, coping with changes, new identities, and threats is in fact the outcome of the assimilation–accommodation and evaluation processes that, in order to achieve appropriate levels of continuity, self-efficacy, self-esteem, and distinctiveness, revise and build the structure of one's identity.

Snapshot 5: Theory of Integrated Value Systems

The content of values is differentiated according to the type of motivational goal that the values express. Schwartz's (1992, 1996) crosscultural research identified ten different categories of values:

1 *Power:* controlling people and resources, obtaining social status and prestige.
2 *Achievement:* achieving personal success.
3 *Hedonism:* pleasure and enjoyment in life.
4 *Stimulation:* having a challenging life, novelty.
5 *Self-direction:* agency, creativity, independent thinking, and choice of actions.
6 *Universalism:* pursuing the welfare of other people and of the environment.
7 *Benevolence:* pursuing the welfare of people with whom one is in contact (e.g., friends).
8 *Tradition:* respecting cultural and religious traditions.
9 *Conformity:* avoiding the violation social norms and expectations.
10 *Security:* pursuing the harmony and stability of the social environment and the self.

The values included in each category serve different motivational goals:

1 Social superiority and esteem (Power and Achievement).
2 Self-centeredness (Achievement and Hedonism).
3 Desire for affectively pleasant arousal (Hedonism and Stimulation).
4 Agency and openness to change (Stimulation and Self-direction).
5 Reliance upon one's judgment and comfort with diversity (Self-direction and Universalism).
6 Concern for others and going beyond self-interests (Universalism and Benevolence).
7 Concern for one's group (Benevolence and Conformity/Tradition).
8 Conservation of order (Conformity/Tradition and Security).
9 Uncertainty avoidance and control over resources (Security and Power).

According to the theory, some motivations cannot be pursued simultaneously. For example, the pursuit of achievement values can conflict with benevolence values.
   The structure of values can be organized according to two dimensions:

1 *Openness to change* (Self-direction and Stimulation) vs. *conservation* (Conformity/Tradition and Security).
2 *Self-enhancement* (Power and Achievement) vs. *self-transcendence* (Universalism and Benevolence).

Hedonism constitutes a special case, as it shares elements of openness to change and of self-enhancement. Values that are on opposite poles tend to differ and conflict with each other, whereas values that are close to one another are similar.

Snapshot 6: Cultural Orientations: The HERMES Survey and the Individualism/Collectivism Dimension

The idea that cultures can be classified along a dimension called individualism/collectivism originates with Hofstede (1980), who surveyed the work-related values of the employees of a multinational company, HERMES (a pseudonym), in 40 countries. Hofstede analyzed his data on a country level rather than an individual level. He concluded that the different countries can be classified according to the following criteria:

- *Power distance:* characterized by the amount of respect and deference expressed in hierarchical relationships.
- *Uncertainty avoidance:* characterized by the degree of organization and planning to avoid uncertainties.
- *Individualism/collectivism:* characterized by the priority given to the self or to the group.
- *Masculinity/femininity:* characterized by the degree of importance of interpersonal relations and harmony.

Individualism/collectivism (I-C) has attracted the interest of researchers, who set out to clarify further its characteristics. This body of research (Markus and Kitayama 1991; Triandis et al. 1985; Triandis 1994, 1995, 1996) claims that in individualistic cultures:

- priority is given to personal goals and achievements;
- people's behavior is thought to relate to their attitudes;
- people's self-concept is built independently of social relationships;
- there is an emphasis on individual differences;
- social relationships are characterized by competition.

Whereas in collectivistic cultures:

- priority is given to cultural norms;
- behavior results from compliance with the norms of the group;
- people's self-concept reflects its interdependence with roles and social relationships;
- there is an emphasis on positions/roles;
- social relationships are characterized by cooperation.

Researchers have investigated how individualism/collectivism relates to self-esteem (Tafarodi, Lang, and Smith 1999), self-efficacy (Earley, Gibson, and Chen 1999), values (Schwartz 1990; Oishi et al. 1998), self-descriptions, personality traits, and moods (Grimm et al. 1999), interpersonal behavior (Adamopoulos 1999), cooperation in social dilemmas (Probst, Carnevale, and Triandis 1999), and sociopsychological adjustment (Watson, Sherbak, and Morris 1998). However, researchers have also criticized the use of I-C to explain cultural and individual variation. For example, it has been suggested that these orientations may coexist within cultures (Raeff 1997) and be elicited according to the situations people face (Arikawa and Templer 1998). Research on emotional expressions in Japan and the US showed that even if individualism and collectivism are supported at a cultural level, only weak evidence can be found at an individual level (Stephan et al. 1998). It is possible that I-C can be meaningful when connected to a culture's philosophical tradition and framed in terms which are familiar to people (Lu 1998).

In an interesting analysis of data from 29 cultures, Green-Staerklé (2002) discusses I-C at different levels of analysis and studies the relationships between these constructs and such macro-social measures as GDP. She concludes that other dimensions, such as "success," "auto-reliance," and "interdependence," might be as successful in distinguishing national groups. Thus, a dichotomous categorization in terms of individualism and collectivism might not be the best way to study the complexities of cultural variation.

Snapshot 7: Classic Theories of Attribution

The starting point of attribution theory is commonly considered to be Heider's (1958) book on interpersonal relations, which studied how people understand their environment in order to predict and control it. Heider suggested that people act as *naive psychologists* and try to attribute causes to events. The process of attribution of causes to events is called *social attribution*. Like psychologists, people seek to establish permanent but not directly observable structures that explain directly observable effects. Through this process of attribution they construct the environment as something stable and coherent. This construction enables them to build expectations, make predictions, and react to events. Heider suggested that people commonly use causes that fall into two categories:

- internal "dispositional" causes, which refer to the personal characteristics of the person acting (abilities, mood, attitudes, etc.);
- external causes, which are factors external to the actor (the characteristics of the situation, the influence of others, luck, etc.).

Following Heider's work, Jones and Davis (1965) developed the theory of correspondent inference in order to understand how people attribute stable characteristics (dispositions) by observing their behavior. In other words, they wanted to understand how people make inferences about the correspondence between behaviors and dispositions. They suggested that in order to infer that a person's behavior *corresponds* to a disposition (a stable characteristic of the actor) the observer needs to perceive that:

1 the person acting had the abilities to perform the action and that he or she was conscious of the effects of this action;
2 the person's action was not driven by social desirability;
3 the person acted freely, choosing from among different options;
4 the act had a direct impact on the observer;
5 the act seemed to be intended to affect the observer.

An attribution to a disposition is then made based on the specific effects of the chosen action, the characteristics that this action does not share with the other possible alternatives, the *uncommon characteristics*.

Kelley (1967) proposed a covariation model, according to which people analyze all the potential causes linked to a particular behavior and then attribute the behavior to the cause that is present when the behavior is present and absent when the behavior is absent (the cause covaries with the behavior). To do this, people need three types of information:

1 *Consistency information:* is the behavior consistent over time?
2 *Distinctiveness information:* is the behavior distinctive (specific to this situation)?
3 *Consensus information:* are other people behaving in the same way in this situation?

The behavior needs to be consistent (high consistency) in order for people to associate with it the person who acted. If consistency is high and the behavior is highly distinctive (particular to the situation) and the consensus is high (other people behave similarly), then the cause is to be attributed to the situation (external). However, when consistency is high but the distinctiveness and the consensus are low (this behavior is not particular to the situation and other people do not behave like that), then the behavior is likely to be attributed to personal dispositions. For Kelley, people appear to analyze information about events rather like statisticians do when they use the analysis of variance, a statistical technique, to analyze covariance.

Other models of attribution focus on attributions of success or failure (Weiner 1979) or on self-attributions (Bem 1972). To find out more about theories of attribution, read Deschamps (1977a, 1983), Deschamps and Clemence (1990), and Hewstone (1989).

Snapshot 8: Relative Deprivation Theory

Relative deprivation is a feeling of frustration, resentment, injustice, and dissatisfaction. It is not the mere reflection of "objective" social conditions: people do not necessarily feel relatively deprived when the conditions of their life are bad. Rather, it is the outcome of a discrepancy between what one has and what one believes one deserves; or between what one believes one deserves and what is obtainable. It is a discrepancy between actual conditions and expectations. Relative deprivation depends on social comparisons (TS2) that are made between the present situation and past ones (intrapersonal), between other people and oneself (interpersonal), between one's ingroup and an outgroup or in relation to an ideal (Guimond and Tougas 1994). Feelings of relative deprivation will prompt actions (strategies) to change the situation. In particular, relative deprivation is considered one of the basic preconditions for protest (Gurr 1970). Runciman (1966) distinguished between *egoistic* relative deprivation that occurs in comparison to other similar individuals, and *fraternalistic* relative deprivation that is the outcome of comparisons with dissimilar others and groups.

Intrapersonal relative deprivation is likely to be very strong when people's attainments fall short of their rising expectations. This feeling will lead to social unrest (Davies 1971). When living conditions steadily improve, the expectations of people rise. A sudden change to this pattern maximizes feelings of relative deprivation and as a consequence the probability of unrest.

Crosby's (1976) model focuses on the determinants of *interpersonal (or egoistic) relative deprivation*, its preconditions, and its consequences. According to this model, feelings of relative deprivation are determined by personality characteristics, the personal past, the immediate environment, societal norms, and the importance of the object of desire for survival. Five preconditions of relative deprivation were identified: one needs to see that others possess the lacked object, to desire it, to feel that one deserves it, to feel no responsibility for not having it, and to think that obtaining it is feasible. If these five preconditions are met, relative deprivation is likely to occur. However, whether this feeling will lead to stress symptoms or efforts of self-improvement, violence against society, or constructive societal change, depends (according to the model) on different factors. It depends on whether people feel that they have high or low personal control over the situation, whether they feel that opportunities are open or closed for them, and whether as individuals they are internalizing or externalizing their feelings of resentment. This model is particularly good in predicting relative deprivation in professional settings.

It is mostly *intergroup (fraternalistic) relative deprivation* that is likely to lead to collective social unrest and social change. This feeling of deprivation stems from the comparison between groups. If social inequalities are linked to a general feeling of dissatisfaction, to a feeling that structural social conditions are illegitimate and unjust, then the likelihood of protest is higher even if people are not touched personally.

Feelings of deprivation and resentment and perceptions of justice have a key role in societal cohesion (Deutsch 1975; Lind and Tyler 1988).

Snapshot 9: A Five-Stage Model of Intergroup Relations

Although intergroup relations differ according to the sociohistorical conditions in which they take place, Taylor and McKirnan (1984) suggested that all intergroup relations follow a five-stage temporal path accompanied by the social psychological processes of social attribution and social comparison (TS2). The passage from one stage to another depends on how members of disadvantaged groups evaluate their status position and attribute the responsibility for it.

Stage 1 involves clearly stratified intergroup relations. The stratification of society and the power asymmetries between groups are justified by means of *ascribed characteristics* such as race or language. The power of the advantaged group dictates the stratification and members of the disadvantaged group are led to believe that because of their ascribed characteristics they are in a socially disadvantaged position. Thus, there is no basis for questioning the legitimacy of the stratification. In terms of social comparison theory (TS2), disadvantaged group members will not seek comparison with members of the other group, as they are too dissimilar. Thus, individualistic or intragroup comparisons are developed. Further, responsibility for one's status is attributed to one's ascribed characteristics, which can explain phenomena of self-hate. Individualistic and intragroup comparisons, and attribution to one's characteristics, are encouraged by the advantaged group so as to maintain the status quo.

Stage 2 involves the emergence of an individualistic social ideology. This is likely to happen when socioeconomic conditions such as those in modern industrial societies encourage the valuing of individual characteristics. Stratification on the basis of ascribed characteristics is questioned and individual achievement is valued. Stratification on the basis of ascribed characteristics is no longer legitimate and the attribution of responsibility for one's status is based on individual characteristics. This shift constitutes the basis of the ideology of meritocracy and emphasizes individual mobility. However, there is still a strong correlation between individual abilities and group membership. The comparisons encouraged remain at an intragroup level or between members of different groups as individuals. Again, the stratification of society remains unchanged.

Stage 3 is characterized by the same ideology and attempts at individual social mobility. Those members of the disadvantaged group who are more skilled and feel that they have the individual characteristics that can give them access to the high-status group attempt to acquire this membership. The pattern of status attribution becomes more complex. People believe that group membership is responsible for their status. However, individual efforts and abilities will enable them to escape this status. Those who cannot manage this escape are thought to be lacking the abilities. Nevertheless, intragroup and intergroup individual comparisons are encouraged and the stratification between groups is left unchanged.

Stage 4 results from the unsuccessful attempts of disadvantaged group members to move upwards and is characterized by consciousness raising. Those high-skilled individuals that fulfilled individually the criteria of membership in the high-status group, but who did not manage to become members of that group, begin to question the system. They attribute responsibility for their status to their group membership and to the discriminatory actions of the high-status group that block their passing. Intergroup comparisons are then made. Disadvantaged group members conclude that their personal status will change only if the conditions of their group as a whole are changed through collective action.

Stage 5 is characterized by competitive intergroup relations. Disadvantaged group members try to alter the stratification. Social comparisons at a group level are maintained and attributions of responsibility are more dual. Responsibility for the past situation of the group is attributed to discrimination, whereas future responsibility is attributed to collective action.

Snapshot 10: Behaving Against One's Intentions, Perceptions, or Beliefs: Two Classic Social Psychological Studies of Social Influence

When faced with an obviously wrong solution or with a moral dilemma how will people behave?

Conformity to majority pressure

Solomon Asch (1951, 1952, 1956) thought that if people were sure and confident about their judgment they would not be influenced by others. Asch sought to study the conditions that induce individuals to remain independent or yield to group pressure when others' positions seem to contradict the facts. His concern was to understand the social psychological basis of Nazi propaganda. He thought that individuals would not submit to group pressures when it was obvious that they were contrary to objective facts. If the object of judgment is unambiguous, then people's behaviors and perceptions cannot be influenced by disagreements and alternative positions. Asch devised a series of experiments to test this idea.

A group of 7–9 individuals, all college students, were gathered in a classroom. The experimenter explained that they would be shown lines differing in length and that their task would be to match lines of equal length. He presented the task as a perceptual test. Then the experimenter showed two white cards with vertical black lines. On the card on the left there was a single line, the standard. The card on the right had three lines differing in length, one of which was equal to the standard line on the other card.

The experiment proceeded normally, the discriminations were simple and obvious, and each individual called out the same judgment. Suddenly this harmony was broken. At the third trial, an individual on the seat from the end disagreed with all the others, who had unanimously called out another line. This incident was repeated twelve times, making the individual feel uncomfortable as he began to realize that he was different from the rest of the group.

Now I have to mention an important element of this experiment: the member of the group who disagreed with the others was in fact the only real participant in the experiment. All the others were experimental confederates, instructed to provide unanimously wrong judgments at specific times.

How did participants respond to the unanimous opposition of the majority? Did they remain independent or did they display a tendency to yield to the majority?

Results showed that 25 percent of participants gave correct answers and remained independent of the majority. However, 50 percent gave wrong answers six or more times and 5 percent conformed every time that the majority gave a wrong answer. The average conformity rate was 33.2 percent. Another group, called the control group, performed the same task but this time participants gave their answers in writing. In this group, where there was no process of influence, the percentage of wrong answers was only 7.4 percent.

What can we conclude from these results?

1 Most of the estimates were correct and independent despite majority pressure.
2 There was a significant movement towards the wrong judgments of the majority. The conformity rate was not negligible.

When Asch asked his participants why they followed the majority, most of them replied that they perceived which line was correct but felt they might be wrong and the others right. Others admitted that although they knew that the answer was wrong they conformed in order to avoid standing out and being disapproved of. Very few said they gave the answer that they believed to be correct. It seems that the participants in this experiment were under *normative influence:* they conformed to avoid punishment or gain rewards – in other words, to avoid social disapproval.

In a variation of this experiment Asch increased the contraction by making the error much more obvious. Although it decreased, the average conformity rate was still high at 28 percent. In another variation Asch confronted a naive subject with only one experimental confederate. In this situation only 3 out of 70 estimates were errors and only one was identical with that of the experimental confederate. In another variation only one confederate, seated in the middle, gave a wrong answer. All the other participants were naive. In this condition the estimates of the naive majority were not altered and the confederate was ridiculed.

When he increased the size of the majority, Asch found that the conformity rate increased to a certain point and then decreased slightly. It seems that conformity reaches its full strength with a 3–5 person majority and additional members have little effect. This is an important point because it means that we do not need to face huge numbers of people in order to conform to a unanimous majority. In a further variation Asch wanted to break the unanimity of the majority. Indeed one of the confederates, usually seated just before the subject, gave the correct answer. Under these conditions the effect of the majority was weakened. Only 5.5 percent of the estimates were identical to the majority errors. In this condition the partner not only gave support, but also broke the unanimity of the majority. In another variation there were two naive participants. In this case the frequency of errors was 10.4 percent. In another variation, in which a partner was introduced during the experiment, one of the confederates changed and gave the correct answer: the frequency of errors was 8.7 percent. However, when the partner was retrieved the frequency of errors rose to 28.5 percent. In order to have conformity, it is important that the majority remains unanimous and that responses are made publicly. These experiments show that even when people are faced with obviously incorrect judgments they might yield to the pressures of a unanimous group.

Asch's experiments concerned a majority contradicting people's visual perceptions. What would happen when people faced a moral dilemma?

Obedience to authority

Milgram (1974) studied obedience when it becomes a dilemma for the individual and when there are important consequences attached to the decision to conform or to remain independent. Like Asch, his preoccupation also concerned the psychological basis of Nazism. In the Nuremberg trials after World War II and in reports of other trials, war criminals appeared very ordinary individuals, gentle and polite, who claimed they had participated in the extermination of millions of people simply because they were ordered to do it.

Milgram devised an experiment to investigate the power of an authority's orders. He used advertisements to recruit men to participate in a study supposed to investigate the effect of punishment on human learning. They were paid US$4 for their participation. The men arrived in pairs and were told that the study needed a teacher and a student. They drew lots to determine their roles. The student had to learn a list of paired words, such as blue–box, nice–day, wild–duck, etc. The teacher read these series of word pairs to the student who was supposed to learn them. Then, in the testing sequence, he would read "blue: sky, ink, box, lamp" and the student would have to indicate which of the four terms had originally been paired with the first word, blue. The teacher was told to administer an electric shock to the student each time he gave a wrong answer. Moreover, the teacher was instructed to move one level higher on the shock generator each time the student gave a wrong answer. The shocks went from 15 to 450 volts and the scale was also labeled from "slight shock" (15–75 volts) to "danger" or "XXX." As an example to the teacher, a 45-volt shock was administrated to him.

What the teacher participant didn't know was that the student was an experimental confederate – a middle-aged man instructed in how to act – and no electric shocks were actually administered. Under all conditions, the student gave a predetermined set of responses to the word-pair test – let's say, one wrong answer for three correct ones. The student didn't indicate discomfort until the 75-volt shock, when he would grunt a little. His protests continued rising until 150 volts, when he would scream "Get me out of here!" At 180 volts he screamed that he could not stand the experiment any longer and at 300 volts he stopped answering. The teacher was instructed to consider his silence as a wrong answer and to administer the punishment.

At different points during the experiment the teachers became stressed because they realized they had been torturing their fellow and expressed the intention of stopping. When this happened, the experimenter replied consistently and progressively, first, "Please continue," then, "The experiment requires that you continue," and then, "It is absolutely essential that you continue" or "You have no other choice, you must go on." The teachers were trapped between the demands of the experimenter and the protests of the student.

Milgram wanted to observe the teachers' reactions. Would they drop out, ending the "torture" of the student despite the orders of the experimenter? At what point would they stop? Would the orders of the experimenter effect the participants' behavior? Milgram measured the point at which the participant stopped administering the shocks, indicated by the voltage of the final shock.

A panel of 110 experts on human behavior, asked to predict how far a non-pathological human being would go, thought that only about 10 percent would exceed 180 volts and nobody would conform to the end. In fact, 62.5 percent of the participants continued to the end of the scale: 450 volts.

There were many variations of this experiment in which the proximity of teacher to student changed. Under all conditions there were still people who administered the highest voltage, although the closer the teacher and the student, the lower the percentage of people who used the highest voltage. In one condition, where the teacher had to readjust the fake electrodes on the hands of the student, only 30 percent of people continued to the end. When the original experiment was reproduced outside the prestigious University of Yale, the level of obedience dropped to 48 percent. When the authority giving the orders became more distant, the percentage dropped to 20.5 percent, and it was only when two authority figures gave contradictory orders that no one continued to the end.

The percentages of people continuing to the end in these experiments are quite high. Why did this happen? Milgram wrote:

> The person entering an authority system no longer views himself as acting out of his own purposes but rather comes to see himself as an agent for executing the wishes of another person. Once an individual conceives his action in this light, profound alterations occur in his behavior and his internal functioning. These are so pronounced that one may say that this altered attitude places the individual in a different state from the one he was in prior to integration into hierarchy. I shall term this the *agentic state*, by which I mean the condition a person is in when he sees himself as an agent for carrying out another person's wishes. This term will be used in opposition to that of autonomy, that is, when a person sees himself as acting on his own.   (Milgram 1974: 133)

There are four crucial factors in this situation:

1 The experimenter is a legitimate authority.
2 The administering of the shocks is progressive and it is only in the middle of their actions that teachers discover that someone is suffering. The recurrent nature of the action creates binding forces. If the participant breaks off he has to acknowledge that what he has done until that point is bad. One form of justification is to go on to the end. It was found that it was easier to break at earlier stages of the process. After a certain level it was more difficult to break the process and participants were psychologically trapped.
3 The loss of responsibility. In this situation the person feels responsible to the authority directing him, but feels no responsibility for the content of the actions that the authority prescribes.
4 In the original experiment the victim was invisible. This is often a feature of authoritarian structures: bureaucracy is introduced so that individuals do not feel close to those they victimize and responsibility is diffused.

What are the implications of Milgram's experiment? Most importantly, it makes us realize that everybody could "press the button" and torture somebody under specific conditions. This is a phenomenon linked to the type of relationship between the individual and a legitimate authority. The second implication concerns the authority of the researcher. It appears that individuals were ready to torture a fellow human being just because a scientist required it. It is an illustration of how powerful the position of science is for the general public.

The third implication involves ethical considerations. Although Milgram debriefed his participants after the experiment and followed them up with the assistance of a psychiatrist, and although a vast majority declared that they were happy to have participated, ethical questions remain. The participants were deceived and put through a stressful experience. Each time research requires deception and putting people in difficult situations one should

- consider whether the importance of the experiment justifies the deception;
- give participants the chance to withdraw whenever they want;
- debrief them thoroughly at the end of the study.

This experiment helps us understand what happens in situations where an authority asks somebody to commit an act that goes against their moral beliefs (as in wartime). Social psychology does not excuse or justify these acts, but tries to understand how they are psychologically possible.

Snapshot 11: Personality and Individual Differences Approaches to Prejudice: The Authoritarian Personality

Basic hypothesis

Adorno et al. (1950) hypothesized that people's political attitudes are an expression of their personality. Prejudice is a manifestation of a pathological type of personality.

Assumptions

Personality differences are rooted in childhood experiences of the family setting. Influenced by psychodynamic theories, it is believed that during their socialization children repress and redirect their feelings and drives. If they are socialized in a family with strict codes of behavior and harsh disciplinary methods, children develop a binary and simplistic way of thinking in terms of right and wrong. Also, afraid of the consequences, they are unable to display natural feelings of aggression towards their parents. These feelings might be redirected later towards other people, who serve as scapegoats. People raised in these environments develop a rigid personality that looks for clear boundaries between categories and shows inflexibility about what is right or wrong. People with this type of personality are overly deferential to authority and are more positive towards people that belong to their group. This type of personality is labeled authoritarian.

Measures

To check their assumptions, Adorno et al. conducted extensive psychometric tests and constructed a scale that measured pre-fascist orientations and the various aspects of the authoritarian personality: the F-Scale. In order to validate the assumptions about the link between personality and childhood experiences, extensive interviews have since been conducted with high scorers and low scorers on the F-Scale. The family life of people who scored high on the F-Scale tended to reflect the assumptions of Adorno and colleagues.

There are studies that show the link between authoritarian personality and prejudice, as well as criticisms of this approach both as methodology and theory (see Brown 1995). One of the criticisms is that this approach deals mainly with right-wing authoritarianism. Rokeach (1956, 1960) has addressed this issue.

The dogmatic personality or "closed minds"

Basic hypothesis

It is important to distinguish between the content of prejudiced beliefs and the groups towards which these beliefs are directed, and the relationships between these beliefs; in other words, their structure. Rokeach believed that prejudiced people had a cognitive structure that allowed contradictory beliefs to be held if these beliefs were isolated from each other. These rigid or dogmatic personalities were closed to new information that contradicted their beliefs: they were closed minds.

Assumptions

As with authoritarian personalities, the roots of dogmatic personalities are to be found in early childhood and in relationships with parents.

Measure

Rokeach devised a scale of intolerance – the Opinionation Scale – and a scale of content-free authoritarianism: the Dogmatism Scale.

There is some empirical support for Rokeach's ideas, as well as methodological and theoretical criticisms (see Brown 1995). One of the main issues concerns the fact that the measures used are not neutral but ideologically driven (Billig 1976). To equate right-wing and left-wing extremists and subtract the content of their beliefs is not only ideologically dangerous, but can also mask the meaning and function of prejudice.

Right-wing authoritarianism (Altemeyer 1981, 1994)

Right-wing authoritarianism can be defined as the covariation of three attitudinal clusters:

1 *Authoritarian submission:* high degree of obedience to legitimate authorities.
2 *Authoritarian aggression:* general feelings of aggressiveness, believed to be endorsed by authorities.
3 *Conventionalism:* commitment to traditions and social conventions believed to be endorsed by authorities.

A scale called RWA has been devised to measure right-wing authoritarianism.

Social dominance orientation (Pratto et al. 1994)

Basic hypothesis

In an attempt to minimize conflict, societies create hierarchy-legitimizing myths that promote the superiority of one group over another, maintain inequalities, and legitimize oppression.

Assumption

A significant factor that leads to the acceptance of such ideologies is an individual-difference variable called social dominance orientation (SDO).

Measure

The SDO Scale has been widely used to assess the desire for social dominance. However, the belief that social and political attitudes are thought to be predicted by an individual-difference variable has been criticized. It might be worthwhile to look further at how hierarchy-legitimizing myths are created and sustained before looking at who might be more prone to accept them.

Snapshot 12: Self-Categorization Theory (Turner et al. 1987; Oakes, Haslam, and Turner 1994; McGarty 1999; Turner and Onorato 1999)

Self-categorization theory states that people categorize themselves in the same way that they tend to categorize other stimuli. According to the theory, the self consists of cognitive representations that take the form of self-categorizations constructed according to the general principles of categorization (McGarty 1999). As a result, in particular contexts, the self is considered as identical to a group of people and different from another group of people.

Self-categorizations are part of a hierarchical system. People can categorize themselves at different levels of abstraction that follow principles of hierarchical inclusion. People can categorize themselves at an:

- *interindividual* level as unique individuals different from other individuals (e.g., two friends);
- *intergroup* or intermediate level on the basis of similarities and differences between individuals characterized by their memberships of different social groups or categories (men vs. women; black people vs. white people; two football teams);
- *interspecies* or superordinate level, which is a more inclusive level focusing on similarities between people.

The process of comparison that determines the level of categorization is defined by the meta-contrast principle. According to this principle, self-categories are formed by comparisons that emphasize the relative differences among stimuli. These comparative relationships are expressed via the meta-contrast ratio:

$$\frac{\text{The average perceived difference between stimuli belonging to different categories (Mean of intercategory differences)}}{\text{The average perceived difference between stimuli belonging to the same category (Mean of intracategory differences)}}$$

The larger this ratio the more likely it is that the compared stimuli belong to the same category (few intracategory differences).

Self-categorization reflects a process of self-stereotyping. When Self-categorization occurs at the intermediate/intergroup level, individuals perceive themselves as interchangeable entities within the group. This depersonalization is responsible for intergroup behavior.

The salience of a self-categorization is context-dependent. It is based on how accessible a category is for the individual (perceiver readiness to use the category based on chronic or situational demands) and how much this category fits the context. The fit of a self-category has a comparative component (described by the meta-contrast ratio) and a normative component that includes the social constraints that guide the perception of similarities and differences.

Snapshot 13: Prejudice and Intergroup Relations: The Summer Camp Experiments

According to Campbell (1965), who reviewed different human and social science theories, prejudice is a reflection of intergroup relationships. Group conflicts are based on competition for scarce resources and people's attitudes express these negative relationships. The most famous researches in social psychology embracing this perspective are the field experiments of Sherif and colleagues (Sherif et al. 1954; Sherif 1966). These classic experiments are known as the Summer Camp Experiments or Robbers' Cave.

Basic hypothesis

When a situation between two groups is negatively interdependent (it is possible for only one group to win) it is likely that hostile attitudes and behaviors will be produced.

1 When individuals with no established relationships are brought together to interact in group activities with common goals, they produce a group structure consisting of hierarchical positions and roles. The group structure tends to generate by-products or norms peculiar to the group, such as common attitudes, positive ingroup identifications, nicknames, etc.
2 If two groups thus formed are brought into a functional relationship, positive or negative outgroup attitudes and appropriate friendly or hostile actions in relation to the outgroup and its members will arise, depending on the harmony or friction between the goals of the two groups. The testing of this hypothesis involves in prototype form the process of the creation of group stereotypes.

These experiments took place at a summer camp. The participants were schoolboys unaware of the research. The experiment initially involved three stages. At the beginning (stage 1) the boys were free to engage in activities and form spontaneous groupings. After a while (stage 2) the researchers split the boys into two groups, taking care to separate friendships formed during stage 1. The two groups were separated and boys engaged in activities only with members of their ingroup (ingroup formation). At a later moment (stage 3) the two groups engaged in competitive activities and games (negatively interdependent intergroup relations).

Results

The researchers observed that at the end of stage 2 a well-defined ingroup organization and structure was formed. The boys named their teams (Bull Dogs and Red Devils), leaders and norms emerged. They readily forgot their old friendships and new ones were formed. After the introduction of competition at stage 3, hostile attitudes emerged, ingroup preferences were strengthened, and the internal structure of the group changed. The groups became more cohesive and elected more aggressive leaders. In one of the experiments, attitudes became so hostile that the experimenters had to stop the camp.

In one of the subsequent experiments another stage was introduced. At that stage (stage 4) a number of superordinate goals were introduced. These are goals desired by both groups, which neither could achieve without the other's cooperation (for example, the need to join forces to rescue a truck that was bringing them food). These goals transformed the competitive and negatively interdependent relationships between the groups into cooperative and positive ones. Only after the introduction of a series of such goals did relations between the two groups improve.

A major conclusion of these studies is that in order to understand prejudice and discrimination it is important to analyze the functional relationships between groups.

Snapshot 14: Minimal Group Paradigm:
(Tajfel et al. 1971; Billig and Tajfel 1973)

What are the minimal necessary and sufficient conditions to produce group discrimination and ingroup favoritism? Perhaps if groups were minimal and artificially
created, ingroup favoritism would not occur. Tajfel and colleagues created *minimal
groups* according to the following principles:

1 Groups should be formed on a random basis.
2 There should be no history of conflicts of interest or competition between the
   groups.
3 There should be complete anonymity, both at the individual level and the group
   level. Participants should only know to which group they belong.
4 There should be no interaction whatsoever between members of the same or
   different groups.
5 There should be no instrumental links between the personal interest of the
   participants and their group membership. Participants will never allocate resources to themselves personally.

It was thought that under these circumstances people might not display ingroup
favoritism.

Participants were British schoolboys. In the initial (now classic) experiment
known as the Klee/Kandinsky experiment, the boys were shown on a screen a series
of paintings painted either by Klee or Kandinsky. The boys were not in a position to
identify the artist correctly. All they were asked to do was indicate on a piece of
paper which one of the two paintings they preferred. After completion of the task
each boy was told secretly that he preferred one or the other artist and were led to
believe that they belonged to the Klee or the Kandinsky group. In fact, the boys were
randomly allocated to a group. The boys did not know who belonged to each group.
All they knew was to which group they, themselves, belonged. They were then asked
to distribute points between two members of their ingroup, between two members of
the outgroup, or between one member of the ingroup and one member of the
outgroup. They never allocated points to themselves. To allocate the points they
had to choose a pair of numbers on a series of matrices proposed by the researchers.
These matrices were carefully constructed to represent different strategies.

These were the strategies proposed:

Fairness (F)	Equal distribution of points between the groups.
Maximum joint profit (MJP)	Allocate the maximum joint profit to both recipients irrespective of which recipient receives most.
Maximum ingroup profit (MIP)	Allocate the maximum number of points to the ingroup.

Maximum difference (MD)	Maximizing the difference between groups in favor of the ingroup.
Favoritism (FAV)	Joint use of MIP and MD.

Two different types of matrices were proposed. Type A matrices combined MIP and MD strategies (in other words, favoritism) and separated them from the strategy of MJP. Type B matrices separated the strategy of MD from the other strategies. Fairness strategies were located at the midpoint of the matrices.

Examples of the matrices used:

Type A
FAV

MIP + MD						F					MJP	
IN	19	18	17	16	15	14	13	12	11	10	9	8	7
OUT	1	3	5	7	9	11	13	15	17	19	21	23	25

Type B
MD

MD					F					MJP + MIP	
IN	7	8	9	10	11	12	13	14	15	16	17	18	19
OUT	1	3	5	7	9	11	13	15	17	19	21	23	25

Results

Using Type A matrices:

- When allocating to members of the same category (ingroup or outgroup): the cells in the middle (Fairness) were chosen.
- When allocating to members of different categories (ingroup vs. outgroup): the cells on the left side of the matrices were chosen (FAV).

Using Type B matrices:

- When allocating to members of the same category (ingroup or outgroup): the cells on the right side (MJP and MIP) were chosen.
- When allocating to members of different categories (ingroup vs. outgroup): the cells on the left side of the matrices were chosen (MD).

In general, participants favored their ingroup. In particular, they were seeking to obtain the maximum possible difference between ingroup and outgroup, even if that meant that they had to sacrifice absolute gains for the ingroup.

Conclusion

Mere categorization into two groups is sufficient and necessary to create discriminatory behaviors. People tend to favor their ingroup at the expense of the outgroup. They do this in the absence of interaction with others, without having a personal interest, and in favor of groups recently constructed, without previous history. Group membership, however minimal, is at the origin of intergroup behavior.

Snapshot 15: Key Moments in Research on Stereotypes

Since the publication in 1922 of Lippmann's book *Public Opinion*, research on stereotypes has gone through different phases. Key points in this research (now considered classic) are described below.

1933: Katz and Braly

This research was among the first to examine the link between stereotypes and prejudice. It used what we call a checklist technique and asked Princeton University undergraduates to choose 5 adjectives from a list of 84 to describe different social groups: Americans, Blacks, Chinese, English, Germans, Irish, Italians, Japanese, Jews, and Turks. What their research has shown is that there was a clear consensus among participants about the typical characteristics of each group. For example, there was consensus in describing blacks as "superstitious," "lazy," and "happy-go-lucky," whereas Americans were described as "industrious," "intelligent," and "materialistic." Katz and Braly concluded that participants' beliefs and the high consensus they displayed could not be the result of first-hand experience with these groups. They proposed that stereotypes are linked to prejudiced beliefs and are "public fictions."

This research focused on the content of stereotypes and their link to prejudice.

1936: Sherif

Using a visual illusion (autokinesis), Sherif asked participants to evaluate the movement of a dot of light in a very dark room. The autokinesis constitutes an illusory perception that a spot of light in an absolute dark place is moving when in fact the light stays still. Sherif, interested in the formation of norms, wanted to see how people would make these evaluations in the absence of any point of reference. He observed that people started to make evaluations that were erratic, but after a while their evaluations converged towards a "standard," a personal reference. Furthermore, if after establishing their personal norm individuals are placed in a group and asked to perform the same task, they progressively abandon their own norm and establish a new group norm. In addition, those people who performed the task in groups before being asked to do so individually used the group norm to guide their evaluations. Sherif's research suggest that norms are formed progressively over time to provide people and groups with the means to make sense of their environment and to make evaluations. They constitute the point of reference that organizes perceptions. The same process, Sherif believed, is at the origins of stereotypes. In particular, in the Robbers' Cave experiments (TS13), Sherif (1966) observed that groups progressively produce stereotypes that reflect functional relationships between groups.

This research concerns the formation of stereotypes within the context of intergroup relations.

1950: Adorno and colleagues

Adorno et al. (1950) suggested that stereotypes are the characteristics of rigid authoritarian personalities.

This research considers the link between stereotypes and prejudice and proposes a view of stereotypes linked to personality characteristics (TS11).

1954: Allport

Allport's *Nature of Prejudice* highlighted the importance of categorization processes in understanding prejudice. He was one of the first theorists to suggest that stereotypes are linked to cognitive processes. However, he considered stereotypes to be erroneous beliefs.

His thoughts contribute to the discussion about the formation of stereotypes and their links to prejudice.

1961/1976: Moscovici

Moscovici studied the transformation of psychoanalysis from a scientific discourse to commonsense discourse (TS1). He observed that those groups that used a specific way of communicating their beliefs about psychoanalysis (namely, propaganda) were producing stereotypes: beliefs characterized by a binary view of reality in terms of right or wrong.

This research highlights the importance of modes of communication in producing different types of cognitive organizations.

1963: Tajfel and Wilkes

Tajfel and Wilkes showed people lines of different length and asked them to judge their length. There were three experimental groups.

For the first group, the longer lines were labeled with the letter A and the shorter with the letter B. In this case there was a correspondence between the length of the line and the labeling. For the second group, the lines were labeled A and B randomly. The third group viewed lines without any labeling. In other words, in the last two conditions there was no correspondence between the length of the line and the labels.

The authors found that participants in the first group increased the differences between the lines labeled A and the lines labeled B. They also minimized the differences between the lines labeled A as a whole and between the lines labeled B. In other words, the participants in the condition where there was a correspondence between the length of the line and the label evaluated the lines that had the same label (A or B) as more similar to each other and considered that the lines with different labels were more different. They *accentuated* the similarities between lines that seemed to be categorized under the same label and *contrasted* them with those having a different label. The participants in the other two conditions did not behave in the same way.

The authors concluded that when people are asked to make an evaluative judgment, instead of focusing on the dimension they have to judge (here, the length of the line) they focus on peripheral dimensions (such as the label of the line). Thus, the fact that stimuli seem to belong to different categories in accordance to their length encourages people to use this information when they make their judgments. According to Tajfel and Wilkes, this is the process by which stereotypes are formed. In knowing that somebody belongs to a particular social group, people will use this information when making judgments about this person. They will accentuate the similarities between this person and others belonging to the same social group and they will contrast this person with people belonging to different groups.

This research focuses on the processes of stereotype formation and highlights the importance of categorization for their formation.

1976: Hamilton and Gifford

Hamilton and Gifford proposed the illusory correlation effect. According to this hypothesis, the fact that people form stereotypes about minority groups is due to an erroneous perception of a co-occurrence of rare events. Thus, although there is no link between being a minority and the occurrence of undesirable behaviors, people perceive such a link. In their paradigm, Hamilton and Gifford asked participants to read information about two groups, A and B. The information concerned different behaviors performed by members of each group that were presented either as positive or negative. Group A seemed to be larger than group B. Furthermore, two thirds of the behaviors in each group were positive, whereas one third were negative. Participants were then shown the behaviors and asked to recall whose group member performed each one. Although the same proportion of negative behaviors was associated with each group, participants tended to overestimate the number of undesirable behaviors performed by group B. Even in the absence of any link between the type of behavior and group membership, people will make an illusory correlation. They will associate the two rare events (the number of undesirable behaviors and the number of members of the group B).

This research focuses on the cognitive processes at the origin of stereotypes and considers their formation as the result of heuristics – quick and economical strategies of reasoning that are normally efficient but could result in shortcomings.

Snapshot 16: Social Constructionism and Discursive Psychology

Social constructionism is a theoretical orientation that underpins a critical movement in social psychology that has been developed recently. During the 1970s social psychologists started challenging the cognitive approach (Gergen 1985, 1989) and introduced such ideas into psychology. Approaches that share this stand are labeled critical psychology, discursive psychology, deconstruction, or poststructuralism.

Inspired by Gergen (1985), Burr (1995: 3) proposed four ideas that together claim a social constructionist approach:

1 *A critical stance towards taken-for-granted knowledge.* Social constructionists challenge the idea that knowledge is based on objective observations that reveal the "true" nature of the world. What we observe is what we perceive to be and knowledge is a social construction. Therefore, social categories are constructions that should not be left unchallenged.
2 *Historical and cultural specificity.* Social constructionists believe that social knowledge is historically and culturally bound and that the ways we understand the world are relative to the historical period and the culture in which we live. Understanding the world in terms of nations, for example, is historically and culturally specific.
3 *Knowledge is sustained by social processes.* Knowledge is constructed by people in social interactions in everyday life. Language plays an important role in constructing and sustaining knowledge.
4 *Knowledge and social action go together.* The different constructions of the social world are not free from social consequences. On the contrary, each construction is linked to specific actions. For example, the construction of the nation-state based on homogeneity and ethnicity is linked to actions that exclude ethnic minorities from its membership.

Following these ideas, Burr continues by identifying seven points that differentiate social constructionism from other approaches in social psychology.

1 *Anti-essentialism:* there is no inherent nature (essences) to the world or to people.
2 *Anti-realism:* knowledge is not a direct perception of reality and therefore the pursuit of "truth" becomes problematic
3 *Knowledge is historically and culturally specific:* the theories and concepts of psychology are time bound and culturally bound.
4 *Language as a precondition for thought:* culturally specific concepts and categories are learned and reproduced through language that becomes a precondition for thought.

5 *Language as a form of social action:* the world is constructed through language. Thus, language constitutes a form of action, constructing the world.

6 *A focus on interaction and social practices:* instead of looking at individuals' properties to explain social phenomena, social constructionism focuses on the social practices and the interactions of people and locates the explanations in the interactive processes.

7 *A focus on processes:* the emphasis of the social investigation is on the processes that produce the phenomena, in other words on what people do together. Knowledge is considered to be the outcome of such collective actions.

The publication of *Discourse and Social Psychology* by Potter and Wetherell in 1987 laid the foundations for a discursive psychology. This approach conceptualizes psychological phenomena, not as cognitive phenomena, but as discursive actions (Willig 2001). People draw on "discourses" (Parker 1992) or "interpretative repertoires" (Potter and Wetherell 1987) to construct a version of events. This approach is not just another way of analyzing qualitative data and should not be separated from its epistemology (Coyle 2000). According to Willig (2001: 91), "psychological concepts such as prejudice, identity, memory or trust become something people do rather than something people have. The focus of analysis in Discursive Psychology is on how participants use discursive resources and with what effects. In other words, discursive psychologists pay attention to the action orientation of talk." The focus of the analysis is on the use of rhetorical strategies that fulfill particular social functions. The task of the researcher is to "identify what functions are being performed by the linguistic material that is being analyzed and to consider how these functions are performed (Coyle 2000: 254).

An important part of social constructionism and discourse analysis is the emphasis on power. Power, within this perspective, is not only the access people have to material and symbolic resources that build social inequalities, but also the power of language and discourse to construct, uphold, and sustain particular forms of social life (e.g., racism, sexism, homophobia, equality). In some respects it is the power to produce knowledge – commonsense knowledge (see also TS1 on social representations and TS17 on social influence).

Snapshot 17: Social Debates, Persuasion, and Processes of Social Influence: How Does Society Change?

We have defined social psychology as the discipline that is interested in understanding how individuals change society and how they are transformed by societal processes; as the discipline that is interested in understanding how people produce knowledge and culture. There is no other area of social psychology that better exemplifies this definition than social influence.

"Phenomena of social influence concern the processes by which the individuals and the groups form, maintain, diffuse, and modify their way of thinking and their behavior, when they are in the presence of direct or symbolic social interactions" (Mugny 1995: 195). When we talk about phenomena of social influence we are interested in both the change in individual beliefs, thoughts, and feelings and in the way these changes are made at a collective level to produce widespread social change.

We have already seen these processes in action when we discussed obedience to authority and conformity to the majority (TS10) and in relation to Sherif's (1936) work on norm formation (TS13). We have seen how people modify their way of thinking and behavior to obey a legitimate authority and how they yield to majority pressure and give an answer that they know is wrong. At a more societal level, Sherif's (1936) autokinetic experiment showed that when people do not have a frame of reference to make judgments they tend to establish one: they form norms. These collective constructions are the product of mutual influence between people of equal status.

There is a trend in research interested in producing changes in *individual* beliefs and attitudes that is labeled *persuasion*. Models have been developed to understand when a particular message will convince people to change their pre-existing attitudes. Following World War II, interest developed in understanding propaganda. Hovland and colleagues (Hovland, Janis, and Kelley 1953) at Yale University developed a model of persuasion now known as the *Yale communication model*. According to this model, the key to understanding how people ultimately accept a message is to focus on the characteristics of the source of the message (the communicator), the characteristics of the message, and the characteristics of the target or recipient of this message (the audience). Numerous studies have investigated the factors that impact on each of these three key aspects of persuasion phenomena.

More recently, research has focused on the cognitive processes that enable people to attend (or not) to the content of a message. The main argument of this tradition is that in order for a message to be persuasive, people must attend to the message and have the opportunity to elaborate on it. According to Petty and Cacioppo (1986), who proposed the *elaboration likelihood model*, there are two cognitive routes to the elaboration of a message: a central route is used when the argument is attended to closely and is scrutinized, whereas a peripheral route is followed when the argument is not attended to carefully. If the central route is followed, persuasion depends on the quality of the argument. However, if the argument takes the peripheral route, persuasion depends on the presence of persuasion cues. Chaiken (1987) suggested a similar model, the *heuristic model of persuasion*. This model distinguishes between systematic processing of the message (careful scrutiny of the information) and heuristic processing (the elaboration of the message based on the use of heuristics, cognitive strategies that function as rules of thumb to process information quickly and efficaciously). These models are called *dual process models of persuasion* because they suggest two routes of information processing. Despite the fact that these models occupy a large area in social psychological research, I will not discuss them further (for recent theoretical and empirical developments on persuasion see Maio and Olson 2000). The reason is that in my opinion attitudes need to change at a collective level if one wants to change the way people view immigrants, ethnic minorities, and multicultural societies. Although they might seem like individual opinions, decisions about the inclusion or exclusion of others in a society are made symbolically at a collective level.

In the early stages of social psychology the prevailing idea among social psychologists was that groups are nothing more than an aggregate of individual opinions. Thus, it would be sufficient to know what each member of a group thought to predict the collective opinion. To his surprise, Stoner (1961) uncovered a different image of *collective decision-making* when he found that, after discussion, groups made more risky decisions than individual members did previously. The well-established phenomenon of *risky shift* gave rise to numerous studies. One of the findings of this research is that sometimes these shifts of the collective decision are not towards greater risk but towards caution (Stoner 1968). Inspired by these findings and keen to explore this phenomenon beyond risk taking, Moscovici and Zavalloni (1969) established that the tendency towards extremization in collective decisions concerns all attitudinal objects (not only risk) and proposed the term *polarization* to account for the phenomenon.

Subsequent research on the polarization of collective decisions showed that the shift was not necessarily made towards the predominant opinion within the discussion group, but towards the opinion that reflected the spirit of the times (the *zeitgeist*) (Paicheler 1988). Furthermore, what leads to the polarization of the decision is the quality of the discussion, where everybody participates and where conflicts are not resolved without debate. Thus, Moscovici and Doise (1992), in an influential book, suggest that discussion and debate, participation and expression of disagreements are the "ingredients" of consensus. Debate, participation, and free expression of disagreements enable people to make a decision that is not a compromise but a decision where everybody feels part of (and therefore committed to) its enactment. They suggest that these are the processes that allow societies to create new norms, to develop and change. The direction of change is not random. It follows the norm to which people adhere.

Self-categorization theorists (Turner et al. 1987; Turner 1991) focused on the psychological processes that make consensus not only possible but also acted upon. Following self-categorization principles (TS12), they suggest that the important vehicle of influence is *social identification*: the perception of oneself as a group member. The process of self-categorization, that distinguishes between ingroups and outgroups, is at the origin of processes of influence. During discussion, people form a representation of what the group norm is and differentiate it from the norms that characterize other groups. Their identification with the group "guarantees" their adherence to the norm. Thus, polarization of the collective decision is the outcome of the willingness of group members to uphold and sustain the norm created during discussion. Individuals adopt positions that are closer to the stereotypical position of the group to which they belong. Thus, influence lies with those who can provide information about the ingroup norm (*referent informational influence*).

Do those who we consider to be part of our group only influence us? Societal ideas develop through the struggle for influence between different people and groups. Asch (1951, 1952, 1956) showed that numerical majorities have the power to influence people. What about minorities? Do they have the power to exert influence? History is full of examples. The question is not *whether* they can but *how*. Minority members face a number of challenges. They are few in number, have no power/status, and they challenge the status quo. By expressing a different opinion they create diversity and conflict. By insisting on this opinion, minorities not only create conflict but they also intensify it. Minorities posit their own judgments and opinions as having the same value, as being equivalent to those of the majority, and they demonstrate that they do not have any intention of conceding.

One of the pioneering experiments in minority influence performed by Moscovici, Lage, and Naffrechoux in 1969 tried to investigate the type of influence that a minority exerts and how a minority could succeed in communicating its message. In this experiment four naive participants were confronted with two confederates in a perceptual task. Blue slides were projected to each group of people. The slides varied only in intensity. When judgment began, the experimental confederates consistently named the slides green instead of blue. Results showed that 8.24 percent of the estimations of the naive subjects followed the confederates and claimed a green answer, whereas in the control group, formed only by naive participants, only 0.25 percent of the responses was green. In total, 33 percent of the people gave at least one green response. These results showed that a minority could have a direct influence. In an extension of this experiment a second task was introduced in order to measure the latent effects of minority influence. In other words, does a minority change the perceptual code of people?

At the end of the first phase the experimenter thanked the participants and asked them whether they would like to participate in another independent study on the effects of exercise on vision phenomena. The task consisted of judging the color of disks individually and privately on a sheet of paper. The material consisted of disks in the blue-green zone, six of which were absolutely unambiguous (clearly blue or green), whereas the rest might appear ambiguous. The results showed that the participants who were under minority influence in the previous phase described more slides as green than the participants who were previously in the control condition. The influence of the minority was latent. This experiment started a series of researches known as the blue/green paradigm (see also Moscovici and Lage 1976, 1978; Moscovici and Personnaz 1980).

These results suggest that majorities and minorities exert different types of influence. Majorities exert direct public influence, whereas minorities bring about indirect latent and private change. Moscovici and his colleagues believed that this depends upon the behavioral style that each source of influence adopts.

Whereas majorities should be unanimous in order to influence, minorities have to be consistent. So, the power of a minority relies upon its consistency. Majority influence is linked to stability and preservation of the status quo, whereas minority influence is linked to social change and innovation. By being consistent a minority produces uncertainty and doubt, draws attention to itself as an entity, proposes an alternative point of view, shows commitment to this point of view, and implies that the only possible solution to this conflict is to espouse its point of view. Thus, minorities need to be consistent, to appear involved and committed, and to appear autonomous and flexible.

When somebody proposes a different view about reality a conflict is created between the source and the target of influence. Moscovici (1976, 1980) proposed a *conversion theory* of social influence according to which individuals confronted with an influence source have two reactions. The first is to compare their response to that of the source. They are concerned to know whether their response – what they see or think – agrees or disagrees with that of the source of influence. In this case the object or the content itself doesn't have any importance. Therefore, once the public interaction is over and they are left to themselves again they see and think what they did before the interaction. This is why they comply publicly only if the source of influence is present, but they do not change their mind. When faced with a majority – because they think that two pairs of eyes are better than one – people will compare their responses to those of the majority and will be worried. Why do they not see the same thing? In this case the first tendency will prevail and so the influence will lead to public compliance.

The second possibility is to try to validate the response given by the source of influence by comparing it to the real object and examining its content. They will try to find out why the others give a different answer. Their mental activity is directly related to the stimulus and results in a change in what they perceive and think. Therefore, after the public interaction is over the change that has been initiated will be maintained and may sometimes even be amplified. They now see the reality differently. When faced with a minority that says something unbelievable, people will try to validate this response by confronting it with reality. They will concentrate on the stimulus and therefore the influence will lead to conversion.

To summarize: when deviant information is presented by a majority, the responses of the source appear to be legitimate, common, and accepted as "true" information about reality. When there is a divergence, each individual compares his or her judgement with that proposed by the majority, without necessarily reconsidering the object to which that judgment refers. This is the process of *social comparison*.

On the other hand, the opinion of a minority is immediately considered as illegitimate, wrong, or contrary to commonsense and reality. So the first reaction is to doubt it. Then if the minority is consistent and persists, some people will think that the deviant response may contain some truth. Therefore, they will try to validate the minority response by confronting it with the stimulus. During interaction it is difficult to adopt such a deviant point of view. Therefore the direct, manifest influence is not very important. However, in a private situation, when they can evaluate the question again, they perceive it differently because during the interaction a process of *validation* took place (they were trying to verify or falsify the opinion of the minority). So, according to Moscovici, direct influence (compliance) is a property of majority influence because people, when faced with a majority, are bound to be involved in a social comparison process. They do not care about the argument but they want to avoid exclusion from the majority. However, indirect influence (conversion) is a property of minority influence because when they are faced with a minority people examine closely the properties of the object under dispute and try to validate their opinion.

Other researchers (Nemeth and Wachtler 1983; Nemeth 1986) suggest that when confronted by a majority, people develop a *convergent form of thinking*. The fear of being seen as deviant by a majority induces great stress, leading people to focus exclusively on the majority's position. This implies that the majority's positions will be adopted – or used as a frame of reference – to the detriment of any other alternative perspectives. Conversely, minority influence favors a *divergent type of thinking*. Minority dissent leads people to consider multiple perspectives, and not only that of the minority, thus inducing the discovery of novel solutions.

The difference between this theory and conversion theory is that in Nemeth's formulation the nature of the source determines the modes of thinking (convergent vs. divergent) and not the levels of influence (direct vs. latent). It follows in particular that a minority influence does not consist in adopting, even at a latent level, the minority position. Instead, what happens is that new responses are formed which are potentially original or creative.

Another theory was proposed to account for manifest and latent minority influences in attitudes and opinions. This theory was proposed by Perez and Mugny (Pérez and Mugny 1990; Mugny and Pérez 1991) and in its latest version also integrates majority influence. The underlying hypothesis is that indirect influence is only possible when subjects sociocognitively dissociate the social comparison activity from the validation activity. The basic assumption of *Dissociation Theory* is that latent influence is possible only if the processing of the message content can be dissociated from the social comparison with the source. This is particularly true for tasks involving opinions. In this type of task people resent accepting another point of view because they do not want to be associated with the source. So a message is influential when the subjects have dissociated the content from the source of the message. Perez and Mugny propose that even a majority in some cases could exert latent influence if the subjects are involved in what they call a *normative conflict*. This conflict places the subjects in a deviant position in relation to the collective norm. In this case the individual has to elaborate personally the conflict between his or her own position and that of the majority. So, if the individual is opposed to the group and cannot deny the divergence, influence at an indirect level may occur.

However, Pérez and Mugny (1993) observed that in these studies the researchers used different types of tasks. Research using the blue/green paradigm was based on objective, non-ambiguous tasks involving numerical majorities/minorities. Nemeth's research was based on aptitudes confronting expert and non-expert sources of influence. Finally, dissociation theory concerned opinions where sources were categorized into ingroups and outgroups.

Hence, Perez, Mugny, and colleagues (Pérez and Mugny 1993, 1996; Mugny et al. 1995) suggested that manifest or latent influence is a function of the interaction between the nature of the task and the nature of the source in a way that almost any source under appropriate circumstances can produce any pattern of influence.

What is important is the way people give meaning to the divergence existing between them and the source of influence, the way they elaborate the conflict. The new *Conflict Elaboration Theory* has three basic hypotheses:

1 Even when the levels of divergence are the same and the tasks are of the same nature, but the influence is exerted by two different sources, the conflict will be differently elaborated.
2 Even when the levels of divergence are the same and the sources are of the same nature, but the tasks are different, the conflict will be differently elaborated.
3 Different conflict elaboration will lead to different types of influence.

The types of tasks can be classified according to whether they are ambiguous (not just one correct answer) or not (just one correct answer) and whether they are socially implicating (accepting this opinion means that I am part of a group or I have specific characteristics) or not. Crossing these dimensions provide us with a four-type classification:

1 Objective non-ambiguous tasks which are non-socially implicating (Asch, and Moscovici).
2 Ambiguous tasks which are non-socially implicating (Sherif).
3 Objective non-ambiguous tasks which are socially implicating – aptitudes (Nemeth).
4 Ambiguous tasks which are socially implicating – opinions (Perez and Mugny).

Each type of task implies a different conflict elaboration:

1 People know that only one answer is correct and they know the answer. Because judgments are facts and are not dependent on social divisions they expect unanimity. Anyone who does not agree will introduce a conflict. Faced with conflict people query why the source prevents unanimity. When the source is a majority because of fear of being ridiculed, disapproved, or rejected, the conflict is of a *relational* nature. Social comparison processes are taking place as people look for consensus at a manifest level, whereas at the latent level they gain their autonomy (as in Asch). When the source is a minority they are faced with an *epistemic* conflict (validation). They need to reconstruct the properties of the object in order to maintain its uniformity, now anchored in the point of view of the minority source. At a manifest level they do not comply, but they are influenced at a latent level (e.g., blue/green experiments).

2 These tasks involve personal opinions that are not socially implicating. Judgments do not have consequences for people's self-image, responses are not related to specific aptitudes or to specific memberships. There are no expectations of reaching consensus and thus there is no conflict (conflict of *avoidance*).

3 People believe that there are correct answers or answers which are more valid than others, but they do not initially know the correct answer. They are concerned to increase the correctness of their judgments and/or to present their best self-image in terms of their own abilities. The conflict becomes a conflict of *uncertainty*. When the source is perceived as high status or competent (majority) people will take for granted that the opposing point of view is more valid than their own and will adopt it or imitate it directly. When the source is of low status or not particularly competent people will develop a divergent type of thinking (Nemeth)

4 There is no objective way to determine what is right or wrong concerning opinion tasks. What is expected is a direct correspondence between different opinions and relevant social differentiations because a particular opinion assigns people to a determined group or social category. What is important for people is to determine whether the source belongs to the same group or social category with them and then to maintain the categorical differentiation. They are facing a conflict of *identity*. When the source is an ingroup they are faced with normative and identification conflicts. They need to understand why they seem to transgress the group norm and how they will keep their positive image and maintain the cohesion of the group. They are pushed towards conformity. When the source is an outgroup they are faced with *intergroup conflict*. At a manifest level there is social differentiation. However, if they dissociate the source from the content and if a process of validation occurs, they might be influenced at a latent level.

To learn more about social influence see Butera and Mugny (2001), Moscovici, Mucchi-Faina, and Maass (1994), and Mugny and Pérez (1991).

Snapshot 18: Justice Concerns

Concerns about what is fair and just constitute a central issue in social psychology. We have seen, for example, that relative deprivation (TS8) – in other words, feelings of entitlement – are related to prejudice and social protest. Beliefs and social norms that are shared among members of different social groups govern what is perceived to be fair and just. These beliefs can concern the outcome of a decision as well as the procedures used to make the decision.

The area concerned with the criteria that ensure an outcome is perceived as just is *distributive justice* (Deutsch 1975, 1985, 2000). Three principles have been identified as governing decisions about the fair distribution of outcomes:

- *Equity principle* (Adams 1965; Walster, Walster, and Berscheid 1978): an outcome is judged as fair if it corresponds with the contribution of the person or group that obtains it. In other words, the benefits are proportional to one's contribution and those who contribute more should receive more.
- *Equality principle:* benefits should be equally distributed to members of the group.
- *Need principle:* distribution should match the needs of members. Thus, the more needy members should receive more.

Deutsch suggested that different social contexts emphasize different principles. Where economic productivity is salient, the equity principle will prevail. When social harmony is salient, cohesiveness and positive relations are the goal the equality principle governs decisions. Finally, needs are taken into consideration when emphasis is put on personal welfare. However, it is possible that not only the goals prevailing in the social context but also the nature of the resources to be distributed and the relative status of the recipients might impact on the principles of justice that are activated (Chryssochoou 1996a).

The area concerned with the criteria that govern the procedures by which decisions are made is *procedural justice*. According to the *control model* proposed by Thibaut and Walker (1975), people are concerned about the fairness of the procedures that ultimately govern their outcomes. In particular, they are concerned about the level of control they have over these procedures. Thibaut and Walker distinguish two types of control: *process control* concerns control over the process of presentation of their case and *decision control* concerns the level of control over the decision made. The model is based on instrumental concerns about the decision. Thibaut and Walker suggest that people see procedures as a means to an end, namely to a fair outcome. However, they also note that people are equally interested in preserving interaction with the other parties in order to solve the dispute or make the distribution.

Lind and Tyler (1988) proposed the *group-value model*, suggesting that people are concerned about the relationship they have with the third party or authority involved in the decision-making. Thus, their judgments about the procedures are also governed by relational concerns. In particular, people are concerned about how they are treated by the authorities responsible for the procedures (Tyler 1989; Tyler and Smith 1998). They have three relational concerns: the *neutrality* of the authority, the *trustworthiness* of the authority, and *status recognition* – whether they feel they have been treated with dignity, whether their rights are respected, and whether they are valued. The more people believe that decisions are made in a neutral and unbiased arena, that the parties involved can be trusted, and that they are respected and valued, the more likely it is that they will find the procedures just.

According to this model, therefore, if people are to find the procedures of a decision as fair and just they must feel that the authorities are following the principles of relational justice and they should identify with the group that includes both themselves and the authorities.

The scope of justice

It is important to stress that it is implicit in many theories of justice that justice concerns are restricted within the boundaries of the group. As Deutsch (1985, 2000) puts it, justice concerns indicate who is entitled to fair outcomes and treatment, in other words who is part of one's moral community. This is what is called the *scope of justice*. Opotow (1990: 1) talks about a process of moral exclusion, according to which some "individuals and groups are perceived to be outside the boundary in which moral values, rules, and considerations of fairness apply." She defines the scope of justice as "the psychological boundary within which considerations of fairness and moral rules govern our conduct" (Opotow 1993: 72). The scope of justice is of great importance for multicultural societies, as it is part of the processes of inclusion and exclusion of social groups from the wider society.

Snapshot 19: How Do People Form Impressions About Others?

Asch (1946) proposed a configural model of impression formation, principally asking two questions:

1 Are we able to form a coherent and "total" impression of a person from different pieces of information, and is this image socially shared?
2 Are all pieces of information equally important?

Asch asked his students to read a description of a fictitious person. The descriptions of the person were exactly the same, with one exception. Half of the participants read that the person was *warm* whereas the other half read that the person was *cold*. Then the participants were asked to evaluate this person on a series of other dimensions. The table below shows how the person described as warm was also thought to be more generous, wise, happy, etc. than when he was described as cold. In a subsequent experiment when the words *warm* and *cold* were replaced by the words *polite* and *blunt* no significant differences were found between the two descriptions.

Group A	Group B
Intelligent	Intelligent
Skilful	Skilful
Industrious	Industrious
Warm	*Cold*
Determined	Determined
Practical	Practical
Cautious	Cautious

	Warm	Cold	Polite	Blunt
Generous	*91*	*8*	56	58
Wise	*65*	*25*	30	50
Happy	*90*	*34*	75	65
Good natured	*94*	*17*	87	56
Humor	*77*	*13*	71	48
Sociable	*91*	*38*	83	68
Popular	*84*	*28*	94	56
Reliable	94	99	95	100
Important	88	99	94	96
Humane	*86*	*31*	59	77
Good looking	77	69	93	79
Persistent	100	97	100	100
Serious	100	99	100	100

Restrained	*77*	*89*	82	77
Altruistic	*69*	*18*	29	46
Imaginative	*51*	*19*	33	31
Strong	98	95	100	100
Honest	98	94	87	100

Asch concluded that people form impressions about others as a "whole." These impressions are based on some elements that are more central than others (warm/cold are central, whereas polite/blunt are peripheral).

Implicit theories of personality

Bruner and Tagiuri (1954) suggested that people form implicit theories of personality which are lay theories about the co-occurrence of the traits used to describe people. In other words, these theories consist of a set of beliefs that suggest that if somebody has the trait X he or she must also have the trait Y but must not have the trait Z. Implicit theories of personality are systems of beliefs about the relationships between characteristics. These theories are shared among people of the same cultural group.

Snapshot 20: Attitudes and Behavior: Is There a Link?

Attitudes are evaluations. They denote a person's orientation to some object, or attitude referent. Referents may be specific and tangible like "George W. Bush," "Martin Luther King," "immigrants," "fox hunting," and "meat." They can also be abstract and intangible like "social psychology" or "Iraq."

Attitudes are expressed in the language of like/dislike, approach/avoid, good/bad; they are *evaluative*. Having an attitude about something is associating an evaluation with an object. Putting emphasis only on the evaluative dimension of attitudes corresponds to the *one-component model* of attitudes. Another definition of attitudes is that they are mental states that guide evaluations and predispose actions. This definition corresponds to a *two-component model*.

Zanna and Rempel (1988: 319) define attitudes as follows: "We regard an attitude as the categorization of a stimulus object along an evaluative dimension based upon, or generated from, three general classes of information: cognitive information, affective/emotional information and/or information concerning past behaviors or behavioral intentions." In other words, people evaluate an object based on what they know about it, how they feel about it, and what they have done in the past or what they intend to do in the future about it. This definition states that an attitude is a combination of three conceptually distinguishable reactions to a certain object. These reactions are:

- *affective:* hate/love, like/dislike;
- *cognitive:* beliefs, opinions, ideas;
- *conative/behavioral:* intentions or behavioral tendencies.

This is known as a *three-component model* of attitudes.

Why are attitudes important?

1 Attitudes are believed to influence social thought, to give people a way to react to their social environment.
2 Attitudes are believed to influence behavior.

What are the functions of attitudes?

According to Katz (1960), there are four attitudinal functions:

- *Knowledge* function: attitudes help us explain and understand the world around us.
- *Utilitarian/instrumentality* function: attitudes helps us gain rewards and avoid punishments.

- *Value-expressive* function: attitudes are sometimes public statements of what a person believes or identifies with.
- *Ego-defensive* function: attitudes can help people defend their self-esteem.

Attitudes also serve social functions:

- Attitudes serve to position the individual within the social environment. The expression of attitudes supports social cohesion and evaluation. Members of a particular group cannot remain silent about matters important for this group. They ought to take a position.
- Attitudes are also a mechanism for the transmission of social beliefs. Public expression of attitudes provokes reactions. Public reaction engages both the individual and the public in dialogue. Positions and beliefs are exchanged and there is a debate.
- Attitudes play an explanatory, justificatory role in orienting the individual within the social world. For example, expressing an attitude towards refugees confers a position (status) on this social group. Attitudes help to explain as well as to justify, reproduce the social system, and defend the individual's own social position.

Attitudes serve more than one function and may be held or expressed for different reasons at different times.

Do attitudes actually influence behavior?

Social psychologists spend a lot of time and energy in research trying to identify the links between attitudes and behavior.

The work of LaPiere (1934) showed how difficult it is to predict the link between attitudes and behavior. For several months, LaPiere traveled around the United States with a young Chinese couple in a period when Chinese people were seen very negatively in the US. During this journey they stopped at 184 restaurants and 66 hotels and motels. In general, they were treated with courtesy and they were refused service only once. When they returned, LaPiere wrote to all the places they had visited and asked them whether they would offer service to Chinese visitors (of course, he did not mention that they had been there before). Surprisingly, 92 percent of the restaurants that replied and 91 percent of the hotels and motels that replied said that they would not offer service to Chinese visitors! This contradicted their previous behavior. Thus, knowing the prejudiced attitudes of the hotel owners would not allow us to predict their behavior towards the Chinese couple.

After LaPiere's study a lot of researchers tried to explore the attitude/behavior relationship. It was difficult to provide strong evidence for this link. In an early review of this research (Wicker 1969) it was noted that only 2 percent of variance in behavior is accounted for by attitudes. Important situational constraints and social norms may undermine the link between attitudes and behavior. Fishbein and Ajzen

(1975) proposed a model of attitudes and behavior that incorporates social norms. This model is called the theory of reasoned action (TRA)

According to TRA, what determines behavior is not the attitude but the *intention* to perform or not perform the behavior. This is an internal declaration to act. This behavioral intention is influenced by two factors:

1   The attitude towards the behavior. This is a function of the *expectation* or belief that this behavior will have certain *consequences* and the *value* attached to these consequences. Therefore, we call this model an expectancy-value model.
2   The subjective norm. This means the person's judgment of what others expect him or her to do. This subjective norm is determined by two factors: *normative beliefs* (what other important persons are expecting the individual to do) and the person's *motivation to comply* with these expectations.

An extended version of this model introduced another factor called the *perceived volitional control*. Perceived volitional control is the extent to which the person believes it is easy or difficult to perform the act. This can include past experiences or present obstacles. This factor was added to the original model because some behaviors are less under people's control than others. This new model is called the theory of planned behavior (TPB).

A general criticism of both TRA and TPB is that they assume that attitudes are rational and that socially significant behaviors are intentional, reasoned, and planned. This may not always be the case.

Sometimes actions shape people's attitudes and not vice versa. The process that underlies such effects is known as *cognitive dissonance* (Festinger 1957; Festinger and Carlsmith 1959). People feel tension when two thoughts or beliefs or ideas are psychologically inconsistent. In order to reduce this unpleasant tension people will adjust their thinking. The fox who couldn't reach the grapes and then decided that they were in fact "sour" experienced cognitive dissonance.

Festinger and Carlsmith (1959) conducted the following (now classic) experiment. For an hour they asked people to perform very dull tasks, such as turning wooden knobs again and again. At the end of the task the experimenter told participants that this study concerns how expectations affect performance. The experimenter asked the participant to create a positive expectation about the experiment for the next participant. To do so the participants were asked to lie and say that they found the task interesting. The experimenter offered either $1 or $20 to the participant to lie. The participant accepted and tried to create a positive expectation in the next participant, who was in fact an experimental confederate. After having done that, another experimenter supposedly interested in how people react in experiments asked the participant questions about the previous task and how much they enjoyed it.

Under which condition would people agree to tell the little lie and under which condition would people state in the questionnaire that in fact they enjoyed the experiment very much? When they are paid $1 or $20? Festinger and Carlsmith hypothesized that when people are paid only $1 to lie this is insufficient to justify their behavior. Therefore, they would experience more tension, more cognitive dissonance. Thus, they would be more motivated to believe what they have done was more interesting than those who received $20, an amount that could justify a little lie. The results confirmed their predictions. People are motivated to adjust their attitudes (how interesting they found the task) to their actions (the lie), so they therefore change their attitudes in order to be consistent with what they have done.

References

Abrams, D., and Hogg, M. A. (1999). *Social Identity and Social Cognition*. Oxford: Blackwell.

Abric, J.-C. (1993). Central system, peripheral system: Their functions and roles in the dynamics of social representations. *Papers on Social Representations*, 2, 75–78.

Abric, J.-C. (2001). A structural approach to social representations. In K. Deaux and G. Philogene (eds.), *The Representations of the Social* (pp. 42–7). Oxford: Blackwell.

Adamopoulos, J. (1999). The emergence of cultural patterns of interpersonal behaviour. In J. Adamopoulos and Y. Kashima (eds.), *Social Psychology and Cultural Context*. Thousand Oaks, CA: Sage.

Adams, J. S. (1965). Inequity in socal exchange. In L. Berkowitz (ed.), *Advances in Experimental Social Psychology* (pp. 266–99). New York: Academic Press.

Adorno, T. W., Frenkel-Brunswik, E., Levinson, D. J., and Sanford, R. N. (1950). *The Authoritarian Personality*. New York: Harper.

Allport, G. W. (1954). *The Nature of Prejudice*. Reading, MA: Adison-Wesley.

Altemeyer, B. (1981). *Right-Wing Authoritarianism*. Winnipeg: University of Manitoba Press.

Altemeyer, B. (1988). *Enemies of Freedom: Understanding Right-Wing Authoritarianism*. San Francisco, CA: Jossey-Bass.

Altemeyer, B. (1994). *Reducing Prejudice in Right-Wing Authoritarians*. In M. P. Zanna and J. M. Olson (eds.), *The Psychology of Prejudice: Ontario Symposium on Personality and Social Psychology* (pp. 131–48). Hove: Lawrence Erlbaum Associates.

Amir, Y., and Sharon, I. (1987). Are social-psychological laws cross-culturally valid? *Journal of Cross-cultural Psychology*, 18, 383–470.

Anderson, B. (1983). *Imagined Communities: Reflections on the Origins and Spread of Nationalism*. London: Verso.

Apostolidis, T. (2001). *Penser le rapport au sexuel à l'epoque du SIDA*. Lille: Presses Universitaires du Septentrion.

Arikawa, H., and Templer, D. I. (1998). Comparison of Japanese and American college students on collectivism and social context of decision-making. *Psychological Reports*, 83, 577–8.

Asch, S. E. (1946). Forming impressions of personality. *Journal of Abnormal and Social Psychology*, 41, 258–90.

Asch, S. E. (1951). Effects of group pressure upon the modification and distortion of group judgements. In H. Guetzkow (ed.), *Groups, Leadership and Men* (pp. 177–90). Pittsburgh: Carnegie Press.

Asch, S. E. (1952). *Social Psychology*. Englewood-Cliffs, NJ: Prentice-Hall.

Asch, S. E. (1956). Studies of independence and conformity: A minority of one against a unanimous majority. *Psychological Monographs: General and Applied*, 70:1–70.

Ashmore, R. D., and Jussim, L. (1997). *Self and Identity: Fundamental Issues*. New York: Oxford University Press.

Augoustinos, M. (1998). Social representations and ideology: towards the study of ideological representations. In U. Flick (ed.), *The Psychology of the Social* (pp. 156–69). New York: Cambridge University Press.

Augoustinos, M., and Quinn, C. (2003). Social categorization and attitudinal evaluations: Illegal immigrants, refugees or asylum seekers? *Nouvelle Revue de Psychologie Sociale/New Review of Social Psychology*, 2, 29–37.

Augoustinos, M., and Reynolds, K. J. (2001). *Understanding Prejudice, Racism and Social Conflict*. London: Sage.

"Australian Multiculturalism." www.immi.gov.au/multicultural/ australian/index.htm

Ayduk, O., Mendoza-Denton, R., Mischel, W., Downey, G., Peake, P. K., and Rodriguez, M. (2000). Regulating the interpersonal self: Strategic self-regulation for coping with rejection sensitivity. *Journal of Personality and Social Psychology*, 79, 776–92.

Bangerter, A. (2000). Transformation between scientific and social representationsof conception: The method of serial reproduction. *British Journal of Social Psychology*, 39, 521–35.

Bar Tal, D. (1990a). *Group Beliefs: A Conception for Analysing Group Structure, Processes and Behaviour*. New York: Springer Verlag.

Bar Tal, D. (1990b). Causes and consequences of delegitimization. *Journal of Social Issues*, 46, 65–81.

Bar Tal, D. (1993). Patriotism as fundamental beliefs of group members. *Politics and the Individual*, 4, 45–62.

Bar Tal, D. (2000). *Shared Beliefs in a Society: Social Psychological Analysis*. Thousand Oaks, CA: Sage.

Bar Tal, D., and Staub, E. (1997). *Patriotism in the Lives of Individuals and Nations*. Chicago, IL: Nelson-Hall Publishers.

Barrett, M. (1996). English children's acquisition of a European identity. In G. M. Breakwell and E. Lyons (eds.), *Changing European Identities: Social Psychological Analyses of Social Change* (pp. 349–70). Oxford: Butterworth-Heinemann.

Barrett, M. (in press). Children's knowledge beliefs and feelings about nations and national groups. Hove: Psychology Press.

Barrett, M., Lyons, E., and del Valle, A. (in press). The development of national identity and social identity processes: Do social identity theory and self-categorization theory provide useful heuristic frameworks for developmental research? In M. Bennett and F. Sani (eds.), *The Development of the Social Self*. Hove: Psychology Press.

Bauer, M. W., and Gaskell, G. (1999). Towards a paradigm for research on social representations. *Journal for the Theory of Social Behaviour*, 29, 163–86.

Bauer, T., Lofstrom, M., and Zimmermann, K. F. (2000). Immigration policy, assimilation of immigrants and natives' sentiments towards immigrants: Evidence from 12 OECD countries. *Swedish Economic Policy Review*, 7, 11–53.

Beaton, A. M., and Tougas, F. (2001). Reactions to affirmative action: Group membership and social justice. *Social Justice Research*, 14, 61–78.

Beauvois, J.-L., and Dubois, N. (1988). The norm of internality in the explanation of psychological events. *European Journal of Social Psychology*, 18, 299–316.

Bem, D. J. (1972). Self-perception theory. In L. Berkowitz (ed.), *Advances in Experimental Social Psychology* (pp. 1–62). New York: Academic Press.

Berry, J. W. (1980). Social and cultural change. In H. C. Triandis and R. W. Brislin (eds.), *Handbook of Cross-Cultural Psychology* (pp. 211–79). Boston, MA: Allyn and Bacon.

Berry, J. W. (1990). Psychology of acculturation: Understanding individuals moving across cultures. In R. W. Brislin (ed.), *Applied Cross-Cultural Psychology*. Newbury Park, CA: Sage.

Berry, J. W. (1992). Acculturation and adaptation in a new society. *International Migration*, 30, 69–85.

Berry, J. W. (1997a). Immigration, acculturation and adaptation. *Applied Psychology: An International Review*, 46, 5–34.

Berry, J. W. (1997b). Constructing and expanding a framework: Opportunities for developing acculturation research. *Applied Psychology: An International Review*, 46, 62–8.

Berry, J. W. (1998). Acculturative stress. In P. B. Organista and K. M. Chum (eds.), *Readings in Ethnic Psychology* (pp. 117–22). London: Taylor and Francis/Routledge.

Berry, J. W. (1999). Intercultural relations in plural societies. *Canadian Psychology*, 40, 12–21.

Berry, J. W. (2001). A psychology of immigration. *Journal of Social Issues*, 57, 615–31.

Berry, J. W., Kim, U., Minde, T., and Mok, D. (1987). Comparative studies of acculturative stress. *International Migration Review*, 21, 491–511.

Billig, M. (1976). *Social Psychology and Intergroup Relations*. London: Academic Press.

Billig, M. (1978). *Fascists: A Social Psychological View of the National Front*. London: Harcourt and Brace Jovanovich.

Billig, M. (1979). *Psychology, Racism and Fascism*. Birmingham: Searchlight and AFR Publications.

Billig, M. (1981). *L'Internationale Raciste*. Paris: Maspero.

Billig, M. (1995). *Banal Nationalism*. London: Sage.

Billig, M., and Tajfel, H. (1973). Social categorization and similarity in intergroup behaviour. *European Journal of Social Psychology*, 3, 27–52

Blanz, M., Mummendey, A., Mielke, R., and Klink, A. (1998). Responding to negative social identity: A taxonomy of identity management strategies. *European Journal of Social Psychology*, 28, 687–729.

Blumer, H. (1955). Reflections on theory of race relations. In A. W. Lind (ed.), *Race Relations in World Perspective* (pp. 3–21). Honolulu: University of Hawaii Press.

Blumer, H. (1958). Race prejudices as a sense of group position. *Pacific Sociological Review*, 1, 3–7.

Bobo, L. D. (1998). Race, interests and beliefs about affirmative action. *American Behavioural Scientist*, 41, 985–1003.

Bobo, L. D. (1999). Prejudice as group position: Microfoundations of a sociological approach to racism and race relations. *Journal of Social Issues*, 55, 445–72.

Bochner, S. (1986). Coping with unfamiliar cultures: Adjustment or culture learning? *Australian Journal of Psychology*, 38, 347–58.

Bond, M. H. (1998). Unity in diversity: Orientations and strategies for building a harmonious multicultural society. In J. Adamopoulos and Y. Kashima (eds.), *Social Psychology and Cultural Context* (pp. 17–40). Thousand Oaks, CA: Sage.

Boneva, B. S., and Frieze, I. H. (2001). Toward a concept of a migrant personality. *Journal of Social Issues*, 57, 477–91.

Bourhis, R. Y. (1994). Power, gender and intergroup discrimination: Some minimal group experiments. In M. P. Zanna and J. M. Olson (eds.), *The Psychology of Prejudice: The Ontario Symposium* (pp. 171–208). Hillsdale NJ: Lawrence Erlbaum Associates.

Bourhis, R. Y., Moïse, L. C., Perreault, S., and Senécal, S. (1997). Towards an interactive acculturation model: A social psychological approach. *International Journal of Psychology*, 32, 369–86.

Branscombe, N. R., and Ellemers, N. (1998). Coping with group-based discrimination: Individualistic versus group level strategies. In J. K. Swim and C. Stangor (eds.), *Prejudice: The Target's Perspective* (pp. 244–66). San Diego, CA: Academic Press.

Branscombe, N. R., Ellemers, N., Spears, R., and Doosje, B. (1999). The context and content of social identity threat. In N. Ellemers, R. Spears, and B. Doosje (eds.), *Social Identity* (pp. 35–58). Oxford: Blackwell.

Breakwell, G. M. (1986). *Coping with Threatened Identities*. London: Methuen.

Breakwell, G. M. (1993). Social representations and social identity. *Papers on Social Representations*, 2, 198–217.

Breakwell, G. M. (2001). Social representational constraints upon identity Processes. In K. Deaux and G. Philogene (eds.), *Representations of the Social* (pp. 271–84). Oxford: Blackwell.

Breakwell, G. M., and Lyons, E. (1996). *Changing European Identities: Social Psychological Analyses of Social Change*. Oxford: Butterworth-Heinemann.

Brewer, M. (1991). The social self: On being the same and different at the same time. *Personality and Social Psychology Bulletin*, 17, 475–82.

Brewer, M. B. (1999). Multiple identities and identity transition: Implications for Hong Kong. *International Journal of Intercultural Relations*, 23, 187–97.

Brewer, M. B. (2000). Superordinate goals versus superordinate identity as bases of intergroup cooperation. In D. Capozza and R. Brown (eds.), *Social Identity Processes* (pp. 117–32). London: Sage.

Brewer, M. B., and Miller, N. (1984). *Groups in Contact: The Psychology of Desegregation*. New York: Academic Press.

Brewer, M. B., and Miller, N. (1996). *Intergroup Relations*. Buckingham: Open University Press.

Brislin, R. W., Landis, D., and Brandt, M. (1983). Conceptualizations of intercultural behaviour and training. In D. Landis and R. W. Brislin (eds.), *Handbook of Intercultural Training* (pp. 1–35). New York: Pergamon.

Brown, R. (1995). *Prejudice: Its Social Psychology*. Oxford: Blackwell.

Brown, R. (2000). Social identity theory: Past achievements, current problems and future challenges. *European Journal of Social Psychology*, 30, 745–78.

Brown, R., Hinkle, S., Ely, P. G., Fox-Cardamone, L., Maras, P., and Taylor, L. A. (1992). Recognizing group diversity: Individualist–collectivist and autonomous–relational social orientations and their implications for intergroup processes. *British Journal of Social Psychology*, 31, 327–42.

Brown, R., and Middendorf, J. (1996). The underestimated role of temporal comparison: A test of the life-span model. *Journal of Social Psychology*, 136, 325–31.

Bruner, J. S., and Tagiuri, R. (1954). The perception of people. In G. Lindzey (ed.), *Handbook of Social Psychology* (pp. 634–54). Reading, MA: Addison-Wesley.

Burr, V. (1995). *An Introduction to Social Constructionism*. London: Routledge.

Bush, G. W. (2003). The State of the Union Address. Speech to the US Congress. www.white-house.gov/news/releases/ 2003/01/20030128-22.htlm

Butera, F., and Mugny, G. (eds.) (2001). *Social Influence in Social Reality*. Bern: Hogrefe and Huber Publishers.

Campbell, C., and Jovchelovitch, S. (2000). Health, community and development: Towards a social psychology of participation. *Journal of Community and Applied Social Psychology*, 10, 255-70.

Campbell, D. T. (1958). Common fate, similarity and other indices of the status of aggregates of persons as social entities. *Behavioral Science*, 3, 14-25.

Campbell, D. T. (1965). Ethnocentric and other altruistic motives. In D. Levine (ed.), *Nebraska Symposium on Motivation* (pp. 283-311). Lincoln: University of Nebraska Press.

"Canadian Multiculturalism." www.pch.gc.ca/progs/multi/ policy/act_e.cfm

Capozza, D., and Brown, R. (2000). *Social Identity Processes*. London: Sage.

Castles, S., and Davidson, A. (2000). *Citizenship and Migration: Globalization and the Politics of Belonging*. London: Macmillan.

Chaiken, S. (1987). The heuristic model of persuasion. In M. P. Zanna, J. M. Olson, and C. P. Herman (eds.), *Social Influence: The Ontario Symposium, Vol. 5*. Hillsdale, NJ: Lawrence Erlbaum Associates.

Chryssochoou, X. (1996a). L'Identité sociale. La construction identitaire nationale et Européenne de Français et de Grecs. Université René Descartes-Paris V; PhD thesis.

Chryssochoou, X. (1996b). How group membership is formed: Self-categorization or group beliefs? The construction of a European identity in France and Greece. In G. M. Breakwell and E. Lyons (eds.), *Changing European Identities: Social Psychological Analyses of Social Change* (pp. 297-314). Oxford: Butterworth and Heinemann.

Chryssochoou, X. (2000a). Multicultural societies: Making sense of new environments and identities. *Journal of Community and Applied Social Psychology*, 10, 343-54.

Chryssochoou, X. (2000b). Memberships in a superordinate level: Rethinking European Union as a multinational society. *Journal of Community and Applied Social Psychology*, 10, 403-20.

Chryssochoou, X. (2000c). How superordinate identity is formed? The case of the European. *European Psychologist*, 5, 269-77.

Chryssochoou, X. (2003). Studying identity in social psychology: Some thoughts on the definition of identity and its relation to action. *Language and Politics*, special issue: Conceptual and methodological issues on the study of collective identity. A. Triandafyllidou guest editor, 2: 2, 225-42.

Chryssochoou, X., and Sanchez-Mazas, M. (2000). Modèle ou renégat? Une étude sur la perception de la "personne-alibi" dans un contexte méritocratique. *Cahiers Internationaux de Psychologie Sociale*, 47-8, 34-43.

Chryssochoou, X., and Volpato, C. (2002). The genesis of collective action: an analysis of the rhetorical strategies in the Communist Manifesto. Paper submitted for publication.

Chulvi, B., and Pérez, J. A. (2003). Ontologisation Vs discrimination d'une minorité ethnique (les gitans). *Nouvelle Revue de Psychologie Sociale/New Review of Social Psychology*, 2, 6-15.

Cinnirella, M. (1997). Towards a European identity: Interactions between the national and European social identities manifested by university students in Britain and Italy. *British Journal of Social Psychology*, 36, 19-31.

Clark, K. B., and Clark, M. P. (1947). Racial identification and preference in negro children. In H. Proshansky and B. Seidenberg (eds.), *Basic Studies in Social Psychology*. New York: Holt Rinehart and Winston.

Clemence, A. (2001). Social positioning and social representations. In K. Deaux and G. Philogene (eds.), *Representations of the Social* (pp. 83–95). Oxford: Blackwell.

Codol, J.-P. (1975). "Effet PIP" et conflit des normes. *L' Année Psychologique*, 75, 127–46.

Condor, S. (1996). Unimagined community? Some social psychological issues concerning English national identity. In G. M. Breakwell and E. Lyons (eds.), *Changing European Identities: Social Psychological Analyses of Social Change* (pp. 41–68). Oxford: Butterworth-Heinemann.

Condor, S. (2000). Identity management in English people's talk about 'this country'. *Discourse and Society*, 11, 175–205.

Condor, S. (2001). Nations and nationalisms: Particular cases and impossible myths. *British Journal of Social Psychology*, 40, 177–81.

Coon, H. M., and Kemmelmeier, M. (2001). Cultural orientations in the United States: (Re)examining differences among ethnic groups. *Journal of Cross-cultural Psychology*, 32, 348–64.

Cousins, S. D. (1989). Culture and self-perception in Japan and the United States. *Journal of Personality and Social Psychology*, 56, 124–131.

Coyle, A. (2000). Discourse analysis. In G. M. Breakwell, S. Hammond, and C. Fife-Schaw (eds.), *Research Methods in Psychology* (pp. 251–68). London: Sage.

Crisp, R. J., and Hewstone, M. (2000). Multiple categorization and social identity. In D. Capozza and R. Brown (eds.), *Social Identity Processes* (pp. 149–66). London: Sage.

Crocker, J., and Major, B. (1989). Social stigma and self-esteem: The self-protective properties of stigma. *Psychological Review*, 96, 608–30.

Crocker, J., Major, B., and Steele, C. (1998). Social stigma. In D. T. Gilbert, S. T. Fiske, and G. Lindzey (eds.), *The Handbook of Social Psychology* (pp. 504–53). Boston, MA: McGraw-Hill.

Crosby, F. (1976). A model of egoistical reative deprivation. *Psychological Review*, 83, 85–113.

Cross, S. E., Bacon, P. L., and Morris, M. L. (2000). The relational-interdependent self-construal and relationships. *Journal of Personality and Social Psychology*, 78, 791–808.

Cunningham, F. (1987). *Democratic Theory and Socialism*. Cambridge: Cambridge University Press.

Davies, J. C. (1971). Toward a theory of revolution. In J. C. Davies (ed.), *When Men Revolt and Why: A Reader in Political Violence and Revolution*. New York: Free Press.

De Rosa, A. S. (1996). Reality changes faster than research: National and supranational identity in social representations of the European Community in the context of changes in international relations. In G. M. Breakwell and E. Lyons (eds.), *Changing European Identities: Social Psychological Analyses of Social Change* (pp. 381–402). Oxford: Butterworth and Heinemann.

Deaux, K. (1992). Personalizing identity and socializing the self. In G. M. Breakwell (ed.), *Social Psychology of Identity and the Self Concept* (pp. 9–34). Kingston-upon-Thames: Surrey University Press.

Deaux, K. (2000a). Surveying the landscape of immigration: Social psychological perspectives. *Journal of Community and Applied Social Psychology*, 10, 421–31.

Deaux, K. (2000b). Models, meanings and motivations. In D. Capozza and R. Brown (eds.), *Social Identity Processes* (pp. 1–14). London: Sage.

Deaux, K. (2001). Meaning and making: Some comments on content and process. In K. Deaux and G. Philogene (eds.), *Representations of the Social* (pp. 312–17). Oxford: Blackwell.

Deflem, M., and Pampel, F. C. (1996). The myth of postnational identity: Popular support for the European unification. *Social Forces*, 75, 119–43.

Deschamps, J.-C. (1977a). L'Attribution et la catégorisation sociale. Berne: Peter Lang.

Deschamps, J.-C. (1977b). Effect of crossing category memberships on quantitative judgement. *European Journal of Social Psychology*, 7, 517–21.

Deschamps, J.-C. (1980). L'Identité et les rapports de domination. *Revue Suisse de Sociologie*, 6, 111–21.

Deschamps, J.-C. (1983). Social attribution. In J. Jaspars, F. D. Fincham, and M. Hewstone (eds.), *Attribution Theory and Research: Conceptual, Developmental and Social Dimensions* (pp. 223–40). London: Academic Press.

Deschamps, J.-C., and Brown, R. (1983). Superordinate goals and intergroup conflict. *British Journal of Social Psychology*, 22, 189–95.

Deschamps, J.-C., and Clemence, A. (1990). *L'Explication quotidienne. Perspectives psychosociologiques*. Fribourg: Del Val.

Deschamps, J.-C., and Doise, W. (1978a). L'Effet du croisement des appartenances catégorielles. In W. Doise (ed.), *Expériences entre groupes*. Paris: Mouton.

Deschamps, J.-C., and Doise, W. (1978b). Crossed category memberships in intergroup relations. In H. Tajfel (ed.), *Differentiation Between Social Groups: Studies in the Social Psychology of Intergroup Relations* (pp. 141–58). London: Academic Press.

Deschamps, J.-C., Lorenzi-Cioldi, F., and Meyer, G. (1982). *L'Échec scolaire. Elève modèle ou modèles d'élèves? Approche Psychosociologique de la division sociale à l'école*. Lausanne: Pierre Marcel Favre.

Deutsch, M. (1958). Trust and suspicion. *Journal of Conflict Resolution*, 2, 265–79.

Deutsch, M. (1975). Equity, equality and need : What determines which value will be used as the basis of distributive justice? *Journal of Social Issues*, 31, 137–49.

Deutsch, M. (1985). *Distributive Justice: A Social Psychological Perspective*. New Haven, CT: Yale University Press.

Deutsch, M. (2000). Justice and conflict. In M. Deutsch and P. T. Coleman (eds.), *The Handbook of Conflict Resolution: Theory and Practice* (pp. 41–64). San Francisco, CA: Jossey-Bass.

Devine, P. (1989). Stereotypes and prejudice: Their automatic and controlled components. *Journal of Personality and Social Psychology*, 56, 5–18.

Diamond, J. (1997) *Guns, Germs and Steel: The Fates of Human Societies*. New York: Norton.

Dixon, J. (2001). Contact and boundaries: "Locating" the social psychology of intergroup relations. *Theory and Psychology*, 11, 587–608.

Doise, W. (1978). *Expériences entre groupes*. Paris: Mouton.

Doise, W. (1984). Social representations, intergroup experiments and level of analysis. In R. Farr and S. Moscovici (eds.), *Social Representations* (pp. 255–68). Cambridge: Cambridge University Press.

Doise, W. (1986). *Levels of Explanation in Social Psychology*. Cambridge: Cambridge University Press.

Doise, W. (1990). Les Représentations sociales. In R. Guiglione, C. Bonnet, and J.-F. Richard (eds.), *Traité de psychologie cognitive 3*. Paris: Presses Universitaires de France.

Doise, W. (1992). L'Ancrage sur les études sur les représentations sociales. *Bulletin de Psychologie*, 405, 189–95.

Doise, W. (1997). Organizing social psychological explanations. In C. McGarty and S. A. Haslam (eds.), *The Message of Social Psychology* (pp. 63–76). Oxford: Blackwell.

Doise, W. (1998). Social representations in personal identity. In S. Worchel, J. F. Morales, D. Paez, and J.-C. Deschamps (eds.), *Social Identity: International Perspectives* (pp. 13–23). London: Sage.

Doise, W. (2001). *Droits de l'homme et force des idées*. Paris: Presses Universitaires de France.

Doise, W., Clemence, A., and Lorenzi-Cioldi, F. (1993). *The Quantitative Analysis of Social Representations*. London: Harvester Wheatsheaf.

Doise, W., and Devos, T. (1999). Identité et interdépendance: pour une psychologie sociale de l'Union Européenne. *Psychologie et Société*, 1, 11–27.

Doise, W., and Herrera, M. (1994). Déclaration universelle et représentations sociales des droits de l'homme: une étuide à Genève. *Revue Internationale de Psychologie Sociale*, 7, 87–107.

Doise, W., and Lorenzi-Cioldi, F. (1991). L'Identité comme représentation sociale. In V. Aebisher, J.-P. Deconchy, and E. M. Lipiansky (eds.), *Idéologies et représentations sociales*. Delval: Cousset.

Doise, W., and Mugny, G. (1981). *Le Développement social de l'intelligence*. Paris: Inter-Editions.

Doise, W., Spini, D., and Clemence, A. (1999). Human rights studied as social representations in a cross-national context. *European Journal of Social Psychology*, 29, 1–29.

Doise, W., Spini, D., Jesuino, J. C., Ng, S. H., and Emler, N. (1994). Values and perceived conflicts in the social representations of human rights. *Swiss Journal of Psychology*, 53, 240–51.

Dovidio, J. F., and Gaertner, S. L. (1991). Changes in the nature and expression of racial prejudice. In H. Knopke, J. Norrell, and R. Rogers (eds.), *Opening Doors: An Appraisal of Race Relations in Contemporary America* (pp. 201–41). Tuscaloosa: University of Alabama Press.

Dovidio, J. F., and Gaertner, S. L. (1996). Affirmative action, unintentional racial biases, and intergroup relations. *Journal of Social Issues*, 52, 51–75.

Dovidio, J. F., and Gaertner, S. L. (1998). On the nature of contemporary prejudice: The causes, consequences and challenges of aversive racism. In J. L. Eberhardt and S. T. Fiske (eds.), *Confronting Racism: The Problem and the Response* (pp. 3–32). Thousand Oaks, CA: Sage.

Dovidio, J. F., and Mullen, B. (1992). Race, physical handicap and response amplification. Unpublished manuscript cited in Dovidio and Gaertner 1998.

Downey, G., Freitas, A. L., Michaelis, B., and Khouri, H. (1998). The self-fulfilling prophecy in close relationships: Rejection sensitivity and rejection by romantic partners. *Journal of Personality and Social Psychology*, 75, 545–60.

Durkheim, E. (1898). Représentations individuelles et representations collectives. *Revue de Métaphysique et Morale*, 6, 273–302.

Duveen, G. (1997). Psychological development as a social process. In L. Smith, J. Dockrell, and P. Tomlinson (eds.), *Piaget, Vygotsky and Beyond*. London: Routledge.

Duveen, G. (2001). Representations, identity, resistence. In K. Deaux and G. Philogene (eds.), *Representations of the Social* (pp. 257–70). Oxford: Blackwell.

Duveen, G., and Lloyd, B. (1990). Introduction. In G. Duveen and B. Lloyd (eds.), *Social Representations and the Development of Knowledge*. Cambridge: Cambridge University Press.

Eagly, A. H. (1987). *Sex Differences in Social Behavior: A Social-Role Interpretation*. Hillsdale, NJ: Lawrence Erlbaum Associates.

Earley, P. C., Gibson, C. B., and Chen, C. C. (1999). "How did I do?" versus "How did we do?" Cultural contrasts of performance feedback use and self-efficacy. *Journal of Cross-cultural Psychology*, 30, 594–619.

Eberhardt, J. L., and Fiske, S. T. (1998). *Confronting Racism: The Problem and the Response*. Thousand Oaks, CA: Sage.

Echebarria-Echabe, A., Elejabarrieta, F., Valencia, J., and Villareal, M. J. (1992). Représentations sociales de l'Europe et identités sociales. *Bulletin de Psychologie*, 45, 280–8.

Echebarria-Echabe, A., and Gonzales Castro, J. L. (1996). Images of immigrants: A study on the xenophobia and permeability of intergroup boundaries. *European Journal of Social Psychology*, 26, 341–52.

Elejabarrieta, F. (1994). Social positioning: A way to link social representations and social identity. *Social Science Information*, 33, 241–53.

Ellemers, N. (1993). The influence of socio-structural variables on identity enhancement strategies. *European Review of Social Psychology*, 4, 27–57.

Ellemers, N., Doosje, B., Van Knippenberg, A., and Wilke, H. (1992). Status protection in high status minority groups. *European Journal of Social Psychology*, 22, 123–40.

Ellemers, N., Spears, R., and Doosje, B. (1999). *Social Identity*. Oxford: Blackwell.

Esses, V. M., Dovidio, J. F., Jackson, L. M., and Armstrong, T. L. (2001). The immigration dilemma: The role of perceived group competition, ethnic prejudice and national identity. *Journal of Social Issues*, 57, 389–412.

Esses, V. M., and Gardner, R. C. (1996). Multiculturalism in Canada: Context and current status. *Canadian Journal of Behavioural Science*, 28, 1–11.

Esses, V. M., Jackson, L. M., and Armstrong, T. L. (1998). Intergroup competition and attitudes toward immigrants and immigration: An instrumental model of group conflict. *Journal of Social Issues*, 54, 699–724.

Esses, V. M., Jackson, L. M., Nolan, J. M., and Armstrong, T. L. (1999). Economic threat and attitudes towards immigrants. In S. Halli and L. Drieger (eds.), *Immigrant Canada: Demographic, economic and social challenges* (pp. 212–29). Toronto: Toronto University Press.

Ethier, K. A., and Deaux, K. (1994). Negotiating social identity when contexts change: Maintaining identification and responding to threat. *Journal of Personality and Social Psychology*, 67, 243–51.

European Union Final Treaty, Maastricht (1992) http://europa.eu.int/en/ record/mt/top.html

Faranda, J. and Gaertner, S. L. (1979). The effects of inadmissible evidence introduced by the prosecution and the defense and the defendant's race on the verdicts by high and low authoritarians. Paper presented at the annual meeting of the Eastern Psychological Association, March, New York.

Federico, C. M., and Sidanius, J. (2002). Sophistication and the antecedents of Whites' racial policy attitudes: Racism, ideology and affirmative action in America. *Public Opinion Quarterly*, 66, 145–76.

Festinger, L. (1954). A theory of social comparison processes. *Human Relations*, 7, 117–40.

Festinger, L. (1957). *A Theory of Cognitive Dissonance*. Stanford, CA: Stanford University Press.

Festinger, L., and Carlsmith, J. M. (1959). Cognitive consequences of forced compliance. *Journal of Abnormal and Social Psychology*, 58, 203–10.

Finlay, W. M. L., and Lyons, E. (2000). Social categorizations, social comparisons and stigma: Presentations of self in people with learning difficulties. *British Journal of Social Psychology*, 39, 129–46.

Fishbein, M., and Ajzen, I. (1975). Belief, attitude intention and behaviour: An introduction to theory and research. Reading, MA: Addison-Wesley.

Fiske, A. P. (1991). *Structures of Social Life: The Four Elementary Forms of Human Relations*. New York: Free Press.

Fiske, A. P. (1992). The four elementary forms of sociality: Framework for a unified theory of social relations. *Psychological Review*, 99, 689–723.

Fiske, A. P., Kitayama, S., Markus, H. R., and Nisbett, R. E. (1998). The cultural matrix of social psychology. In D. T. Gilbert, S. T. Fiske, and G. Lindzey (eds.), *The Handbook of Social Psychology, Vol. 2* (pp. 915–81). Boston, MA: McGraw-Hill.

Fiske, S. T. (1998). Stereotyping prejudice and discrimination. In D. T. Gilbert, S. T. Fiske, and G. Lindzey (eds.), *The Handbook of Social Psychology* (pp. 357–411). New York: McGraw-Hill.

Fiske, S. T. (2000). Interdependence and the reduction of prejudice. In S. Oskamp (ed.), *Reducing Prejudice and Discrimination*. Mahwah, NJ: Lawrence Erlbaum Associates.

Fiske, S. T., and Neuberg, S. L. (1990). A continuum of impression formation, from category-based to individuating processes: Influences of information and motivation on attention interpretation. *Advances in Experimental Psychology*, 23, 1–74.

Fiske, S. T., Xu, J., Cuddy, A. C., and Glick, P. (1999). (Dis)respecting versus (dis)liking: Status and interdependence predict ambivalent stereotypes of competence and warmth. *Journal of Social Issues*, 55, 473–89.

Freeman, M. A. (2001). Linking self and social structure: A psychological perspective on social identity in Sri Lanka. *Journal of Cross-cultural Psychology*, 32, 291–308.

Furnham, A., and Bochner, S. (1986). *Culture Shock: Psychological Reactions to Unfamiliar Environments*. London: Methuen.

Gaertner, S. L., and Dovidio, J. F. (1977). The subtlety of white racism, arousal, and helping behaviour. *Journal of Personality and Social Psychology*, 35, 691–707.

Gaertner, S. L., and Dovidio, J. F. (1986). The aversive form of racism. In J. F. Dovidio and S. L. Gaertner (eds.), *Prejudice, Discrimination, and Racism* (pp. 61–89). Orlando, FL: Academic Press.

Gaertner, S. L., Dovidio, J. F., Anastasio, P. A., Bachman, B. A., and Rust, M. C. (1993). The common ingroup identity model: Recategorization and the reduction of intergroup bias. In W. Stroebe and M. Hewstone (eds.), *European Review of Social Psychology, Vol. 4* (pp. 1–26). Chichester: Wiley.

Gaertner, S. L., Dovidio, J. F., Nier, J. A., Banker, B. S., Ward, C., Houlette, M., and Loux, S. (2000). The common ingroup identity model for reducing intergroup bias: Progresses and challenges. In D. Capozza and R. Brown (eds.), *Social Identity Processes* (pp. 133–48). London: Sage.

Gaertner, S. L., Dovidio, J. F., Rust, M. C., Nier, J. A., Banker, B. S., Ward, C., Mottola, G. R., and Houlette, M. (1999). Reducing intergroup bias elements of intergroup cooperation. *Journal of Personality and Social Psychology*, 76, 388–408.

Gaunt, R., Leyens, J.-P., and Demoulin, S. (2002). Intergroup relations and the attribution of emotions: Control over memory for secondary emotions associated with the ingroup and outgroup. *Journal of Experimental Social Psychology*, 38, 508–14.

Gellner, E. (1997). *Nationalism*. London: Weidenfeld and Nicolson.

General Assembly of the United Nations (1951). Geneva Convention relating to the Status of Refugees. 429 (V) 14/12/1950, http://www.unchr.ch/ htlm/menu3

Gergen, K. J. (1985). The social constructionist movement in modern psychology. *American Psychologist*, 40, 266–75.

Gergen, K. J. (1989). Warranting voice and the elaboration. In J. Shotter and K. J. Gergen (eds.), *Texts of Identity*. London: Sage.

Gerstle, G. (1999). Liberty, coercion and the making of Americans. In C. Hirschman, P. Kasinitz, and J. De Wind (eds.), *Handbook of International Migration* (pp. 275–93). New York: Russell Sage Foundation.

Glick, P., and Fiske, S. T. (2001). Ambivalent stereotypes as legitimizing ideologies: Differentiating paternalistic and envious prejudice. In J. T. Jost and B. Major (eds.), *The Psychology of Legitimacy: Emerging Perspectives on Ideology, Justice and Intergroup Relations* (pp. 278–306). New York: Cambridge University Press.

Gordon, M. M. (1964). *Assimilation in American Life*. New York: Oxford University Press.

Gould, S. J. (1981). *The Mismeasure of Man*. New York: Norton.

Green-Staerklé, E. (2002). Individualisme/collectivisme. Une analyse de leurs significations dans 29 pays. PhD thesis, Université de Lausanne.

Greenfield, P. M. (1997). Culture as a process: Empirical methods for cultural psychology. In J. W. Berry, Y. H. Poortinga, and J. Pandey (eds.), *Handbook of Cross-Cultural Psychology*, 2nd edn. Boston, MA: Allyn and Bacon.

Grimm, S. D., Church, A. T., Katigbak, M. S., and Reyes, J. A. S. (1999). Self-described traits, values and moods associated with individualism and collectivism: Testing I-C theory in an individualistic (US) and a collectivistic (Philippine) culture. *Journal of Cross-cultural Psychology*, 30, 466–500.

Guimelli, C. (1994). *Structures et transformations des représentations sociales.* Neuchâtel: Delachaux Niestlé.

Guimelli, C. (1998). Differentiation between the central core elements of social representations. *Swiss Journal of Psychology*, 57, 209–24.

Guimond, S., and Dambrun, M. (2002). When prosperity breeds intergroup hostility: The effects of relative deprivation and relative gratification on prejudice. *Personality and Social Psychology Bulletin*, 28, 900–12.

Guimond, S., and Tougas, F. (1994). Sentiments d'injustice et actions collectives: la privation relative. In R. Y. Bourhis and J.-P. Leyens (eds.), *Stéréotypes, discrimination et relations intergroupes* (pp. 201–32). Liège: Mardaga.

Gurr, T. R. (1970). *Why Men Rebel.* Princeton, NJ: Princeton University Press.

Halabi, S. (1999). Reactions to receiving assumptive help from an ingroup vs an outgroup helper. MSc thesis, Tel Aviv University.

Hamberger, J., and Hewstone, M. (1997). Interethnic contact as a predictor of blatant and subtle prejudice: Test of a model in four West European countries. *British Journal of Social Psychology*, 36, 173–90.

Hamilton, D. L. (1981). *Cognitive Processes in Stereotyping and Intergroup Behavior.* Hillsdale, NJ: Lawrence Erlbaum Associates.

Hamilton, D. L., and Gifford, R. K. (1976). Illusory correlation in intergroup perception: A cognitive basis of stereotypic judgements. *Journal of Experimental Social Psychology*, 12, 392–407.

Harré, R. (1987). The social constructions of selves. In K. Yardley and T. Honess (eds.), *Self and Identity: Psychosocial Perspectives* (pp. 41–52). Chichester: John Wiley and Sons.

Harré, R. (1998). *The Singular Self: An Introduction to the Psychology of Personhood.* London: Sage.

Haslam, N., Rothschild, L., and Ernst, D. (2000). Essentialist beliefs about social categories. *British Journal of Social Psychology*, 39, 113–27.

Haslam, N., Rothschild, L., and Ernst, D. (2002). Are essentialist beliefs associated with prejudice? *British Journal of Social Psychology*, 41, 87–100.

Haslam, S. A., Turner, J. C., Oakes, P. J., Reynolds, K. J., and Doosje, B. (2002). From personal pictures in the head to collective tools in the world: How shared stereotypes allow groups to represent and change social reality. In C. McGarty, V. Y. Yzerbyt, and R. Spears (eds.), *Stereotypes as Explanations: The Formation of Meaningful Beliefs About Social Groups* (pp. 157–85). Cambridge: Cambridge University Press.

Hegarty, P., and Pratto, F. (2001). The effects of social category norms and stereotypes on explanations for intergroup differences. *Journal of Personality and Social Psychology*, 80, 725–35.

Heider, F. (1958). *The Psychology of Interpersonal Relations.* New York: Wiley.

Herzlich, C. (1973). *Health and Illness: A Social Psychological Analysis.* London: Academic Press.

Hewstone, M. (1986). *Understanding Attitudes to the European Community: A Social-Psychological Study in Four Member States.* Cambridge: Cambridge University Press.

Hewstone, M. (1989). *Causal Attribution: From Cognitive Processes to Collective Beliefs.* Oxford: Blackwell.

Hewstone, M., and Brown, R. (1986). Contact is not enough: An intergroup perspective on the contact hypothesis. In M. Hewstone and R. Brown (eds.), *Contact and Conflict in Intergroup Encounters* (pp. 1–44). Oxford: Blackwell.

Hilton, D. J., Erb, H.-P., Dermot, M., and Molian, D. J. (1996). Social representations of history and attitudes to European unification in Britain, France, and Germany. In G. M. Breakwell and E. Lyons (eds.), *Changing European Identities: Social Psychological Analyses of Social Change* (pp. 275–96). Oxford: Butterworth-Heinemann.

Hinkle, S., and Brown, R. (1990). Intergroup comparisons and social identity: Some links and lacunae. In D. Abrams and M. A. Hogg (eds.), *Social Identity Theory: Constructive and Critical Advances* (pp. 48–70). London: Harvester Wheatsheaf.

Hobsbawm, E. J. (1990). *Nations et nationalisme depuis 1780.* Paris: Gallimard.

Hofstede, G. (1980). *Culture's Consequences: International Differences in Work Related Values.* Beverly Hills, CA: Sage.

Hogg, M. A. (2000). Subjective uncertainty reduction through self-categorization: A motivational theory of social identity. *European Review of Social Psychology*, 11, 223–55.

Hogg, M. A. (2001). A social identity theory of leadership. *Personality and Social Psychology Bulletin*, 5, 184–200.

Hogg, M. A., and Abrams, D. (1988). *Social Identifications: A Social Psychology of Intergroup Relations and Group Processes.* London: Routledge.

Hogg, M. A., and Abrams, D. (1990). *Social Identity Theory: Constructive and Critical Advances.* London: Harvester Wheatsheaf.

Hopkins, N. (2001). National identity: Pride and prejudice? *British Journal of Social Psychology*, 40, 183–6.

Hopkins, N. and Kahani-Hopkins, V. (in press). Identity construction and British Muslims' political activity: Beyond Rational actor theory. *British Journal of Social Psychology.*

Hopkins, N., and Reicher, S. (1996). The construction of social categories and processes of social change: Arguing about national identities. In G. M. Breakwell and E. Lyons (eds.), *Changing European Identities: Social Psychological Analyses of Social Change* (pp. 69–94). Oxford: Butterworth-Heinemann.

Hopkins, N., Reicher, S., and Levine, M. (1997). On the parallels between social cognition and the "new racism." *British Journal of Social Psychology*, 36, 305–29.

Horenczyk, G. (1997). Immigrants' perceptions of host attitudes and their reconstruction of cultural groups. *Applied Psychology: An International Review*, 46, 34–8.

Hornsey, M. J., and Hogg, M. A. (2000). Assimilation and diversity: An integrative model of subgroup relations. *Personality and Social Psychology Review*, 4, 143–56.

Hovland, C. I., Janis, I. L., and Kelley, H. H. (1953). *Communication and Persuasion.* New Haven, CT: Yale University Press.

Huddy, L. (2001). From social to political identity: A critical examination of social identity theory. *Political Psychology*, 22 (1), 127–56.

Huici, C., Ros, M., Cano, I., Hopkins, N., Emler, N., and Carmona, M. (1997). Comparative identity and evaluation of socio-political change: Perceptions of the European Community as a function of the salience of regional identities. *European Journal of Social Psychology*, 27, 97–113.

Human Resources Development Canada www.info.load_otea.hrdc-drhc.ca/workplace_equality/information/history.shtml

Hunter, J. A., Stringer, M., and Watson, R. P. (1991). Intergroup violence and intergroup attributions. *British Journal of Social Psychology*, 30, 261–6.

Hutnik, N. (1991). *Ethnic Minority Identity: A Social Psychological Perspective*. Oxford: Clarendon Press.

Hyman, H. H. (1942). The psychology of status. *Archives of Psychology*, 269.

Hyman, H. H. (1960). Reflections of reference groups. *Public Opinion Quarterly*, 24, 389–96.

Isin, E. F., and Turner, B. S. (2002). *Handbook of Citizenship Studies*. London: Sage.

Jackson, L. M., and Esses, V. M. (2000). Effects of perceived economic competition on people's willingness to help empower immigrants. *Group Processes and Intergroup Relations*, 3, 419–35.

Jacobson, J. (1997). Perceptions of Britishness. *Nations and Nationalism*, 3, 181–99.

Jahoda, G. (1984). Do we need the concept of culture? *Journal of Cross-cultural Psychology*, 15, 139–51.

Jahoda, G. (1986). Nature, culture and social psychology. *European Journal of Social Psychology*, 16, 17–30.

Jahoda, G. (1988). J'accuse. In M. H. Bond (ed.), *The Cross-Cultural Challenge to Social Psychology*. Newbury Park, CA: Sage.

Janis, I. L. (1972). *Victims of Groupthink: A Psychological Study of Foreign Policy Decisions and Fiascoes*. Boston, MA: Houghton Mifflin.

Janoski, T., and Gran, B. (2002). Political citizenship: Foundations of rights. In E. F. Isin and B. S. Turner (eds.), *Handbook of Citizenship Studies*. London: Sage.

Jodelet, D. (1984). Représentation sociale: Phenomène, concept a théorie. In S. Moscovici (ed.), *Psychologie sociale*. Paris: Presses Universitaires de France.

Jodelet, D. (1989). Représentations sociales: Un domaine en expansion. In D. Jodelet (ed.), *Les Représentations sociales*. Paris: Presses Universitaires de France.

Jodelet, D. (1991). *Madness and Social Representations*. Berkeley: University of California Press.

Jodelet, D. (1993). Indigeneous psychologies and social representations of the body and the self. In U. Kim and J. W. Berry (eds.), *Indigeneous Psychologies: Research and Experience in Cultural Context*. Newbury Park, CA: Sage.

Joffe, H. (1999). Risk and "the other." New York: Cambridge University Press.

Joffe, H., and Haarhoff, G. (2002). Representations of far-flung illnesses: The case of Ebola in Britain. *Social Science and Medicine*, 54, 955–69.

Jones, E. E., and Davis, K. E. (1965). From acts to dispositions: The attribution process in person perception. In L. Berkowitz (ed.), *Advances in Experimental Social Psychology* (pp. 219–66). New York: Academic Press.

Jost, J. T., and Banaji, M. R. (1994). The role of stereotyping in system-justification and the production of false consciousness. *British Journal of Social Psychology*, 33, 1–27.

Jost, J. T., and Major, B. (2001). *The Psychology of Legitimacy: Emerging Perspectives on Ideology, Justice and Intergroup Relations*. Cambridge: Cambridge University Press.

Jovchelovitch, S., and Gervais, M.-C. (1999). Social representations of health and illness: The case of the Chinese community in England. *Journal of Community and Applied Social Psychology*, 9, 247–60.

Kagitçibasi, C. (1997). Whither multiculturalism? *Applied Psychology: An International Review*, 46, 44–52.

Kashti, Y. (1997). Patriotism as identity and action. In D. Bar Tal and E. Staub (eds.), *Patriotism in the Lives of Individuals and Nations* (pp. 151–64). Chicago, IL: Nelson-Hall Publishers.

Katz, D. (1960). The functional approach to the study of attitudes. *Public Opinion Quarterly*, 24, 163–204

Katz, D., and Braly, K. (1933). Racial stereotypes of one hundred college students. *Journal of Abnormal and Social Psychology*, 28, 280–90.

Katz, I., and Hass, R. G. (1988). Racial ambivalence and American value conflict: Correlational and priming studies of dual cognitive structures. *Journal of Personality and Social Psychology*, 55, 893–905.

Kelley, H. H. (1967). Attribution theory in social psychology. In D. Levine (ed.), *Nebraska Symposium on Motivation* (pp. 192–238). Lincoln: University of Nebraska Press.

Kelman, H. C. (1997). Nationalism, patriotism, and national identity: Social-psychological dimensions. In D. Bar Tal and E. Staub (eds.), *Patriotism in the Lives of Individuals and Nations* (pp. 165–89). Chicago, IL: Nelson-Hall Publishers.

Kessler, T., Mummendey, A., and Leisse, U.-K. (2000). The personal–group discrepancy: Is there a common information basis for personal and group judgement? *Journal of Personality and Social Psychology*, 79, 95–109.

Knafo, A., and Schwartz, S. (2001). Value socialization in families of Israeli-born and Soviet-born adolescents in Israel. *Journal of Cross-cultural Psychology*, 32, 213–28.

Kramer, R. M. (1999). Trust and distrust in organizations: Emerging perspectives, enduring questions. *Annual Review of Psychology*, 50, 569–98.

Kroeber, A. L., and Kluckholm, C. (1952). *Culture: A Critical Review of Concepts and Definitions*. Cambridge, MA: Peabody Museum.

Kuwahara, Y., and Chryssochoou, X. (2002). Representation of society in individualistic and collectivistic countries: A cross-cultural qualitative study with British and Japanese women. Presentation at the Sixth International Conference on Social Representations, August, 2002.

Lalonde, R. N., and Cameron, J. E. (1993). An intergroup perspective on immigrant acculturation with a focus on collective strategies. *International Journal of Psychology*, 28, 57–74.

LaPierre, R. T. (1934). Attitudes vs actions. *Social Forces*, 13, 230–7.

Laungani, P. (1999). Cultural influences on identity and behavior: India and Britain. In Y. Lee and C. R. Clark (eds.), *Personality and Person Perception Across Cultures* (pp. 191–212). Mahwah, NJ: Lawrence Erlbaum Associates.

LeCouteur, A., and Augoustinos, M. (2001). The language of prejudice and racism. In M. Augoustinos and K. J. Reynolds (eds.), *Understanding Prejudice, Racism and Social Conflict* (pp. 215–30). London: Sage.

Lemaine, G. (1974). Social differentiation and social originality. *European Journal of Social Psychology*, 4, 17–52.

Lemaine, G., Kastersztein, J., and Personnaz, B. (1978). Social differentiation. In H. Tajfel (ed.), *Differentiation Between Social Groups: Studies in the Social Psychology of Intergroup Relations*. London: Academic Press.

Lerner, M. J. (1977). The justice motive: Some hypotheses as to its origins and forms. *Journal of Personality*, 45, 1–52.

Lerner, M. J. (1980). *The Belief in a Just World: A Fundamental Delusion*. New York: Plenum.

Leyens, J.-P., Paladino, P. M., Rodriguez-Torres, R., Vaes, J., Demoulin, S., Rodriguez-Perez, A., and Gaunt, R. (2000). The emotional side of prejudice: The attribution of secondary emotions to ingroups and outgroups. *Personality and Social Psychology Review*, 4, 186–97.

Leyens, J.-P., Rodriguez, A. P., Rodriguez, R. T., Gaunt, R., Paladino, P. M., Vaes, J., and Demoulin, S. (2001). Psychological essentialism and the differential attribution of uniquely human emotions to ingroups and outgroups. *European Journal of Social Psychology*, 31, 395–411

Leyens, J.-P., Yzerbyt, V. Y., and Schandron, G. (1994). *Stereotypes and Social Cognition*. London: Sage.

Licata, L. (2001). Identitées représentées et représentations identitaires: effets des contextes comparatifs et socio-politique sur la signification psychologique des appartenances géopolitiques. PhD thesis, Université Libre de Bruxelles.

Licata, L., and Klein, O. (2002). Does European citizenship breed xenophobia? European identification as a predictor of intolerance towards immigrants. *Journal of Community and Applied Social Psychology*, 12, 323–37.

Lind, E. A., and Tyler, T. R. (1988). *The Social Psychology of Procedural Justice*. New York: Plenum.

Lippmann, W. (1922). *Public Opinion*. New York: Harcourt and Brace.

Lloyd, B., and Duveen, G. (1990). A semiotic analysis of social representations of gender. In G. Duveen and B. Lloyd (eds.), *Social Representations and the Development of Knowledge*. Cambridge: Cambridge University Press.

Lloyd, B., and Duveen, G. (1992). *Gender Identities and Education*. London: Harvester Wheatsheaf.

Lorenzi-Cioldi, F. (1988). *Individus dominants, groupes dominés. Images masculines et feminines*. Grenoble: Presses Universitaires de Grenoble.

Lorenzi-Cioldi, F. (1995). The self in collection and aggregate groups. In R. Lubeck, G. Van Hezewijk, G. Petherson, and C. W. Tolman (eds.), *Trends and Issues in Theoretical Psychology*. New York: Springer.

Lorenzi-Cioldi, F., and Clemence, A. (2001). Group processes and the construction of social representations. In M. A. Hogg and R. S. Tindale (eds.), *Blackwell Handbook of Social Psychology* (group processes) (pp. 311–33). Oxford: Blackwell.

Lorenzi-Cioldi, F., and Doise, W. (1994). Identité sociale et identité personelle. In R. Y. Bourhis and J.-P. Leyens (eds.), *Stéreotypes, discrimination et relations intergroupes* (pp. 69–96). Liège: Mardaga.

Lu, X. (1998). An interface between individualistic and collectivistic orientations in Chinese cultural values and social relations. *Howard Journal of Communications*, 9, 91–107.

Luhmann, N. (1979). *Trust and Power*. Chichester: John Wiley and Sons.

Lyons, E., and Chryssochoou, X. (2000). Cross-cultural research methods. In G. M. Breakwell, S. Hammond, and C. Fife-Schaw (eds.), *Research Methods in Psychology* (pp. 134–46). London: Sage.

McConahay, J. B. (1982). Self-interest versus racial attitudes as correlates of antibusing attitudes in Louisville: Is it the buses or the blacks? *Journal of Politics*, 44, 692–720.

McConahay, J. B. (1986). Modern racism, ambivalence and the modern racism scale. In J. F. Dovidio and S. L. Gaertner (eds.), *Prejudice, Discrimination and Racism* (pp. 91–125). Orlando, FL: Academic Press.

McGarty, C. (1999). *Categorization in Social Psychology*. London: Sage.

McGarty, C., Yzerbyt, V. Y., and Spears, R. (2002). Social, cultural and cognitive factors in stereotype formation. In C. McGarty, V. Y. Yzerbyt, and R. Spears (eds.), *Stereotypes as Explanations: The Formation of Meaningful Beliefs About Groups* (pp. 1–15). Cambridge: Cambridge University Press.

McGarty, C., Spears, R., and Yzerbyt, V. Y. (2002). Conclusion: Stereotypes are selective, variable and contested explanations. In C. McGarty, V. Y. Yzerbyt, and R. Spears (eds.), *Stereotypes as Explanations: The Formation of Meaningful Beliefs About Groups* (pp. 186–99). Cambridge: Cambridge University Press.

Maio, G. R., and Esses, V. M. (1998). The social consequences of affirmative action: Deleterious effects on perceptions of groups. *Personality and Social Psychology Bulletin*, 24, 65–74.

Maio, G. R., and Olson, J. M. (2000). *Why We Evaluate: Functions of Attitudes*. Mahwah, NJ: Lawrence Erlbaum Associates.

Major, B. (1995) Academic performance, self-esteem, and race: The role of disidentification. Meeting of the American Psychological Association, August, New York.

Major, B., Feinstein, J., and Crocker, J. (1994). Attributional ambiguity and affirmative action. *Basic and Applied Social Psychology*, 15, 113–42.

Manganelli, A. M. and Volpato, C. (2001) Forme sottili e manifesti di prejudizio verso gli immigrati. *Giornale Italiano di Psicologia*, 28 (2), 351–75.

Marcus-Newhall, A., Miller, N., Holtz, R., and Brewer, M. B. (1993). Cross-cutting category membership with role assignment. *British Journal of Social Psychology*, 32, 125–46.

Markovà, I. (1999). Sur la Reconnaissance sociale. *Psychologie et Société*, 1, 55–76.

Markovà, I. (2000). Amédée of how to get rid of it: Social representations from a dialogical perspective. *Culture and Psychology*, 6, 419–460.

Markovà, I., and Farr, R. (1995). *Representations of Health, Illness and Handicap*. Langhorne, PA: Harwood Academic Publishers.

Markovà, I., and Foppa, K. (1990). *The Dynamics of Dialogue*. Hemel Hempstead: Harvester Wheatsheaf.

Markovà, I., Graumann, C. F., and Foppa, K. (1995). *Mutualities in Dialogue*. Cambridge: Cambridge University Press.

Markovà, I., Moodie, E., Farr, R., Drozda-Senkowska, E., Eros, F., Plictova, J., Gervais, M.-C., Hoffmannova, J., and Mullerova, O. (1998). Social representations of the individual: A post-communist perspective. *European Journal of Social Psychology*, 28, 797–829.

Markus, H. R., and Kitayama, S. (1991). Culture and the self: Implications for cognition, emotion and motivation. *Psychological Review*, 98, 224–53.

Markus, H. R., Mullally, P. R., and Kitayama, S. (1997). Selfways: Diversity in modes of cultural participation. In U. Neisser and D. A. Jopling (eds.), *The Conceptual Self in Context* (pp. 13–61). Cambridge: Cambridge University Press.

Markus, H. R., and Nurius, P. (1986). Possible selves. *American Psychologist*, 41, 954–69.

Markus, H. R., and Nurius, P. (1987). Possible selves: The interface between motivation and the self-concept. In K. Yardley and T. Honess (eds.), *Self and Identity: Psychological Perspectives* (pp. 157–72). Chichester: John Wiley and Sons.

Martin, D., Deaux, K., and Bikmen, N. (2001). The color line of immigration. Paper presented in the symposium Cultural Diversity and Ethnicity. British Psychological Society Social Section annual conference, June.

Marx, K., and Engels, F. (1848). *The Communist Manifesto*. Oxford: Oxford University Press.

Mead, G. H. (1934). *Mind, Self and Society*. Chicago, IL: Chicago University Press.

Medin, D. L., and Ortony, A. (1989). Psychological essentialism. In S. Vosniadou and A. Ortony (eds.), *Similarity and Analogical Reasoning* (pp. 179–95). New York: Cambridge University Press.

Medin, D. L., and Wattenmaker, W. D. (1987). Category cohesiveness, theories and cognitive archeology. In U. Neisser (ed.), *Concepts and Conceptual Development: Ecological and Intellectual Factors in Categorization.* Cambridge: Cambridge University Press.

Merton, R. K., and Lazersfeld, P. (1950). *Continuities in Social Research: Studies in the Scope and Method of the American Soldier.* New York: Free Press.

Messick, D. M., and Mackie, D. (1989). Intergroup relations. *Annual Review of Psychology*, 40, 45–81.

Milgram, S. (1974). *Obedience to Authority.* London: Tavistock.

Minard, R. D. (1952). Race relationships in the Pocahontas coal field. *Journal of Social Issues*, 8, 29–44.

Mlicki, P. P., and Ellemers, N. (1996). Being different or being better? National stereotypes and identifications of Polish and Dutch students. *European Journal of Social Psychology*, 26, 97–114.

Moghaddam, F. M. (1998). *Social Psychology: Exploring Universals Across Cultures.* New York: W. H. Freeman.

Moghaddam, F. M., Taylor, D. M., and Wright, S. C. (1993). *Social Psychology in Cross-Cultural Perspective.* New York: W. H. Freeman.

Morin, M., and Apostolidis, T. (2002). Contexte social et santé. In G. Fischer (ed.), *Traité de psychologie de la santé.* Paris: Dunod.

Moscovici, S. (1961/1976). *La Psychanalyse son image et son public.* Paris: Presses Universitaires de France.

Moscovici, S. (1976). *Social Influence and Social Change.* London: Academic Press.

Moscovici, S. (1980). Toward a theory of conversion behavior. In L. Berkowitz (ed.), *Advances in Experimental Social Psychology, Vol. 13.* New York: Academic Press.

Moscovici, S. (1984). The phenomenon of social representations. In R. Farr and S. Moscovici (eds.), *Social Representations* (pp. 3–69). Paris: Maison des Sciences de l'Homme; Cambridge: Cambridge University Press.

Moscovici, S. (1988a). Notes towards a description of social representations. *European Journal of Social Psychology*, 18, 211–50.

Moscovici, S. (1988b). Le Domaine de la psychologie sociale. In S. Moscovici (ed.), *Psychologie sociale.* Paris: Presses Universitaires de France.

Moscovici, S. (1988c). *La Machine à faire des dieux.* Paris: Fayard.

Moscovici, S. (1996). *Psychologie des minorités actives.* Paris: Quadrige/Presses Universitaires de France.

Moscovici, S. (1998). The history and actuality of social representations. In U. Flick (ed.), *The Psychology of the Social* (pp. 209–47). Cambridge: Cambridge University Press.

Moscovici, S. (2000). Society and theory in social psychology. In G. Duveen (ed.), *Social Representations: Explorations in Social Psychology* (pp. 78–119). Cambridge: Polity Press.

Moscovici, S. (2001). Why a theory of social representations? In K. Deaux and G. Philogene (eds.), The Representations of the Social (pp. 8–35). Oxford: Blackwell.

Moscovici, S., and Doise, W. (1992). *Dissensions et consensus.* Paris: Presses Universitaires de France.

Moscovici, S., and Lage, E. (1976). Studies in social influence, III: Majority versus minority influence in a group. *European Journal of Social Psychology*, 6, 149–74.

Moscovici, S., and Lage, E. (1978). Studies in social influence. IV: Minority influence in a context of original judgements. *European Journal of Social Psychology*, 8, 349–65.

Moscovici, S., Lage, E., and Naffrechoux, M. (1969). Influence of a consistent minority on the response of majority in a color perception task. *Sociometry*, 32, 365–80.

Moscovici, S., Mucchi-Faina, A., and Maass, A. (eds.) (1994). *Minority Influence*. Chicago, IL: Nelson-Hall Publishers.

Moscovici, S., and Perez, J. A. (1997). Representations of society and prejudice. *Papers on Social Representations*, 6, 27–36.

Moscovici, S., and Personnaz, B. (1980). Studies in social influence, V: Minority influence and conversion behavior in a perceptual task. *Journal of Experimental Social Psychology*, 16, 270–82.

Moscovici, S., and Vignaux, G. (2000). The concept of themata. In G. Duveen (ed.), *Social Representations: Explorations in Social Psychology* (pp. 156–83). Cambridge: Polity Press.

Moscovici, S., and Zavalonni, M. (1969). The group as a polarizer of attitudes. *Journal of Personality and Social Psychology*, 12, 125–35.

Mugny, G. (1995). L'Influence sociale: Guide de lecture. In G. Mugny, D. Oberlé, and J.-L. Beauvois (eds.), *Relations humaines, groupes et influence sociale* (pp. 195–8). Grenoble: Presses Universitaires de Grenoble.

Mugny, G., Butera, F., Sanchez-Mazas, M., and Pérez, J. A. (1995). Judgements in conflict: The conflict elaboration theory of social influence. In B. Boothe, R. Hirsig, A. Helminger, B. Meier, and R. Volkart (eds.), *Perception-Evaluation-Interpretation*. Göttingen: Hogrefe and Huber.

Mugny, G., and Pérez, J. A. (1991). *The Social Psychology of Minority Influence*. Cambridge: Cambridge University Press.

Mugny, G., Sanchez-Mazas, M., Roux, P., and Pérez, J. A. (1991). Independence and interdependence of group judgements: Xenophobia and minority influence. *European Journal of Social Psychology*, 21, 213–23.

Mullin, B. A., and Hogg, M. A. (1999). Motivations for group membership: The role of subjective importance and uncertainty reduction. *Basic and Applied Social Psychology*, 21, 91–102.

Mummendey, A., Kessler, T., Klink, A., and Mielke, R. (1999). Strategies to cope with negative social identity: Predictions by social identity theory and relative deprivation theory. *Journal of Personality and Social Psychology*, 76, 229–45.

Mummendey, A., Klink, A., and Brown, R. (2001a). Nationalism and patriotism: National identification and outgroup rejection. *British Journal of Social Psychology*, 40, 159–72.

Mummendey, A., Klink, A., and Brown, R. (2001b). A rejoinder to our critics and some of their misapprehensions. *British Journal of Social Psychology*, 40, 187–91.

Mummendey, A., and Schreiber, H.-J. (1984). "Different" just means "better": Some obvious and some hidden pathways to ingroup favouritism. *British Journal of Social Psychology*, 23, 363–8.

Mummendey, A., and Simon, B. (1989). Better or just different? III: The impact of importance of comparison dimension and relative ingroup size upon intergroup discrimination. *British Journal of Social Psychology*, 28, 1–16.

Mummendey, A., and Wenzel, M. (1999). Social discrimination and tolerance in intergroup relations: Reactions to intergroup difference. *Personality and Social Psychology Review*, 3, 158–74.

Murphy, G. L., and Medin, D. L. (1985). The role of theories in conceptual coherence. *Psychological Review*, 92, 289–316.

Murrell, A. J., Dietz-Uhler, B. L., Dovidio, J. F., Gaertner, S. L., and Drout, C. (1994). Aversive racism and the resistance to affirmative action: Perceptions of justice are not necessarily color-blind. *Basic and Applied Social Psychology*, 15, 86.

Nadler, A. (2002). Intergroup helping relations as power relations: Maintaining or challenging social dominance between groups through helping. *Journal of Social Issues*, 58,
487–502.

Nauck, B. (2001). Intercultural contact and intergenerational transmission in immigrant families.
Journal of Cross-cultural Psychology, 32, 159–73.

Neisser, U., and Jopling, D. A. (1997). *The Conceptual Self in Context: Culture, Experience, Self-
Understanding*. Cambridge: Cambridge University Press.

Nemeth, C. (1986). Differential contributions of majority and minority influence. *Psychological
Review*, 93, 23–32.

Nemeth, C., and Wachtler, J. (1983). Creative problem solving as a result of majority versus
minority influence. *European Journal of Social Psychology*, 13, 45–55.

Newcomb, T. M. (1943). *Personality and Social Change*. New York: Holt, Rinehart and Winston.

Oakes, P. J., Haslam, S. A., and Turner, J. C. (1994). *Stereotyping and Social Reality*. Oxford:
Blackwell.

Oberg, K. (1960). Culture shock: Adjustment to new culture environments. *Practical Anthropol-
ogy*, 7, 187–92.

Oishi, S., Schimmack, U., Diener, E., and Suh, E. M. (1998). The measurement of values and
individualism–collectivism. *Personality and Social Psychology Bulletin*, 24, 1177–89.

Olson, J. M., and Hafer, C. L. (2001). Tolerance of personal deprivation. In J. T. Jost and B. Major
(eds.), *The Psychology of Legitimacy: Emerging Perspectives on Ideology, Justice and Intergroup
Relations* (pp. 157–75). Cambridge: Cambridge University Press.

Operario, D., and Fiske, S. T. (1998). Racism equals power plus prejudice: A social psychological
equation for racial oppression. In J. L. Eberhardt and S. T. Fiske (eds.), *Confronting Racism: The
Problem and the Response* (pp. 33–53). Thousand Oaks, CA: Sage.

Opotow, S. (1990). Moral exclusion and injustice: An introduction. *Journal of Social Issues*, 46,
1–20.

Opotow, S. (1993). Animals and the scope of justice. *Journal of Social Issues*, 49, 71–85.

Orpwood, G. (2002). The impact of perceptions of homogeneity and industrialization on people's
conception of the nation. BSc dissertation, University of Surrey.

Oyserman, D. (1993). The lens of personhood: Viewing the self and others in a multicultural
society. *Journal of Personality and Social Psychology*, 65, 993–1009.

Oyserman, D., Coon, H. M., and Kemmelmeier, M. (2002). Rethinking individualism and collectivism: Evaluation of theoretical assumptions and meta-analyses. *Pyschological Bulletin*, 128,
3–72.

Paicheler, G. (1988). *The Psychology of Social Influence*. Cambridge: Cambridge University
Press.

Paladino, P. M., Leyens, J.-P., Rodriguez, R. T., Rodriguez, A. P., Gaunt, R., and Demoulin, S.
(2002). Differential association of uniquely and non-uniquely human emotions with the
ingroup and the outgroup. *Group Processes and Intergroup Relations*, 5, 105–18.

Palmonari, A., and Zani, B. (1989). Les Représentations sociales dans le champ des professions
psychologiques. In D. Jodelet (ed.), *Les Représentations sociales* (pp. 299–319). Paris: Presses
Universitaires de France.

Papastamou, S. (1987). Psychologisation et conversion. In S. Moscovici and G. Mugny (eds.),
Psychologie de la conversion. Fribourg: Cousset-Delval.

Papastamou, S. (1989). Psychologisation: erreur individuelle ou strategie collective? In
J.-L. Beauvois, J.-M. Monteil, and R. V. Joule (eds.), *Perspectives cognitives et conduites
sociales*. Fribourg: Cousset-Delval.

Parker, I. (1992). Discourse Dynamics: Critical Analysis for Social and Individual Psychology. London: Routlegde.

Pérez, J. A., Chulvi, B., and Alonso, R. (2001). When a majority fails to convert a minority: The case of gypsies. In F. Butera and G. Mugny (eds.), *Social Influence in Social Reality*. Bern: Hogrefe and Huber Publishers.

Pérez, J. A., Moscovici, S., and Chulvi, B. (2002). Natura y Cultura como principio de classificacion social. Anclaje de representaciones sociales sobre minorias ethnicas. *Revista de Psicologia Social*, 17, 51–67.

Pérez, J. A., and Mugny, G. (1990). Minority influence, manifest discrimination and latent influence. In D. Abrams and M. A. Hogg (eds.), *Social Identity Theory*. Brighton: Harvester Wheatsheaf.

Pérez, J. A., and Mugny, G. (1993). *Influences sociales. La théorie de l'élaboration du conflit*. Neuchâtel: Delachaux et Niestlé.

Pérez, J. A., and Mugny, G. (1996). The conflict elaboration theory of social influence. In E. H. Witte and J. H. Davis (eds.), *Understanding Group Behavior, Vol. 2: Small Group Processes and Interpersonal Relations*. Mahwah, NJ: Lawrence Erlbaum Associates.

Pettigrew, T. F. (1958). Personality and sociocultural factors in intergroup attitudes: A cross-national comparison. *Journal of Conflict Resolution*, 2, 29–42.

Pettigrew, T. F. (1979). The ultimate attribution error: Extending Allport's cognitive analysis of prejudice. *Personality and Social Psychology Bulletin*, 5, 461–76.

Pettigrew, T. F. (1998a). Reactions toward the new minorities of western Europe. *Annual Review of Sociology*, 24, 77–103.

Pettigrew, T. F. (1998b). Intergroup contact theory. *Annual Review of Psychology*, 49, 65–85.

Pettigrew, T. F. (2002). Relative deprivation as a key social psychological concept. In I. Walker and H. J. Smith (eds.), *Relative Deprivation: Specification, Development and Integration* (pp. 351–73). New York: Cambridge University Press.

Pettigrew, T. F., Jackson, J. S., Ben Brika, J., Lemaine, G., Meertens, R. W., Wagner, U., and Zick, A. (1998). Outgroup prejudice in western Europe. *European Review of Social Psychology*, 8, 241–73.

Pettigrew, T. F., and Meertens, R. W. (1995). Subtle and blatant prejudice in western Europe. *European Journal of Social Psychology*, 25, 57–75.

Pettigrew, T. F., and Tropp, L. R. (2000). Does intergroup contact reduce prejudice? Recent meta-analytic findings. In S. Oskamp (ed.), *Reducing Prejudice and Discrimination* (pp. 93–114). Mahwah, NJ: Lawrence Erlbaum Associates.

Petty, R. E., and Cacioppo, J. T. (1986). *Communication and Persuasion*. New York: Springer-Verlag.

Phalet, K., and Schönpflug, U. (2001). Intergenerational transmission of collectivism and achievement values in two acculturation contexts: The case of Turkish families in Germany and Turkish and Moroccan families in the Netherlands. *Journal of Cross-cultural Psychology*, 32, 186–201.

Philogène, G. (1994). African American as a new social representation. *Journal for the Theory of Social Behaviour*, 24, 89–109.

Philogène, G. (1999). *From Black to African American: A New Social Representation*. Westport, CT: Greenwood-Praeger.

Philogène, G. (2000). Blacks as "serviceable other." *Journal of Community and Applied Social Psychology*, 10, 391–401.

Philogène, G. (2001). From race to culture: The emergence of African-American. In K. Deaux and G. Philogene (eds.), *Representations of the Social*. Oxford: Blackwell.

Phinney, J. S. (1990). Ethnic identity in adolescents and adults: Review of research. *Psychological Bulletin*, 108, 499–514.

Pick, S. (1997). Berry in Legoland. *Applied Psychology: An International Review*, 46, 49–52.

Plotke, D. (1999). Immigration and political incorporation in the contemporary Unitd States. In C. Hirschman, P. Kasinitz, and J. De Wind (eds.), *Handbook of International Migration* (pp. 294–318). New York: Russell Sage Foundation.

Potter, J., and Wetherell, M. (1987). *Discourse and Social Psychology: Beyond Attitudes and Behaviour*. London: Sage.

Pratkanis, A. R., and Turner, M. E. (1996). The proactive removal of discriminatory barriers: Affirmative action as effective help. *Journal of Social Issues*, 55, 787–815.

Pratto, F., Sidanius, J., Stallworth, L. M., and Malle, B. F. (1994). Social dominance orientation: A personality variable predicting social and political attitudes. *Journal of Personality and Social Psychology*, 67, 741–63.

Probst, T., Carnevale, P. J., and Triandis, H. C. (1999). Cultural values in intergroup and single-group social dilemmas. *Organizational Behavior and Human Decision Processes*, 73, 171–91.

Rabbie, J. M., and Horwitz, M. (1969). Arousal of ingroup–outgroup bias by a chance win or loss. *Journal of Personality and Social Psychology*, 13, 269–77.

Rabbie, J. M., and Horwitz, M. (1982). Individuality and membership in intergroup system. In H. Tajfel (ed.), *Social Identity and Intergroup Relations*. Cambridge: Cambridge University Press.

Raeff, C. (1997). Individuals in relationships: Cultural values, children's social interactions and the development of an American individualistic self. *Developmental Review*, 17, 205–38.

Redfield, R., Linton, R., and Herkovits, M. J. (1936). Memorandum on the study of acculturation. *American Anthropologist*, 38, 149–52.

Rehm, J., Waldemar, L., and Van Eimeren, B. (1988). Reduced intergroup differentiation as a result of self-categorization in overlapping categories: A quasi experiment. *Journal of Social Psychology*, 18, 375–9.

Reicher, S. (2001). Studying psychology studying racism. In M. Augoustinos and K. J. Reynolds (eds.), *Understanding Prejudice, Racism and Social Conflict* (pp. 273–98). London: Sage.

Reicher, S., and Hopkins, N. (1996). Seeking influence through characterizing self-categories: An analysis of anti-abortionist rhetoric. *British Journal of Social Psychology*, 35, 297–311.

Reicher, S., and Hopkins, N. (2001). *Self and Nation*. London: Sage.

Reicher, S., Hopkins, N., and Condor, S. (1997). Stereotype construction as a strategy of influence. In R. Spears, P. J. Oakes, N. Ellemers, and S. A. Haslam (eds.), *The Social Psychology of Stereotyping and Group Life* (pp. 94–118). Oxford: Blackwell.

Rempel, J. K., Holmes, J. G., and Zanna, M. P. (1985). Trust in close relationships. *Journal of Personality and Social Psychology*, 49, 95–112.

Reynolds, K. J., Turner, J. C., Haslam, S. A., and Ryan, M. K. (2001). The role of personality and group factors in explaining prejudice. *Journal of Experimental Social Psychology*, 37, 427–34.

Roccas, S., and Brewer, M. B. (2002). Social identity complexity. *Personality and Social Psychology Review*, 6, 88–106.

Rokeach, M. (1956). Political and religious dogmatism: An alternative to the authoritarian personality. *Psychological Monographs*, 70 (whole issue).

Rokeach, M. (1960). *The Open and Closed Mind*. New York: Basic Books.

Rokeach, M. (1968). *Beliefs, Attitudes and Values: A Theory of Organization and Change*. San Francisco, CA: Jossey-Bass.

Ross, L. D. (1977). The intuitive psychologist and his shortcomings: Distortions in the attribution process. In L. Berkowitz (ed.), *Advances in Experimental Social Psychology, Vol. 10*. New York: Academic Press.

Rotter, J. B. (1971). Generalized expectancies for interpersonal trust. *American Psychologist*, 26, 442–52.

Rouquette, M.-L. (1996). Social representations and mass communication research. *Journal for the Theory of Social Behaviour*, 26, 221–31.

Runciman, W. G. (1966). *Relative Deprivation and Social Justice*. London: Routledge.

Sachdev, I., and Bourhis, R. Y. (1984). Minimal majorities and minorities. *European Journal of Social Psychology*, 14, 35–52.

Sachdev, I., and Bourhis, R. Y. (1985). Social categorization and power differentials in group relations. *European Journal of Social Psychology*, 15, 415–34.

Sachdev, I., and Bourhis, R. Y. (1987). Status differentials and intergroup behaviour. *European Journal of Social Psychology*, 17, 277–93.

Sanchez, G. J. (1999). Face the nation: Race, immigration and the rise of nativism in late twentieth-century America. In C. Hirschman, P. Kasinitz, and J. De Wind (eds.), *The Handbook of International Migration* (pp. 371–82). New York: Russell Sage Foundation.

Sanchez-Mazas, M. (1994). Les Conflits normatifs comme dynamiques de l'influence sociale. PhD thesis, Université de Genève.

Sanchez-Mazas, M., Roux, P., and Mugny, G. (1994). When the outgroup becomes ingroup and when the ingroup becomes outgroup: Xenophobia and social categorization in a resource allocation task. *European Journal of Social Psychology*, 24, 417–23.

Sani, F., and Reicher, S. (1998). When consensus fails: An analysis of schism within the Italian communist party (1991). *European Journal of Social Psychology*, 28, 623–45.

Schatz, R. T., Staub, E., and Lavine, H. (1999). On the varieties of national attachment: Blind versus constructive patriotism. *Political Psychology*, 20, 151–74.

Schönpflug, U. (1997). Acculturation: Adaptation or development? *Applied Psychology: An International Review*, 46, 52–5.

Schwartz, S. (1990). Individualism–Collectivism, Critiques and proposed refinements. *Journal of Cross-cultural Psychology*, 21, 139–57.

Schwartz, S. (1992). Universals in the context and structure of values: Theoretical advances and empirical tests in 20 countries. In M. P. Zanna (ed.), *Advances in Experimental Social Psychology* (pp. 1–65). Orlando, FL: Academic Press.

Schwartz, S. (1994). Are there universal aspects in the structure and content of human values? *Journal of Social Issues*, 50, 19–45.

Schwartz, S. (1996). Value priorities and behavior: Applying a theory of integrated value systems. In C. Seligman, J. M. Olson, and M. P. Zanna (eds.), *The Psychology of Values: The Ontario Symposium, Vol. 8* (pp. 1–24). Mahwah, NJ: Lawrence Erlbaum Associates.

Sears, D. O., and McConahay, J. B. (1973). *The Politics of Violence: The New Urban Blacks and the Watts Riots*. Boston, MA: Houghton-Mifflin.

Sedikides, C., and Brewer, M. B. (2001). *Individual Self, Relational Self, Collective Self*. Hove: Psychology Press.

Sherif, M. (1936). *The Psychology of Social Norms*. New York: Harper.

Sherif, M. (1966). *In Common Predicament: Social Psychology of Intergroup Conflict and Cooperation*. Boston, MA: Houghton-Mifflin.

Sherif, M. (1967). *Social Interaction: Process and Products*. Chicago, IL: Aldine Press.

Sherif, M., White, B. J., Hood, W. R., and Sherif, C. W. (1954). *Study of Positive and Negative Intergroup Attitudes Between Experimentally Produced Groups: Robbers Cave Study.* Norman: University of Oklahoma.

Siegel, A. E., and Siegel, S. (1957). Reference groups, membership groups and attitude change. *Journal of Abnormal and Social Psychology*, 55, 360–4.

Simmel, G. (1950). *The Sociology of George Simmel.* New York: Free Press.

Simon, B. (1998). Individuals, groups and social change: On the relationship between individual and collective self-interpretations and collective action. In C. Sedikides, J. Schopler, and C. A. Insko (eds.), *Intergroup Cognition and Intergroup Behaviour* (pp. 257–82). London: Lawrence Erlbaum Associates.

Simon, B., Loewy, M., Stuermer, S., Weber, U., Freytag, P., Habig, C., Kampmeier, C., and Spahlinger, P. (1998). Collective identification and social movement participation. *Journal of Personality and Social Psychology*, 74, 646–58.

Singelis, T. M. (1994). The measurement of independent and interdependent self-construals. *Personality and Social Psychology Bulletin*, 20, 580–91.

Slovic, P. (1993). Perceived risk, trust and democracy. *Risk Analysis*, 13, 675–82.

Smith, A. D. (1986). *The Ethnic Origins of Nations.* Oxford: Blackwell.

Smith, A. D. (1991). *National Identity.* London: Penguin Books.

Smith, H. J., and Tyler, T. R. (1996). Justice and power: When will justice concerns encourage the advantaged to support policies which redistribute economic resources and the disadvantaged to willingly obey the law? *European Journal of Social Psychology*, 26, 171–200.

Smith, J. A., Osborn, M., and Jarman, M. (1999). Doing interpretative phenomenological analysis in health psychology. In M. Murray and K. Chamberlain (eds.), *Qualitative Health Psychology: Theories and Methods.* London: Sage.

Smith, P. B., and Bond, M. H. (1998). *Social Psychology Across Cultures.* London: Prentice-Hall Europe.

Sollors, W. (1996). Theories of American ethnicity. In W. Sollors (ed.), *Theories of Ethnicity: A Classical Reader* (pp. x–xliv). Houndmills: Macmillan.

Soysal, Y. (1994). *Limits of Citizenship: Migrants and Postnational Membership in Europe.* Chicago, IL: University of Chicago Press.

Spears, R. (2002). Four degrees of stereotype formation: Differentiation by any means necessary. In C. McGarty, V. Y. Yzerbyt, and R. Spears (eds.), *Stereotypes as Explanations: The Formation of Meaningful Beliefs About Groups* (pp. 127–56). Cambridge: Cambridge University Press.

Spini, D. (1997). Valeurs et representations sociales des droits de l'homme: une approche structurale. PhD thesis, Université de Genève.

Spini, D., and Doise, W. (1998). Organizing principles of involvement in human rights and their social anchoring in value priorities. *European Journal of Social Psychology*, 28, 603–22.

Staerklé, C. (1999). Représentations sociales et jugements symboliques: études experimentales sur les conceptions profanes des rapports entre la societé et l'Etat. PhD thesis, Université de Genève.

Staerklé, C., Clemence, A., and Doise, W. (1998). Representation of human rights across different national contexts: The role of democratic and non-democratic populations and governments. *European Journal of Social Psychology*, 28, 207–26.

Staub, E. (1997). Blind versus constructive patriotism: Moving from embeddedness in the group to critical loyalty and action. In D. Bar Tal and E. Staub (eds.), *Patriotism in the Lives of Individuals and Nations* (pp. 213–28). Chicago, IL: Nelson-Hall Publishers.

Steele, C., and Aronson, J. (1995). Stereotype vulnerability and the intellectual test performance of African-Americans. *Journal of Personality and Social Psychology*, 69, 797–811.

Steele, S. (1990). *The Content of Our Character: A New Vision of Race in America*. New York: St. Martin's Press.

Stephan, C. W., Stephan, W. G., Saito, I., and Barnett, S. M. (1998). Emotional expression in Japan and the United States: The nonmonolithic nature of individualism and collectivism. *Journal of Cross-cultural Psychology*, 30, 620–40.

Stephan, W. G., and Stephan, C. W. (2000). An integrated threat theory of prejudice. In S. Oskamp (ed.), *Reducing Prejudice and Discrimination*. Mahwah, NJ: Lawrence Erlbaum Associates.

Stephan, W. G., Ybarra, O., and Bachman, G. (1999). Prejudice towards immigrants. *Journal of Applied Social Psychology*, 29, 2221–37.

Stickland, N. (2002). Multiple identities: Examining relationships between identities among Muslim men. BSc thesis, University of Surrey.

Stoner, J. A. (1961). A comparison of individual and group decisions involving risk. MSc thesis, MIT School of Industrial Management.

Stoner, J. A. (1968). Risky and cautious shifts in group decision: The influence of widely held values. *Journal of Experimental Social Psychology*, 4, 442–59.

Stryker, S. (1980). *Symbolic Interactionism: A Social Structural Approach*. Menlo Park, CA: Benjamin/Cummings.

Stryker, S. (1992). Identity theory. In E. F. Borgatta and M. L. Borgatta (eds.), *Encyclopedia of Sociology, Vol. 2* (pp. 871–6). New York: Macmillan.

Stryker, S., and Burke, P. J. (2000). The past, present and future of an identity theory. *Social Psychology Quaterly*, 63, 284–97.

Suls, J., and Mullen, B. (1982). From the cradle to the grave: Comparison and self-evaluation across the life-span. In J. Suls (ed.), *Psychological Perspectives on the Self* (pp. 97–125). London: Lawrence Erlbaum Associates.

Sumner, G. A. (1906). *Folkways*. New York: Ginn.

Swim, J. K., Cohen, L. L., and Hyers, L. L. (1998). Experiencing everyday prejudice and discrimination. In J. K. Swim and C. Stangor (eds.), *Prejudice: The Target's Perspective* (pp. 37–60). San Diego, CA: Academic Press.

Tafarodi, R. W., Lang, J. M., and Smith, A. J. (1999). Self-esteem and the cultural trade-off: Evidence for the role of individualism–collectivism. *Journal of Cross-cultural Psychology*, 30, 620–40.

Tajfel, H. (1969). The formation of national attitudes: A social psychological perspective. In M. Sherif and C. W. Sherif (eds.), *Interdisciplinary Relationships in the Social Sciences* (pp. 137–76). Chicago, IL: Aldine Press.

Tajfel, H. (1974). Social identity and intergroup behaviour. *Social Science Information*, 13, 65–93.

Tajfel, H. (1978). *Differentiation Between Social Groups: Studies in the Social Psychology of Intergroup Relations*. London: Academic Press.

Tajfel, H. (1981). *Human Groups and Social Categories: Studies in Social Psychology*. Cambridge: Cambridge University Press.

Tajfel, H. (1982). Social psychology of intergroup relations. *Annual Review of Psychology*, 33, 1–39.

Tajfel, H., Billig, M., Bundy, R. P., and Flament, C. (1971). Social categorization and intergroup behaviour. *European Journal of Social Psychology*, 1, 149–77.

Tajfel, H., and Turner, J. C. (1979). An integrative theory of intergroup conflict. In W. G. Austin and S. Worchel (eds.), *The Social Psychology of Intergroup Relations* (pp. 33–47). Monterey, CA: Brooks/Cole.

Tajfel, H., and Turner, J. C. (1986). The social identity theory of intergroup behaviour. In S. Woschel (ed.), *Psychology of Intergroup Relations*. Chicago, IL: Nelson Hall Publishers.

Tajfel, H., and Wilkes, A. L. (1963). Classification and quantitative jugdement. *British Journal of Psychology*, 54, 101–14.

Tapia, C. (1997). *Les Jeunes face à l'Europe*. Paris: Presses Universitaires de France.

Taylor, D. M., and Jaggi, V. (1974). Ethnocentrism and causal attribution in a south Indian context. *Journal of Cross-cultural Psychology*, 5, 162–71.

Taylor, D. M., and McKirnan, D. J. (1984). A five-stage model of intergroup relations. *British Journal of Social Psychology*, 23, 291–300.

Taylor, D. M., Wright, S. C., Moghaddam, F. M., and Lalonde, R. N. (1990). The personal/group discrimination discrepancy: Perceiving my group, but not myself, to be a target for discrimination. *Personality and Social Psychology Bulletin*, 16, 254–62.

Taylor, D. M., Wright, S. C., and Porter, L. E. (1994). Dimensions of perceived discrimination: The personal/group discrimination discrepancy. In M. P. Zanna and J. M. Olson (eds.), *The Psychology of Prejudice: The Ontario Symposium, Vol. 7* (pp. 233–55). Hillsdale, NJ: Lawrence Erlbaum Associates.

Thibaut, J., and Walker, L. (1975). *Procedural Justice: A Psychological Analysis*. Hillsdale, NJ: Lawrence Erlbaum Associates.

Timotijevic, L., and Breakwell, G. M. (2000). Migration and threat to identity. *Journal of Community and Applied Social Psychology*, 10, 355–72.

Triandafyllidou, A. (2000). The political discourse on immigration in southern Europe: A critical analysis. *Journal of Community and Applied Social Psychology*, 10, 373–90.

Triandis, H. C. (1989). The self and social behaviour in different cultures. *Psychological Review*, 96, 506–20.

Triandis, H. C. (1994). *Culture and Social Behavior*. New York: McGraw-Hill.

Triandis, H. C. (1995). *Individualism and Collectivism*. Boulder, CO: Westview Press.

Triandis, H. C. (1996). The psychological measurement of cultural syndromes. *American Psychologist*, 51, 407–15.

Triandis, H. C. (1997). Where is culture in the acculturation model? *Applied Psychology: An International Review*, 46, 55–8.

Triandis, H. C., Bontempo, R., Villareal, M. J., Asai, M., and Lucca, N. (1988). Individualism and collectivism: Cross-cultural perspectives on self–ingroup relationships. *Journal of Personality and Social Psychology*, 54, 323–38.

Triandis, H. C., Leung, K., Villareal, M. J., and Clark, F. L. (1985). Allocentric versus idiocentric tendencies: Convergent and discriminant validation. *Journal of Research in Personality*, 19, 345–415.

Triandis, H. C., and Vassiliou, V. (1967). Frequency of contact and stereotyping. *Journal of Personality and Social Psychology*, 7, 316–28.

Turner, J. C. (1991). *Social Influence*. Buckingham: Open University Press.

Turner, J. C., and Giles, H. (1981). *Intergroup Behaviour*. Oxford: Blackwell.

Turner, J. C., Hogg, M. A., Oakes, P. J., Reicher, S., and Wetherell, M. S. (1987). *Rediscovering the Social Group: A Self-Categorization Theory*. Oxford: Blackwell.

Turner, J. C., and Onorato, R. S. (1999). Social identity, personality, and the self-concept: A self-categorization perspective. In T. R. Tyler, R. M. Kramer, and O. P. John (eds.), *The Psychology of the Social Self* (pp. 11–46). Mahwah, NJ: Lawrence Erlbaum Associates.

Turner, M. E., and Pratkanis, A. R. (1994). Affirmative action: Insights from social psychological and organizational research. *Basic and Applied Social Psychology*, 15, 1–11.

Tyler, T. R. (1989). The psychology of procedural justice. *Journal of Personality and Social Psychology*, 57, 830–8.

Tyler, T. R., and Smith, H. J. (1998). Social justice and social movements. In D. T. Gilbert, S. T. Fiske, and G. Lindzey (eds.), *The Handbook of Social Psychology* (pp. 595–629). New York: McGraw-Hill.

US Commission on Civil Rights (1977). "Statement on Affirmative Action," October, www.fcnl.org/issues/civ/sup/aff-review.htm

Van Oudenhoven, J. P., Groenewoud, J. T., and Hewstone, M. (1996). Cooperation, ethnic salience and generalization of interethnic attitudes. *European Journal of Social Psychology*, 26, 661.

Van Oudenhoven, J. P., Prins, K. S., and Buunk, B. P. (1998). Attitudes of minority and majority members towards adaptation of immigrants. *European Journal of Social Psychology*, 28, 995–1013.

Vanbeselaere, N. (1987). The effects of dichotomous and crossed social categorizations upon intergroup discrimination. *European Journal of Social Psychology*, 17, 143–56.

Verkuyten, M. (2001). "Abnormalization" of ethnic minorities in conversation. *British Journal of Social Psychology*, 40, 257–78.

Verkuyten, M., and Thijs, J. (2002). Multiculturalism among minority and majority adolescents in the Netherlands. *International Journal of Intercultural Relations*, 26, 91–108.

Vignoles, V. L., Chryssochoou, X., and Breakwell, G. M. (2000). The distinctiveness principle: Identity, meaning and the bounds of cultural relativity. *Personality and Social Psychology Review*, 4, 337–54.

Vignoles, V. L., Chryssochoou, X., and Breakwell, G. M. (2002a). Evaluating models of identity motivation: Self-esteem is not the whole story. *Self and Identity*, 1, 201–18.

Vignoles, V. L., Chryssochoou, X., and Breakwell, G. M. (2002b). Sources of distinctiveness: Position, difference and separateness in the identities of the Anglican parish priests. *European Journal of Social Psychology*, 32, 761–80.

Volpato, C., and Durante, F. (2002). Delegitimization and racism: The social construction of anti-Semitism in Italy. Paper submitted for publication.

Volpato, C., and Manganelli Ratazzi, A.-M. (2000). Prejudizio e immigrazione. Effeti del contatto sulle relazioni interethniche. *Ricerche di Psicologia*, 24, 57–80.

Wagner, W., and Kronberger, N. (2001). Killer tomatoes! Collective symbolic coping with biotechnology. In K. Deaux and G. Philogene (eds.), *Representations of the Social* (pp. 147–64). Oxford: Blackwell.

Walker, I. (2001). The changing nature of racism: From old to new? In M. Augoustinos and K. J. Reynolds (eds.), *Understanding Prejudice, Racism and Social Conflict* (pp. 24–42). London: Sage.

Walster, E., Walster, G. W., and Berscheid, E. (1978). *Equity: Theory and Research*. Boston, MA: Allyn and Bacon.

Ward, C. (1997). Culture learning, acculturative stress and psychopathology: Three perspectives on acculturation. *Applied Psychology: An International Review*, 46, 58–62.

Watkins, D., Akande, A., Fleming, J., Ismail, M., Lefner, K., Regmi, M., Watson, S., Yu, J., Adair, J., Cheng, C., Gerong, A., McInerney, D., Moofu, E., Singh, S. S., and Wondinu, H. (1998).

Cultural dimension: Gender and the nature of self-concept. A fourteen-country study. *International Journal of Psychology*, 33, 17–31.

Watson, P. J., Sherbak, J., and Morris, R. J. (1998). Irrational beliefs, individualism, collectivism and adjustment. *Personality and Individual Differences*, 24, 173–9.

Weiner, B. (1979). A theory of motivation for some classroom experiences. *Journal of Educational Psychology*, 71, 3–25.

Wetherell, M., and Potter, J. (1992). *Mapping the Language of Racism*. New York: Harvester Wheatsheaf.

Wicker, A. W. (1969). Attitudes versus actions: The relationship of verbal and overt behavioral responses to attitude objects. *Journal of Social Issues*, 25, 41–78.

Wicker, H.-R. (1997). Theorizing ethnicity and nationalism. In H.-R. Wicker (ed.), *Rethinking Nationalism and Ethnicity: The Struggle for Meaning and Order in Europe* (pp. 1–42). Oxford: Berg.

Wilder, D. A. (1984). Intergroup contact: The typical member and the exception to the rule. *Journal of Experimental Social Psychology*, 20, 194.

Wilder, D. A. (1986). Social categorization: Implications for creation and reduction of intergroup bias. In L. Berkowitz (ed.), *Advances in Experimental Social Psychology* (pp. 292–355). New York: Academic Press.

Williams, D. R., Jackson, J. S., Brown, T. N., Torres, M., Forman, T. A., and Brown, K. (1999). Traditional and contemporary prejudice and urban whites for affirmative action and government help. *Social Problems*, 46, 503–27.

Willig, C. (2001). *Introducing Qualitative Research in Psychology: Adventures in Theory and Method*. Buckingham: Open University Press.

Wilson, A., and Ross, M. (2000). The frequency of temporal-self and social comparisons in people's personal appraisals. *Journal of Personality and Social Psychology*, 78, 928–42.

Wood, P. (2000). Mata-analysis. In G. M. Breakwell, S. Hammond, and C. Fife-Schaw (eds.), *Research Methods in Psychology* (pp. 414–25). London: Sage.

Worchel, S., Cooper, J., and Goethals, G. R. (1988). *Understanding Social Psychology*. Chicago, IL: Dorsey.

Worchel, S., and Coutant, D. (1997). The tangled web of loyalty: Nationalism, patriotism and ethnocentrism. In D. Bar Tal and E. Staub (eds.), *Patriotism in the Lives of Individuals and Nations* (pp. 190–210). Chicago, IL: Nelson-Hall Publishers.

Wright, S. C. (2001). Restricted intergroup boundaries: Tokenism, ambiguity and the tolerance of injustice. In J. T. Jost and B. Major (eds.), *The Psychology of Legitimacy* (pp. 223–54). Cambridge: Cambridge University Press.

Wright, S. C., and Taylor, D. M. (1998). Responding to tokenism: Individual action in the face of collective injustice. *European Journal of Social Psychology*, 28, 647–67.

Wright, S. C., Taylor, D. M., and Moghaddam, F. M. (1990). Responding to membership in a disadvantaged group: From acceptance to collective action. *Journal of Personality and Social Psychology*, 58, 994–1003.

Yzerbyt, V. Y., Rocher, S. J., and Schandron, G. (1997). Stereotypes as explanations: A subjective essentialistic view of group perception. In R. Spears, P. J. Oakes, N. Ellemers, and S. A. Haslam (eds.), *The Social Psychology of Stereotyping and Group Life* (pp. 20–50). Oxford: Blackwell.

Yzerbyt, V. Y., and Rogier, A. (2001). Blame it on the group: Entitativity, subjective essentialism and social attribution. In J. T. Jost and B. Major (eds.), *The Psychology of Legitimacy: Emerging Perspectives on Ideology, Justice and Intergroup Relations* (pp. 103–34). Cambridge: Cambridge University Press.

Yzerbyt, V. Y., Rogier, A., and Rocher, S. J. (1998). Blaming group membership: The role of subjective essentialism in the emergence of stereotypes. *International Review of Social Psychology*, 11, 1–19.

Yzerbyt, V. Y., and Schandron, G. (1994). Stéréotypes et jugement social. In R. Y. Bourhis and J.-P. Leyens (eds.), *Stéréotypes, discrimination et relations intergroupes* (pp. 127–60). Liège: Mardaga.

Zagefka, H., and Brown, R. (2002). The relationship between acculturation strategies and relatve fit and intergroup relations: Immigrant–majority relations in Germany. *European Journal of Social Psychology*, 32, 171–88.

Zangwill, I. (1909). *The Melting Pot*. New York: Macmillan.

Zanna, M. P., and Olson, J. M. (1994). Power, gender and intergroup discrimination. In M. P. Zanna and J. M. Olson, *The Psychology of Prejudice: The Ontario Symposium* (pp. 171–208). Hillsdale, NJ: Lawrence Erlbaum Associates.

Zanna, M. P., and Rempel, J. K. (1988). Attitudes: A new look at an old concept. In D. Bar Tal and A. W. Kruglanski (eds.), *The Social Psychology of Knowledge* (pp. 315–34). Cambridge: Cambridge University Press.

Zick, A., Wagner, U., Van Dick, R., and Petzel, T. (2001). Acculturation and prejudice in Germany: Majority and minority perspectives. *Journal of Social Issues*, 57, 541–57.

Index